GREAT MODERN POLICE STORIES

GREAT MODERN POLICE STORIES

Edited by Bill Pronzini
and
Martin H. Greenberg

WALKER AND COMPANY
NEW YORK

All the characters and events portrayed in these stories are fictitious.

First published in the United States of America in 1986 by the Walker Publishing Company, Inc.

Published simultaneously in Canada by John Wiley & Sons Canada, Limited, Rexdale, Ontario.

Library of Congress Cataloging-in-Publication Data
Main entry under title:

Great modern police stories.

   1. Detective and mystery stories. I. Pronzini, Bill. II. Greenberg, Martin Harry.
PN6120.95.D45G73   1986   808.83′872   85–29605
ISBN 0–8027–0881–1
ISBN 0–8027–7291–9 (pbk.)

Book Design by Teresa M. Carboni

Printed in the United States of America

10 9 8 7 6 5 4 3 2 1

CONTENTS

Acknowledgments:

"The Detective's Dilemma" by Cornell Woolrich. Copyright © 1940 by the Frank A. Munsey Co. First published in *Detective Fiction Weekly*. Reprinted by permission of Scott Meredith Literary Agency, Inc.

"I Always Get the Cuties" by John D. MacDonald. Copyright © 1954 by Mercury Publications, Inc.; copyright renewed © 1982 by John D. MacDonald Publishing, Inc. First published in *Ellery Queen's Mystery Magazine*. Reprinted by permission of the author.

"H as in Homicide" by Lawrence Treat. Copyright © 1964 by Lawrence Treat. First published in *Ellery Queen's Mystery Magazine*. Reprinted by permission of the author.

"Night Work" by William Campbell Gault. Copyright © 1954 by King-Size Publications, Inc. First published in *The Saint Detective Magazine*. Reprinted by permission of the author.

"The Drowned Men's Inn" by Georges Simenon. Copyright © 1944 by Georges Simenon. Reprinted by permission of the author.

"Captain Heimrich Stumbles" by Frances and Richard Lockridge. Copyright © 1959 by Mercury Publications, Inc. First published in *Ellery Queen's Mystery Magazine*. Reprinted by permission of Curtis Brown Ltd.

"By Child Undone" by Jack Ritchie. Copyright © 1967 by H.S.D. Publications, Inc. First published in *Alfred Hitchcock's Mystery Magazine*. Reprinted by permission of Larry Sternig Literary Agency.

"The King in Pawn" by Michael Gilbert. Copyright © 1960 by Michael Gilbert. First published in the U.S. in *Ellery Queen's Mystery Magazine*, May 1962. Reprinted by permission of the author.

"Captain Leopold Goes to the Dogs" by Edward D. Hoch. Copyright © 1980 by Edward D. Hoch. First published in *Ellery Queen's Mystery Magazine*. Reprinted by permission of the author.

"Hit-and-Run" by Susan Dunlap. Copyright © 1986 by Susan Dunlap. An original story published by permission of the author.

INTRODUCTION

Until the past few decades, the police officer was generally accorded more respect in Europe than in the United States. This is especially true among fiction writers, who have been inclined to venerate the actions of the professional manhunter over there and to sneer at them over here. Which is why, until the relatively recent upsurge of interest in the American police procedural novel, far more British, French, and Scandinavian mysteries featured police detectives than did American mysteries. And why many crime stories written by Americans have had as their protagonists European police detectives. (John Dickson Carr's Henri Bencolin of the Paris police is one of the more well-known examples.)

Part of the reason for this dichotomy is that the modern police agency is European in origin. Prior to the Industrial Revolution, the police function was carried out in European states by agents of the monarch, who owed their primary loyalty to him, not to some abstract notion of "the public." In fact, crime itself was defined almost entirely by who a person was: crimes committed by those of royal birth were almost never punished, especially when perpetrated against "commoners." The typical method of detection, then as now (at least in the real world), was based on tips from individuals who claimed to have witnessed the crime in question, or to possess other evidence that pointed to a particular suspect. This suspect was then seized and subjected to what was called "trial by ordeal"; i.e., the use of torture to extract a confession of guilt.

It was the French Revolution that changed this system, since its slogans of egalitarianism and justice demanded it. The Revolutionary authorities established a Prefecture of Police for the city of Paris to handle non-political crimes, which led to the formation of the Sûreté in 1811. Elsewhere in Europe the process of industrialization was also in full swing and involved the rapid growth of cities; and it was in these cities, where people did not really know each other, that the need for modern police forces was most felt. In England, where reliance had been on the medieval amateur-constable system—and on Henry and John Fielding's "thief-

takers," the Bow Street Runners—Sir Robert Peel organized the
London Metropolitan Police Force in 1829. His "bobbies," as the
officers quickly became known (from the popular version of Peel's
first name), were the model for all police forces in Britain and
eventually throughout the British Empire.

Both the Sûreté and the London bobbies were well-established
when the first American police force was formed in Boston in 1838.
(New York City's was formed six years later. There, the police were
known as "coppers," either because their badges were made of
copper or from the initials C.O.P., which stood for "Constable on
Patrol.") The Paris and London forces, being the pioneer agencies
they were, were also highly romanticized in popular writings of the
time. The adventures of Francois Eugène Vidocq, the reformed
thief and forger who became the first chief of the Sûreté and later
wrote a much-glamourized autobiography called, in the United
States, *Vidocq, The French Police Spy,* were famous on both sides
of the Atlantic and had a profound influence on early writers of
crime fiction, beginning with Poe himself, who more or less mod-
eled C. Auguste Dupin on Vidocq. This influence was not a result
of any deductive skill on Vidocq's part. During his tenure at the
Sûreté, he began a card-index system, took impressions of footprints, and made such observations as that many criminals appeared
to be bowlegged. These were the limit of his contributions to police
procedural methods.

The chief reason the European policeman became such a popular
figure here and abroad in the twentieth century is the European—
and in particular, British—esteem for representatives of law, order,
and the preservation of existing social and moral attitudes. Beginning with the rise of the middle class and the age of Dickens, such
representatives, by their very election or appointment to lofty
positions, were considered to possess any number of virtues, not
the least of which was an acute intelligence. This attitude persisted
until the general disillusionment that followed (or preceded, depending on your point of view) World War II in Europe. When a
detective-story writer introduced a police detective, it was automatically assumed by the reader that he was a man of intellect and
keen capabilities.

The same was not true in this country. Rampant police corruption in the cities, Western peace officers of the Wyatt Earp ilk who were little better than outlaws themselves, the pioneer spirit of self-reliance and personal rather than public code of ethics, and the story weeklies and dime novels that mostly painted law-enforcement officers in unfavorable colors all combined in the late nineteenth century to create a wholly different police image in American minds. By the time the twentieth century arrived, the police were symbols of authority to be feared, scorned, or at best tolerated, but all too seldom to be revered. Mystery writers, naturally, reflected this attitude in their work; private investigators and gifted amateurs were much preferred to hard-working, honest cops as detective heroes. It became standard practice to depict the police as bumbling comic figures or as sadistic halfwits whose primary function was to be outsmarted and made fools of by the private individual.

While to some extent the stereotypical dumb cop, with his penchant for ungrammatical sentences and the third degree, has survived in crime fiction to the present, his breed is rapidly (and happily) dying out. In the forties and fifties, when crusaders of one type or another began to call loudly for police reform, and new laws were passed (such as the famous Miranda decision) to protect an individual's civil rights, the law-enforcement officers of America were pressured into altering some of their methods and improving relations with the public. This in turn led to a much more favorable depiction not only in the news media but also in works of fiction and in the entertainment industry. Such writers as Lawrence Treat and Ed McBain, and such radio (and later TV) shows as "Dragnet" and "Lineup," focused on the humanity and professionalism of working police officers, as well as on their methodology.

Modern police work is much different than it was forty years ago; the same is true of modern police fiction, as the stories in this anthology demonstrate. Realism is the key ingredient here. You won't find any stereotypical buffoons, any anti- or nonheroes with small minds and the behavioral patterns of a gorilla. The cops in these pages are professional crime-busters and puzzle-solvers and, just as importantly, they are men and women you can (and surely will) believe in and care about. Contemporary police officers doing their job, that is the essence of these stories—and doing it so well that their investigations one and all provide a high level of entertainment.

Enjoy.

—Bill Pronzini and
Martin H. Greenberg

October 1985

GREAT MODERN
POLICE STORIES

THE DETECTIVE'S DILEMMA

CORNELL WOOLRICH

*Cornell Woolrich was one of the few writers who treated police-
men with any respect in those halcyon days (some of us consider them halcyon, anyway) when the pulp magazines were
the ruling form of popular fiction. If he sometimes portrayed
the police as employing rather primitive and sadistic methods
(an accurate reflection of some large-city forces in the 1930s),
he also depicted his cop protagonists as intelligent human
beings who were adept at police work. The hero of "The
Detective's Dilemma," Inspector Burke, is very human indeed—
and very good at his job—and that is a large part of what makes
it one of Woolrich's best pulp-era stories and an appropriate
lead entry for this anthology. Woolrich led an unhappy life, but
this fact and its coloration of his outlook is one of the reasons
why his work is so dark and powerful. Such novels as* The Bride
Wore Black, Black Alibi, Phantom Lady *(as by William Irish),
and* The Night Has a Thousand Eyes *(as by George Hopley)
are the most intense and harrowing works of their kind. It is
with perfect justification that Woolrich has been called "the
Poe of the twentieth century and the poet of its shadows."*

He sent his card in to me. We don't get much of that down at
headquarters. Any, you might say. They're either dragged in, or, if
they come of their own accord, they just say who they are by word
of mouth. What was on it made me raise my brows.

Arnoldo, Prince of Iveria.

With a crown over it. We don't get much of *that* either, down at
headquarters. I was so impressed I even talked it over with Crawley,

1

who happened to be in the room at the time, before I did anything about having him shown in. Sort of trying to get my bearings.

"What the hell do you suppose a blue blood like this could want? And he comes to us in person, yet, instead of sending for us to come to him!"

"I suppose the family rubies have been stolen," Crawley snickered.

"In the first place, is he a real prince or is he phony?"

"There is a party by that name," Crawley told me. "I've seen it in the papers once or twice. Wait a minute. I can check, so we'll be that much ahead."

He seemed to know how to go about it; I wouldn't have known myself. He called some book or magazine called *Who's Who*, and also some very swank club, and managed to find out what we wanted, without letting on we were the police. "Get a description while you're at it," I said over his shoulder.

When he got through he said, "The genuine article is about twenty-nine, nearly six feet tall, lean and light haired; looks more English than Latin."

The cop who had brought the card in nodded vigorously and said, "That's who's waiting out there right now!"

"All right, then we don't have to worry about phonies," I said, relieved.

"Here's a thumbnail sketch of the rest of it," Crawley said. "His own country don't exist any more; it was annexed by another country. He's married to an American girl, the former Marilyn Reid. Scads of dough. Her grandfather first invented chocolate bars with peanuts in 'em. They live out at Eastport."

"That ought to do. I hate to have to ask a lot of fool questions with a guy like this. Better not keep him waiting any more, O'Dare."

I was almost stage-frightened by this time. I straightened the knot of my tie, polished the toe of my shoe against the opposite trouser leg, sat down and arranged a lot of papers in front of me, like I was up to my ears in work. "How does this look?" I asked Crawley nervously.

"Phony as hell—to me," he grinned. "But he won't know the difference."

The cop held the door open and there was one of those breathless waits, like in a play on the stage. He came in on a cane. For a

minute I thought it was just swank, but then I could see he seemed
to need it. A little shaky on his legs.

I didn't know how to address him, so I didn't. Just nodded.

Maybe he didn't know how to address me either, because he
nodded back. He said, "Do you mind if I sit down? I'm not—very
strong."

Crawley slid a chair up, and I said, "Sorry we kept you waiting
like that—"

"I don't mind. You see, I had to come to you myself. If I'd sent
for you, it would have defeated the very purpose—for which I've
come to you."

I said, "What can we do for you, your highness?"

He shook his head. "There are no highnesses here. I am taking
out my first papers next month. But, of course, I won't live to
become a full-fledged citizen—"

I looked at Crawley and he looked at me.

Iveria had taken out a hammered gold cigarette case, with a
sapphire clasp. I thought to smoke, but he didn't open it, just passed
it to me. "I may not be able to prevent it coming out that I stopped
in here. In which case I shall say that I came in to report the loss of
this very case. So suppose you keep it in the meantime, as an
excuse. Let us say some honest person found it and turned it in.
You are holding it for me. That will explain my visit here. Is that
all right with you?"

I could have told him that I was a homicide man, and not the
lost-and-found department, but I didn't. "If you want it that way,
yes," I said uncertainly. Again Crawley and I exchanged a look.

"Now, as to what I have actually come here about—" he looked
from one to the other of us—"I am sorry, but I don't intend to
speak about it before more than one person. I want this held
confidential between myself and just one detective or police official. Until the time comes for this one official to act upon what I
have told him today. Then let the whole world know. I will be gone
by then anyway. Now—can that be arranged?"

I didn't answer him right away.

He went on, "It is very painful; it is very personal; it is so subtle
it will require a man of acutest perception and greatest tact."

I said, "Well, would you care to tell Crawley here? He's very
perceptive and tactful—"

He took just one look at him, then he turned back to me. "You have just shown yourself to be the more tactful of the two, by the very fact that you recommended him, he did not recommend you. You are the man I want. You are the man I would like to tell this to, if I may."

"I'm at your disposal," I said.

Crawley took it in good part. He said, "See you later," and eased out.

"And now—"

"Inspector Burke," I supplied.

"And now, Inspector Burke—" He opened his fluffy llama's wool coat, took a thick manila envelope soldered with sealing wax out of its inner pocket. "This is an affidavit, duly notarized, which, however, merely restates what I am about to tell you verbally. It will bear more weight later than a verbal accusation, particularly after I am no longer alive. You will put it away please until the time comes for you to make use of it. Write your own name on it; show it to no one."

I scrawled "Burke, in re Iveria" across it, went over and put it in the safe, along with the cigarette case. Then I came back and waited for him to begin.

He made a steeple out of his hands. "Now it is a very simple matter. Stated in its simplest form—which, however, does not do it justice—it is merely this: I am about to be killed by my wife. But without me, you will not be able to prove that she did such a thing."

"I won't have to prove it, I'll prevent it—" I started to say vigorously.

He flexed his hand at me almost indifferently. "No, neither you nor I will be able to prevent it. It will surely happen. Nothing will be able to prevent it. For it is coming in such a small way. So, for all practical purposes, let us say I am already dead."

"We don't acquiesce in things like that over here—" I started to say, but again he overrode me. "But it is not right that she should do such a thing and remain unpunished, isn't it so? Or at least, enjoy the fruits of her crime, enjoy peace of mind afterwards—with *him*. That is why I have come to you ahead of time. Even so, you will have a very difficult time proving it. Without me, you would never even be able to establish it *was* a murder."

I just sat there eying him unblinkingly. Whatever else I was, I wasn't bored. He had the verbal gift of holding you spellbound. Once the desk phone rang, and I switched the call into another room without even trying to find out what it was.

"Here is the background, so you will understand the thing fully," he went on. "You must realize that it is difficult for me to speak of these things to another man. But for present purposes you are not a man, you are a police official—"

I considered that a dubious compliment at best, but I let it go.

"—So I will hold nothing back. I am descended from a branch of the ruling house of what was formerly Iveria. I therefore bear in my veins both the assets and the liabilities of royalty." He smiled ruefully when he said that, I noticed.

"I met my wife, the former Marilyn Reid, three years ago in St. Moritz, and we were married there. She was supposedly enormously wealthy; both parents dead, sole heiress to the Reid peanut-bar fortune. I have seen American papers which thought it was one of those usual fortune-hunting matches, and didn't hesitate to say so. I gave her the title, for what it was worth; she gave me the use of her money. As a matter of fact it was quite the other way around. I was the wealthier of the two by far, even at the time of our marriage. On the other hand, through bad management and her own extravagance, the enormous estate that had come down to Marilyn from her grandfather was already badly depleted at the time I first met her, and since then has dwindled away to nothing. Naturally, that isn't commonly known. Even if it were, it wouldn't be believed. Say 'exiled aristocracy' to people and they immediately think of poverty.

"The point is, I did not marry Marilyn for her money. When you see her face, you won't have to be told why I did: she was the most beautiful girl in Europe and she still is the most beautiful in America today. Try to keep in mind—when the time comes—that she murdered me. It won't be easy to.

"The rest is rather shabby. I will hurry over it as quickly as I can. I am ill; she married only a shadow of a man. But when a thing is once mine, I keep it. If she wanted freedom only for herself, I would give it to her. But she wants it for this—automobile speed-racer.

"In Cannes we met this Streak Harrison. She'd always had a mania for breakneck driving herself, so that gave him a good head start. What is there about boxers, airplane pilots, dirt-track racers, that makes women lose their heads? After we'd been back six months and he had 'casually' turned up over here himself, she asked me for her freedom. I said no.

"She was tied hand and foot, the decision rested with me, and it has brought murder into her heart. She could not buy me off; *I* had the fortune and she no longer had a dime of her own by that time. She could not get a divorce, because divorce is not recognized in Iveria and my entire estate is there. Nor could she have it annulled on the grounds of my hereditary disability. I took pains to warn her of that before our marriage, and there are documents in existence that will prove that. She went into the marriage with her eyes open.

"I am the last of my line. As my widow—but only as my widow—she would be sole inheritor under Iverian law.

"Now we come to my imminent murder. My affliction is hemophilia, the disease of kings. You know what that is." I did, but he went on to illustrate anyway. "Once the blood begins to flow, there is no checking it. There is imminent death about me all the day long. Things which to you are simply an 'Ouch!' and a suck at the finger, to me can mean death. For instance, I am sitting here in this office with you. There is a nail on the underpart of this chair. I touch it—so—and accidentally make a little puncture on the pad of my finger. Within a few hours, if they can't find a way of stopping it, I am done for."

"Don't do that again, will you?" I gasped, white-faced. I knew that chair, and there *was* a nail under it; Crawley had torn his pants on it once.

He smiled; he saw that he'd gotten his point across.

"But are you sure she contemplates actual murder, Iveria?"

"If I weren't, do you think I would be here?"

"Let me ask you something. Is she a very stupid woman, your wife?"

"She is one of the most keen-witted, diabolically clever women there are to be met with."

"Then why should she need to risk murder? Granting that she wants to be rid of you, wants to marry this Harrison and at the same time enjoy your ancestral fortune, all she needs is a little patience. As you yourself said a few minutes ago, you bear imminent death about with you all day long. All she has to do is sit back and wait—"

"You forget something. I have lived with this blood curse all my life. I know how to guard against it, take care of myself. If you or anyone else were suddenly afflicted with it, you would probably do something that would cause your death within the first twenty-four hours, you wouldn't be used to taking precautions against it. That is the difference between us. I avoid angles and sharp-edged or pointed things. I have my hair singed instead of clipped, my nails sandpapered instead of filed, I don't dance on waxed floors nor walk about my bedroom in carpet slippers, and so on. My father lived to fifty, my grandfather to sixty-four, and both had it. I have lived twenty-nine years with it. What is to prevent my living another twenty-nine? Another thing: she knows that so far, until now, she stands to inherit automatically, under Iverian law, in case of my death. She cannot be sure that tomorrow, I will not give away my entire estate to charity or deed it to the state, a privilege which is mine while I am still alive. She cannot afford to wait, as you think. It is a matter of days, of hours."

That did put a different slant on it; he was winning me over. But I still had to be sure. "In this set-up you have outlined," I said, speaking slowly, "there is invitation enough to murder. But what actual proof have you that she intends doing so?"

"I thought you would ask that, as a police official," he smiled wryly. "I cannot give you phonograph records on which she says at the top of her voice 'I will kill him!' I can only give you little things, which show the way the wind blows. Tiny, trifling things. Each one in itself meaning nothing. But added to one another over a period of time meaning—murder. That is why I said I wanted to tell this to someone who was acutely perceptive, who does not need a brick wall to fall on his head before he senses something. Well, at random, here are some of these trifling things. And I am leaving out as many as I am recalling. When this Streak first came back here from Europe, he seemed very anxious to enjoy my company. He kept asking me to go out driving in his car with him. Since they loved one another, I couldn't understand why he should be concerned with my being present. I unexpectedly agreed one day, simply to find out what it was about. At once a sort of tension came over the two of them. She quickly gave some lame excuse at the last moment, to get out of going with us; apparently it was not part of their plan for her to endanger herself.

"I figured the route he would take, stepped back in the house a moment just as we were ready to leave, and phoned ahead to a gas-station attendant that Marilyn and I both knew. When we reached there he was to tell Streak there'd been a call for him—from a lady—and he was to wait there until she called back. He'd think it was Marilyn of course.

"The mechanic flagged us and Streak fell for it. While he was in the office waiting, I said to the attendant, 'Check over this car thoroughly and find out what's the matter with it.' And I got out and stood clear while he was doing it.

"He went over it quickly but expertly, and when he got through he said, 'It's in fine condition, I can't find anything wrong with it.' Then he took his handful of waste and, from long habit, began polishing up the windshield. It fell through the frame intact and shattered all over the front seat where I'd been until then. The little clamps that held it to the frame had all been unnoticeably loosened, so that any unusual pressure or impact—He would have braked abruptly somewhere along the way, or grazed a tree or a wall or another car—just enough to give it that little shaking out. He would have been with me, of course. Maybe he would have even been more hurt than I was. He could afford a few bloody nicks and gashes. I couldn't have. I went back to our place on foot and left him there in the office still waiting for that non-existent call. I didn't say a word to her; simply that I was not used to being kept waiting at the roadside by anyone and had changed my mind. They couldn't tell if I knew or didn't know.

"But that ended his participation, gave him cold feet. He never came around again, I've never seen him since. I know he's lurking there unseen in the background, waiting for her to do the job and give him the all-clear signal. He may be reckless on the speedway, but he has no stomach for murder.

"All the remaining attempts have come from her. More trivial even than that, as befits the feminine genius. So subtle that—how shall I repeat them to you and make them sound like anything?"

"Let me be the judge," I murmured.

"The other night she attempted to embrace me, wound both arms about my neck. A caress, surely? But the gesture is false, has no meaning any more between us, so I quickly ward it off in the nick of time—for that reason alone. What death lurked in that innocent sign of affection? Then I noticed a heavy slave bracelet, a bangle, that doesn't seem to close properly on her wrist. Its catch is defective, sticks up like a microscopic spur, needs flattening. What could it do to anyone else but graze them, inflict a tiny scratch. 'Ouch!' 'Oh, I'm sorry, dear, I'll kiss it away.' 'Forget it.' But to me it would have brought death. Strange, that only on the night she was wearing that particular ornament did she try to hug me tightly around the neck. The night before, and the night after, she didn't come near me."

He stopped and looked at me. "More?"

"A little more. I'll tell you when to stop."

"In a hundred ways she has tried to draw the single drop of blood from me that will eventually bring death in its wake. She introduced a cat into the house, a pedigreed Persian. Yet I happen to know that she hates the animals herself. Why a cat, then? I soon found out." He shrugged. "You know the feline propensity for stalking, and finally clawing, at anything moving? I sat reading one night before the fire, with the cat there, and finally dozed off, as she must have hoped I would sooner or later. I opened my eyes just in time to find the cat crouched at my feet, tail lashing warningly back and forth, about to spring. My arm was hanging down limp over the side of the chair. Its claws would have raked it in a half-dozen places. A loose piece of string was traveling up my arm, drawn from behind the chair. Luckily there was a cushion behind me. I just had time enough to swing it out in front of me, use it as a buffer. The cat struck it, gashed it to ribbons. When I stood up and turned, she was behind me, holding the other end of the string she had used to bait it. What could I say? 'You tried to kill me just then?' All she seemed to be doing was playing with the cat. Yet I knew she had tried; I knew she must have kept flinging out that piece of string again and again until it trailed across my arm as she wanted it to.

"Whom could I tell such a thing to—and expect to be believed? What bodyguard, what detective, can protect me against such methods?"

He was right about that. I could have sent someone back with him to protect him against a gun, a knife, poison. Not against a woman playing with a cat or twining her arms about his neck. "Why

don't you leave her, then? Why don't you get out while there is still
time? Why stay and wait for it to happen?"

"We Iverias don't give up the things we prize that easily."

That left me kind of at a loss. Here was a man who knew he was
going to be murdered, yet wouldn't lift his little finger to prevent it.

"Any more?"

"What is the use of going ahead? I have either already convinced
you by the few samples I have given, or else there is no hope of my
ever convincing you."

"And now just what is it you want me to do?"

"Nothing. When it happens—maybe tomorrow, maybe next
week—I will call you, while I still have the strength left, and say
'This is it.' But even if I fail to, be sure that it is 'it.' You will read
in the papers, within a day or two after that, that the Prince of
Iveria died from hemophilia. Some slight mishap in the home. A
pin had been left in his freshly laundered shirt.

"There isn't a living soul in the whole world, physician or lay-
man, will believe such a thing *could* have been murder. But you
will know better, Inspector Burke, you will know better after what
I have told you today.

"Take my affidavit out of your safe, go up there, and arrest her.
Force the issue through, so that she has to stand trial for it.
Probably she will never be convicted. That doesn't matter. The
thing will be brought out into the open, aired before the whole
world. His name will be dragged into it. Convicted or acquitted, I
will have succeeded in what I set out to do. *She cannot marry him*
nor go near him, after I am gone, without branding herself a
murderess in the eyes of the whole world."

"So that's it," I said softly. What a revenge.

"That's it. He can't have her and she can't have him. Unless they
are willing to go through a living hell, become outcasts, end by
hating one another. In which case they have lost one another
anyway. I am a Prince of Iveria. What once belonged to me I give
up to no other man."

He'd said his say and he had no more to say. He stood up and
stretched out his hand to me.

"Good-bye, Inspector Burke. We shall probably not see one
another again. Your job is to punish murder. See that you don't
fail to. You'll do what I've asked you to?"

What could I do? Go up there and arrest her, to prevent it? On what charge? Wearing a bracelet with a catch that needed repairing? Playing with a pet cat in the same room he happened to be in? True, he was almost seeking the thing instead of trying to ward it off. But I couldn't compel him to move out of his own home, if he didn't want to. If murder was committed, even though he made no move to avoid it, even though he met it halfway, that didn't make it any the less murder.

He kept looking at me, waiting for my answer.

I nodded gloomily at last, almost against my will. "I'll do—whatever the situation calls for."

He turned and went slowly out through the doorway with the aid of his cane, stiffly erect, just leaning a little sidewise. I never saw him alive again.

It came quicker than I'd expected it to. Too quickly for me to be able to do anything to prevent it. I'd intended paying a visit up there in person, trying to introduce myself into the establishment in some way, to see if I couldn't size up the situation at first hand, form my own conclusions. He hadn't given me any *physical* evidence, remember, that she was attempting to murder him, only oral. All right, granting that he couldn't give me physical evidence, the very nature of the set-up forbade it, he still hadn't convinced me a hundred percent. My own eyes and ears would have helped. But before I had a chance, it was already too late, the thing was over.

The second day after his visit, at nine in the morning, just after I'd gotten in to headquarters, I was hailed. "Inspector Burke, you're wanted on the phone."

I picked it up and a woman's voice, cool and crisp as lettuce, said, "Inspector Burke, this is the Cedars of Lebanon Hospital at Eastport. We have a patient here, the Prince of Iveria, who would like to speak to you."

I waited, squeezing the life out of the thing. There were vague preparatory sounds at the other end. He must have been very weak already. I could hardly hear him at first. Just a raspy breathing sound, like dry leaves rustling around in the wind. They must have been holding him up to the phone. I said, "I can't hear you!"

Then he got words through. Four of them. "Burke? This is it."

I said, "Hello! Hello!" He'd hung up.

I called right back. I couldn't get him again. Just got the hospital switchboard. They wouldn't clear the call. The patient was in no condition to speak further to anyone, they told me. He was—dying.

"You've got to put me through to him again! He was just on the line, so how can an extra thirty seconds hurt?"

Another wait. The hospital operator came back again. "The patient says—there is nothing further to be said." *Click.*

If ever a man embraced death willingly, you might say exultantly, it was he.

I grabbed my hat, I grabbed a cab, and I went straight out there to the hospital myself, then and there. Again the switchboard operator down on the main floor blocked me. She plugged, plugged out again. "Sorry, no one can go up. The Prince of Iveria is in a coma—no longer conscious—sinking fast. I'm afraid there's not much hope left."

That cooled me off. If he couldn't talk, there wasn't much use going up. I said, "I'll wait," and hung around down there in the lobby for the next two hours, having her ring up at intervals to find out. There was always a chance he might rally. What I wanted to hear from him was: *had* she done it or hadn't she. True, the implication of "This is it," was she had; he'd warned me that was all he was going to say when the time came, but I had to have more than that. Probably the only material witness there would ever be against her was slipping through my fingers. I didn't have a nail intact left on my ten fingers, the marble flooring on my side of the reception foyer was swimming with cigarette butts, by the time the two hours were up. I must have driven the poor switchboard girl half-crazy.

Twice, while I was waiting, I saw rather husky-looking individuals step out of the elevator. They were both too hale-looking to be hospital cases themselves. One was counting over a small wad of bills, the second one hitching at his sleeve as though his arm were tender. Without knowing for sure, I had a good hunch they were donors who had been called on to infuse their blood into him.

The operator tried his floor once more, but he was still unconscious so it looked as though it hadn't helped. Even my badge wouldn't have gotten me up—this was a hospital after all—but I didn't want to use it, in any event.

At ten to two that afternoon the elevator door opened and *she* came out—alone. I saw her for the first time. I knew it must be she. He'd said she was the most beautiful girl in Europe or America. He needn't have left out Asia or Africa. She was the most beautiful human being I'd ever seen anywhere in my life. The sort of a face that goes with wings and a halo. She was all in black, but not the black of mourning—yet—the black of fashion. She wasn't crying, just looking down at the floor as if she had a lot to think about. So at least she was no hypocrite, I gave her that much.

As she moved through the foyer the nurse at the switchboard followed her with her eyes, a pair of question marks in them that couldn't be ignored. She—Iveria's wife—felt their insistence finally, looked over at her, nodded subduedly, with a sort of calm sadness. About the same degree of melancholy introspection that would go with the withering away of a pet plant in one's garden, say, or the receipt of bad news from one's stockbroker.

So he'd died.

I didn't accost her, didn't do anything about it right then. She wasn't some fly-by-night roadhouse hostess that you grab while the grabbing's good; she would always be where I could reach her. The patrimony of the House of Iveria, immovably fixed in the ground in mines, farms, forests, castles, would see to that. If she'd done it, plenty of time. If she hadn't, even more time than plenty.

She went on out through the revolving door to a car waiting for her outside. Nobody else was in it but the driver. It skimmed away like a bolt of satin being unrolled along the asphalt.

The switchboard operator turned to me, and whispered unnecessarily, "He's dead."

It was up to me now, I was on my own. All I had was the valueless memory of a conversation and an almost equally valueless affidavit, deposed before the event itself. And my own eyes and ears and good judgment, for whatever they were worth.

There had been a pyramidal hierarchy of medical experience in attendance on him, as was to be expected, but I didn't bother with the lower strata, took a short-cut straight to the apex, and singled out the topmost man. I did it right then and there, as soon as I'd seen her leave the hospital.

His name was Drake, and he'd treated everyone prominent

who'd ever had it, which meant he got about one patient every ten years. And could live nicely on it, at that, to give you a rough idea.

I found him in some sort of a small, pleasant retiring-room reserved for the doctors on the hospital staff—it was a private institution after all—on the same floor Iveria had just died on, but well-insulated from the hospital activities around it. He was having a glass of champagne and bitters and smoking a Turkish cigarette, to help him forget the long-drawn-out death scene he'd just attended. A radio, tuned down almost to the point of inaudibility, was whispering away.

I didn't make the mistake of thinking this was heartlessness. I could tell it wasn't, just by looking at him. He had a sensitive face, and his hands were a little shaky. The loss of the patient had affected him, either professionally or personally or both.

He thought I was a reporter at first, and wasn't having any. "Please don't bother me right now. They'll give you all the necessary details down at the information desk." Then when he understood I was police, he still couldn't understand why there should be any police interest in the case. Which didn't surprise me. Whatever the thing was, I had expected it to look natural, Iveria had warned me it would, so natural I might never be able to break it down.

I didn't give him an inkling what my real purpose was. "This isn't police interest in the usual sense," I glibly explained. "His Highness took me into his confidence shortly before this happened, asked me to have certain personal matters carried out for him in case of his death, that's my only interest."

That cleared away the obstructions. "Wait a minute, is your name Burke?" He put down his champagne glass alertly.

"That's right."

"He left a message for you. He revived for a moment or two, shortly before the end, whispered something to us. The nurse and I jotted it down." He handed me a penciled scrap of paper. "I don't know whether we got it right or not, it was very hard to hear him—"

It said on it: "Burke. Don't fail me. This is a job for you."

Which was a covert way of saying murder. "Yes, you got it right," I assented gloomily and put it in my pocket. "Was his wife present when he whispered this?"

"Not in the room itself, in the outside room."

"Did she see it afterwards?"

"No. He muttered something that sounded like 'Nobody but him,' so we took that to mean he didn't want anyone but you to see it."

"That's right, he didn't."

"Sit down. Have some?" I shook my head. "Swell fellow, wasn't he? Practically doomed from the beginning, though. They always are with that. I tried five transfusions, and I even tried this new cobra-venom treatment. Minute doses, of course. Very efficacious in some cases. Couldn't stop the flow this time, though. You see, that's the worst part of the hellish thing. It's progressive. Each time they're less able to resist than the time before. He was too weak by this time to really be pulled through—"

He'd been under a strain, and he was going to work it off in garrulousness, I could see, if I didn't stop him; so I stopped him. I wasn't interested in the medical aspects of the case, anyway. There was only one thing I wanted. "What brought it on this time?"

"The lesions were all over his forehead and scalp. An unfortunate chain of trivialities led to an accident. They occupied adjoining bedrooms, you know. The communicating door was faced with a large pier glass, a mirror panel. There was a reading chair in Iveria's room with a large, bulky hassock to go with it, on which he habitually rested his feet. There was a bedside light, which should have cast enough light to avoid what happened. At any rate, he was awakened from a sound sleep by his wife's voice crying out a name; evidently she was being troubled by a bad dream. There was such terror and grief in her voice, however, that he could not be sure it was just that and not possibly an intruder. He seized a small revolver he habitually kept bedded under his pillow, drew the chain pull of the bedside light. It refused to go on, the bulb had evidently burned itself out unnoticed since the last time it had been in use. The switch controlling the main overhead lights was at the opposite side of the room, far out of reach. He therefore jumped up without any lights, made for the mirror door by his sense of direction alone, gun in hand. The reading chair and hassock should have been far offside. The chair still was; the hassock had become misplaced, was directly in his path. It threw him. There was not enough space between it and the mirror-faced door to give the length of his prostrate body clearance. His forehead struck the mirror, shattered it; it was only a thin sheeting after all.

"It would have been a serious accident with anyone. It would not have been a fatal accident with anyone else. None of the numerous little gashes were deep enough to require stitches. But he and his wife both knew what it meant, they didn't waste any time. She telephoned me in Montreal where I was attending a medical convention, and I chartered a plane and flew right back. But I doubt that I could have saved him even if I had been right in the same room with him when it happened. I had them remove him to the hospital and summon donors before I even started down. I gave him the first transfusion ten minutes after I arrived, but he failed to rally, continued sinking steadily—"

I wasn't interested in the rest, only in what the original "mishap," the starting point, had been. I thanked him and I left. This was going to be a tricky thing to sift to the bottom of, if there ever was one. Acutely perceptive? You needed to be a magnetized divining rod to know what to do!

I opened the safe and read over his affidavit before I went out there to tackle her. The affidavit didn't bring anything new to bear on the case, simply restated what he had said to me that day in the office, only at greater length and in more detail. The incident of the loosened windshield was there, the cat incident, and several others that he hadn't told me at the time.

. . . I, therefore, in view of the above, solemnly accuse my wife, Marilyn Reid d'Iveria, of having at various times sought to cause my death, by means of the affliction known to her to be visited upon me, and of continuing to seek to do so at the time this deposition is taken, and charge the authorities and all concerned that in case of my death occurring at any time hereafter during her continued presence in my house and proximity to me, to apprehend and detain the said Marilyn Reid d'Iveria with a view to inquiring into and ascertaining her responsibility and guilt for the aforesaid death, and of bringing just punishment upon her.

Arnoldo Amadeo Manfredo d'Iveria

With that final postscript tacked onto it, it was going to be damned effective. Plenty enough to arrest her on, book her for suspicion of murder, and hold her for trial. What went on after that, in the courtroom, was none of my business. I was a detective, not a lawyer.

I put it in my pocket and left to interview the party of the second part—the murderess.

He'd been buried in the morning—privately—and I got out there about five that same afternoon. There was no question of an arrest yet, not on this first visit anyway, so I didn't bother looking up the locals, even though I was out of jurisdiction here. She could slam the door in my face, if she wanted. She wouldn't, if she was smart. It wouldn't help her case any.

It was a much smaller place than I'd expected it to be. White stucco or sandstone or something, I'm not up on those things. I turned in along the driveway on foot. It was dusk by now, and a couple of the ground-floor windows around on the side were lighted, the rest of the house was blacked-out.

There was a high-powered knee-high foreign car outside the entrance. It wasn't the one she had driven away from the hospital in. It looked like the kind of a job that would belong to a professional auto racer—if he could afford it. I whistled soundlessly, thought: "Whew! Already?" It was almost too good to be true. Maybe this case wasn't going to be such a tough baby to crack after all. One sure thing, she was writing herself up a bad press, if things ever got as far as a jury, by doing this sort of thing. They should have at least let Iveria cool off overnight before they got together.

It was probably the sight of the car that kept me from ringing for admittance right away, sent me on a little cursory scouting expedition around to the side those lighted windows were on. She'd probably be sitting there all in black trying to look sorrowful, with him holding her hand trying to look consoling, and each one of them knowing the other was a damn liar.

When I got in line with them, I moved in close enough for what was behind the gauze, or whatever it was backing them, to come into focus. Just close enough, no closer. To try and take a little of the ignominy out of snooping like that, I suppose. Then I stood stock-still there on the well-kept lawn. I couldn't believe what I saw.

It was her, all right. She was dancing around the room in there, without a partner. The way you do when you're overjoyed, can't contain yourself. Arms stretched out wide, in a gesture of release, waltzing, or at least swaying around. She was in a light tan dress, and it billowed out all around her as she went.

He was sitting there, watching her. I got my first look at him. He was dark haired and broad-shouldered, that was about all I could tell from out where I was. I couldn't see much to him, just something to hang a Stetson on. Iveria's words came back to me. "What is there about boxers, plane pilots, auto racers, that makes women lose their heads?" He was holding his head cocked at a slight angle, with an air of proud ownership, as if to say, "Isn't she lovely? Isn't she cute?" To which my own commentary would have been, "She's the cutest little murderess I've seen in an age."

If this was how she was the very afternoon of the day he'd been buried, I couldn't help wondering what she would have been like a week—or a month—afterwards. Probably eating picnic lunches on his grave. Why, there was no difficulty about this case, it was a pushover. I was only sorry I hadn't brought out a warrant with me, made arrangements with the Eastport locals, and gotten it over with then and there. Whether the crime could ever be proven or not was beside the point. She was begging for arrest if anyone ever was, just on grounds of public decency.

I strode around to the front and rang. Peremptorily. A maid opened the door. I said, "I want to see the princess, or whatever she calls herself."

She'd received her orders ahead of time. "She's not at home to anyone—"

I felt like saying, "No, except to Barney Oldfield, Jr., in there." Instead I elbowed her aside without another word and walked down the hall to where they were. The open doorway of the room cut an orange notch across the corridor, and I turned right at it.

She'd just finished her solo dancing. She'd come to a stop before him, but her filmy tan skirt was still swinging around from before. She was leaning her face down toward him, a hand resting on either arm of his chair. Their lips were only inches apart, and in another minute . . .

I just stood there taking it in. Did I say she was beautiful, before? Double it in spades, and you're still short-suited. I couldn't understand why nature should go to town so, all over one face, and let the others all go hang.

She became aware of me, shot up and back like something released from a bowstring. He reared his head and turned and looked at me, around the back of his chair. She said, "Who're you?" with a sort of unintentional matter-of-factness, that came from not raising her voice high enough to suit the situation.

"Sorry to intrude," I said. "I've come out here to see you. You're d'Iveria's widow, I believe?" I eyed the light tan dress she had on, meaningfully.

"Yes, but people don't just walk in here—" She made an abortive gesture toward some service pushbutton or other.

"That won't do any good," I said. "I came here to have a talk with you, and I'm having it."

The Harrison fellow got up at this point, ready to take part in the matter. He was taller than I'd thought. He must have had a hard time tucking away those legs under a racing car hood. He was just a kid, really. I mean, a kid of about twenty-seven. He was pretty clean-cut looking, too, for a—well, call it home wrecker or whatever you want. I was surprised. He looked like he drank milk with his meals, and when he wanted to paint the town red, went to a movie with a bag of salted peanuts in his pocket.

He started toward me, biting off something about, "You'll have the talk when she's ready, and not when you feel like it—"

Suddenly, something made her change her mind. Some second look at me, or more likely, some unspoken thought in her own mind. She wanted the talk right away, it couldn't come fast enough. But without him; she didn't want him to have any part in it, you could see that. Her arm shot out before him, barring his way. "Don't, Streak," she said. "I think I know what this is. You go now, will you? Call me later." And then to me, almost pleadingly, "It's myself you want to speak to, isn't it? Not the two of us. It's all right if—if he goes now, isn't it?"

"Yourself'll do nicely," I said ominously.

Harrison, who wasn't very alert at grasping nuances (a sign of honesty, they say), couldn't get off anything better than: "Well, but—"

She went into high gear, edging and propelling him toward the room door. She kept throwing me appealing looks, as if begging me to keep quiet just a minute longer, until she could get him out of the way. At least, that was the way I translated them; I couldn't be sure. Meanwhile she was almost crowding him out into the hall before her, saying disconnectedly, "You go now. I know what this is. It's all right, it's nothing. Call me later. About ten?"

The only way I could figure it was, either she wanted to hang onto his good opinion of her as long as she could, or she wanted to keep him in the clear and, ostrich-like, thought that by getting him out of here that would do it, or she thought she could handle me better if he wasn't around to cramp her style. One thing was plain, she already knew what was coming up. And if she wasn't guilty, how the hell could she have known? How should such an idea ever enter her head?

I let him go. It made the issue more clear-cut just to deal with her alone. He hadn't been in the picture at all since the windshield incident, according to d'Iveria's own affidavit. I could always get him later, anyway.

The last thing I heard her say, when she got him as far as the front door, was, "Get home all right. Don't drive too fast, Streak, I'm always so worried about those intersections along the way." That was sure love, to be able to think of such a thing at such a time. Well, I suppose even murderesses love someone.

She didn't come right back to the room. She called, "I'll be right with you, Officer!" and then ran up the stairs before I could get out there and stop her. By the time I did, she was already making the return trip down again.She hadn't been up there long enough to do any damage. She was holding some sort of small black folder in her hand, I couldn't quite make out what it was, except that it was no weapon of any sort.

We went back into the room where they had been originally. She was breathing rapidly from the energy she'd used just now in maneuvering him to the door and then running the stairs—or maybe it was from some other cause entirely, I don't know. People's breathing quickens from fear, too.

She began with beautiful directness. "I know what you're going to say. I wanted to get him out of here before you said it. He would have come to blows with you, and gotten in trouble. I can handle it more tactfully. You're going to say I killed Arnold, aren't you? You're the police, aren't you? Only a detective would crash into a room like you did just now. I suppose you looked through the windows first and saw me dancing, because I was happy he was gone. Well, if you didn't, that's what I was doing just before you got here, so now you know anyway. May I see your credentials?"

I showed her my badge.

"I knew he was going to do this to me," she said. "Yes, I'm not wearing black. Yes, I'm glad he's gone; like a prisoner is when his term is up." She had opened the little black folder while she was speaking, torn out a light blue tab. She was writing something on it. "Do you mind giving me your name?" she said, without looking up.

"The name is Nothing-doing-on-that-stuff." I hitched the light blue tab out from under the midget gold fountain pen she had point-down on it, so that the last zero—there were three after the "1"—streaked off in a long diagonal ink line across the face of it. "Keep it up," I said. "You're saving some lawyer-guy lots of hard work." I put it in my pocket; the blank check had Iveria's name printed across one edge in lieu of written endorsement, so it was as incriminating as if she'd signed it.

"Then there's nothing I can do or say that will—avert this thing, this thing that he wanted to happen to me?"

"Not along those lines. What you can do and say, for the present, is sit down quietly a minute and answer a question or two about your husband's death. Would you mind giving me the exact circumstances, in your own words?"

She calmed herself with a visible effort, sat down, lit a cigarette and then forgot to smoke it. "I was asleep—"

"Do you recall having an unpleasant dream that caused you to cry out?"

She smiled. "One often doesn't, even if one did. The unpleasant dream, in my case, was during my waking hours, you see—"

Trying to gain my sympathy, I thought warily. "That has nothing to do with it. Please go on."

"I heard a breakage sound that waked me, I lit the light, I saw the communicating door move slowly inward and his hand trail after it on the knob, to gain my help. It opened inward, and he kept it locked on his side—" Her eyelids dropped. "—as if afraid of me at night. I found him attempting to pick himself up, in a welter of glass shards. I saw a gun there on the floor behind him that had spiraled from his hand when he fell. I took it into my room and hid it in my dressing table—"

"Why?"

"We both knew he was doomed, instantly. I was afraid, to avoid the pain, the lingering death, that was a certainty, he would take a quicker way out."

Which would not look quite so much like an accident? I addressed her silently.

"That's the whole sum and substance of the matter?"

"That's the whole sum and substance."

"May I see this room it happened in?"

"Of course."

I followed her up the stairs. "The local authorities have already examined it?"

"The local authorities have already examined it."

I looked at her. Meaning, "You didn't have much trouble convincing *them,* did you?" She understood the look, she dropped her eyes.

The only vestiges remaining of the "accident" were the spokes of emptiness slashed out of the mirror panel, in sun-ray formation. His head had struck it low; the upper two-thirds were still intact. The inclined reading chair was far out of the way, a good two to three yards offside. The hassock, now, sat directly before it, where it belonged. "Is this the habitual position of this chair?" But I didn't really have to ask her that. The carpet was a soft plush that showed every mark; the chair had stood there a long time, its four supports had etched deep, ineradicable indentations into the nap where it now was. This was a mark against, not for, her. How could a bulky thing like that hassock travel three yards out from where it belonged—unaided?

I asked her that. I said I wondered.

"I don't know," she said with an air of resigned hopelessness. "Unless he may have kicked it away from him, in getting up from the chair to go to bed."

I sat down in it, arched my legs to the hassock. I had to try it three times, myself, before I could land it all the way out in a line with the mirror door. And I had stronger leg muscles than he; he'd had to walk with a cane. Still, he *could* have done it, in a burst of peevishness or boredom.

I looked the bedside light over next. It was just a stick with a bulb screwed in at the top and a shade clamped over that. I hitched the chain pull; the bulb stayed dark.

"How is it he would not have noticed this bulb was defective before getting into bed?" I wondered aloud for her benefit. "Isn't that what bedside lights are for, to be left on until the last?" The wall switch controlling the overheads was all the way across the room, beside the door leading out to the hall.

"I don't know, maybe he did," she shrugged with that same listless manner as before. "What would he want a new bulb for at that hour, if he was on the point of retiring for the night? He would have had to go downstairs for it himself, the help were all in bed by then. Or perhaps it was still in working order up to the time he turned it off. Bulbs have been known to expire passively between the time they were last used and the next time they are turned on."

I removed the clamped shade. I tested the pear-shaped thing gingerly. It vibrated slightly beneath my fingertips, I thought. I gave it a turn or two to the right. It responded. There should have been no give there, if it was fastened as tightly into the socket as it would go. Brilliant light suddenly flooded it.

The bulb was in perfectly good condition; it had simply been given a half-turn or two to the left, sufficient to break the current.

I looked at her, keeping my hand still in it for as long as I could stand the increasing heat. Her eyes had dropped long before then.

"You say the communicating door was kept locked. Was the outside-door, to the hall, also kept locked by your husband, do you know?"

"I believe it was," she said lifelessly. "I believe the butler, in whom my husband had the greatest confidence, used a special key to let himself in in the mornings. We were—rather a strange household."

I noticed an old-fashioned bellpull there by the bed. I reached for it. She stopped me with a quick little gesture. "I can give you the answer to what you are about to ask him, right now, myself; it will save time. He forgot his key that night, left it standing in the outside lock of the door, after he had concluded his duties for the night and left my husband. I noticed it there myself and returned it to him the next day."

"Then anyone else in the house could—"

She wouldn't let me finish. "Yes, anyone else in the house could have entered my husband's room after he had gone to sleep. To do what? Give a bulb a half-turn so it wouldn't light? Shift a hassock out of place? Don't you think that would have been a foolish misuse of such an opportunity?"

"No, I don't!" I crackled at her. I couldn't have made it more emphatic if I'd tried. "If a knife had been left sticking in him, or a fine wire tightened around his throat, that would have been *murder*. But he died of an 'accident.' One little mishap led to another, as inevitably as in a Rube Goldberg freak invention." I drove the point home viciously. "You and I are agreed on that, he died of an 'accident!' " I dropped my voice. "And I'm here to find out who caused it."

She twined and untwined her fingers a few times. "And I cannot defend myself," she shuddered. "It is not that the charge is so hard to prove; it is that it's so hard to disprove. This is what he intended to happen. I saw the smile on his face, even when I first found him lying there in the litter of glass. As if to say, 'This time I've got you.' I beg of you to do this much at least. Send for the maid that cleans this room. Don't ask her any questions about the bedside light, just test her. Just—well, let me do it, may I?"

I nodded, more on guard than ever. She hitched the bellpull a certain number of times, had me replace the lampshade, lit a cigarette and flicked ashes over it.

Within a few minutes a maid appeared, not the same one who had admitted me to the house originally. "Will you dust off this little bedside light?" Iveria's wife said casually. "Don't take extra pains, just do it as you would ordinarily." I noticed her wrists were both trembling slightly.

The girl took a cloth from her waistband, took a swipe around the stick part. Then she began to swivel the cloth around the shade. She was left-handed, she moved the cloth from right to left. Not only that, but she held the little appliance by the stick to steady it, so that the shade was not held fast at all, began to slip unnoticeably around a little under her ministrations. And the wire cleats that gripped the bulb moved with it of course, turning the bulb a little in its socket.

"That will do." The girl stepped back. Iveria's wife said to me, "Try it now."

I jerked the chain pull. The bulb failed to light up.

She looked at me animatedly, hopefully.

"Very interesting," I said dryly. "You were pretty sure it would happen just that way, though, weren't you?"

I saw the hopefulness ebb out of her face little by little; her former listless resignation came back. "Oh, I see," she said quietly, "I'm supposed to have rehearsed her to do it just that way—" She stood up, smiling wanly. "Will you excuse me for a moment? You'll want to question her alone, I'm sure. And even if she tells you I haven't coached her about this lamp at all, you won't believe I didn't anyway. There isn't really anything I can do or say. Arnold has won; he won in life, and now he's won in death."

She opened the marred mirror panel, stepped through to her own room, closed it behind her.

I said to the maid, "Do you always dust off lamps that vigorously?"

She looked undecided for a moment, finally snickered, confessed, "Only when someone's around to see. When no one's around—" She flicked the edge of her cloth at the lampshade and back to show me.

"Tell Mrs. Iveria I'd like to see her again, if she doesn't mind." The girl opened the door, went in there after her, closed it again.

I creased my eyes dissatisfiedly to myself. Every new fact that appeared on one side of the ledger, brought its corollary with it on the opposite side. To a chartered accountant it might have been heaven, to a detective it was hell.

I wondered why she was taking so long to come out. I crossed to the mirror, threw it open without waiting, even though it led to a lady's room. You couldn't knock on the thing any more without risking bringing the rest of the glass down out of its frame.

I didn't see them for a minute; they were over on the side of the room screened by the door, engaged in a breathless, utterly silent, almost motionless hand-to-hand deadlock over a winking little gun—I suppose the one she had taken from him the night of the accident.

I jumped in at them, caught the wrist holding it, turned the skin cruelly around. She dropped it and I caught it in my open palm. The maid stepped back, began to snivel.

I said, "Why didn't you call me, you little fool!"

"I did call you," she snuffled. "Pity you wouldn't come in and find out what was the matter!"

I pocketed the revolver, said to the girl, "We don't need you any more." And to Iveria's wife, "Come on downstairs." She followed me, white as a ghost but calm now once more.

"Do we go now?" she asked at the foot of the stairs.

"You don't suppose I'm going to leave you behind out here, after what you just tried to do."

"That was a momentary impulse. It won't happen again. It wouldn't be fair to Streak, I see that now. It would be giving Arnold his victory too cheaply."

We'd gone back to the room in which I'd first spoken to her.

"Sit down," I said curtly. "Give yourself time to quiet down first."

She looked at me hopelessly. "Is there anything I can do or say that will make you believe me? I had nothing to do with Arnold's death."

I didn't answer—which was answer enough.

"I don't suppose you believe that, do you?" I didn't answer. "You're positive that I meant to kill Arnold, aren't you?" I didn't answer. "He saw to it that you would be. He went to you and told you the story, didn't he? Told it his way."

I didn't see any point in denying that; it was self-evident, by the mere fact of my being here. "Yes, he did."

She let her head slowly droop forward, as if in admission of irretrievable defeat. But then she raised it again a moment afterwards, refusing the admission. "May I have the same privilege? May I tell the *same* story my way?"

"You're going to have that privilege anyway, when the time comes."

"But don't you see it'll be too late by then? Don't you see this is a special case? The mere accusation in itself is tantamount to a conviction. One wisp of smoke, and the damage has been done. Streak and I can never live it down again—not if every court in the land finds insufficient evidence to convict us. That's what he wanted, don't you see? To blast the two of us—"

"But I'm just a detective; I'm not a judge or State's attorney—"

"But he only told it to *you*, no one else at the time—"

This did get a rise out of me. "How do you know that?" I said sharply.

"Dr. Drake showed me the dying message he had them take down; it had your name on it—'Burke'—it was addressed to you personally, no one else. It was easy to see he'd made you the sole repository of his confidences—until the time came to shout the charges from the roof tops. The evidence was too nebulous, there was no other way in which to do it."

"Tell it, then," I assented.

She didn't thank me or brighten up; she seemed to know it would be hopeless ahead of time. She smiled wanly. "I'm sure the external details are going to be the same. He was far too clever to have changed them. He selected and presented each and every one of them so that I cannot deny them—on a witness stand for instance—unless I perjure myself. It's their inner meaning—or rather, the *slant* of the story—that he distorted."

I just sat and waited, noncommittal. I'd been through this once before. Now I was going to get it a second time. But make no mistake, I wanted to hear it. Just to see what she could do with it.

"I met Arnold in St. Moritz, and I felt vaguely sorry for him. Pity is a dangerous thing, you so often mistake it for love. No one told me what was the matter with him."

Here was the first discrepancy. He'd said she knew ahead of time. But he'd said he had *documents* to prove it.

"He proposed to me by letter, from hotel to hotel—although we were both at the same resort. He used the word 'hemophilia' in one of them, said he knew he had no right to ask me to be his wife— I'm not a medical student. I'd never heard the word before. I thought it was some minor thing, like low blood pressure or anemia. I felt the matter was too confidential to ask anyone; after all, the letter was a declaration of love. I wrote back, using the strange word myself; I said it didn't matter, I thought enough of him to marry him whether he was in good health or poor health.

"By the time I actually found out, it was too late. We'd already been married eight months. I stick to my bargains; I didn't welsh. I was married to a ghost. That was all right. But then I met Streak and—I found out my heart was still single. I went to Arnold and I said, 'Now let me go.' He just smiled. And then I saw I hadn't married any ghost, I'd married a devil.

"You don't know what torture really is, the mental kind. You may have beaten up suspects at times. You don't know what it is to have someone hiss at you three times a day: 'You wish I was dead, don't you?' Until finally you *do* wish they were dead.

"We didn't want a cheap undercover affair. If that was all we'd wanted, it could have been arranged. Streak was born decent, and so was I. He wanted to be my husband and I wanted to be his wife. We were meant for each other, and this ghost had to be in the way, this specter.

"Finally I couldn't stand it any more. I said, 'It would be so easy; why should we go on letting him do this to us?' Streak said, 'Don't talk that way. We don't want to get together by building a bridge over someone's dead body.' Streak's not a murderer. Streak's out of this entirely."

Which didn't prove a thing, except how much she loved him.

"They say the female of the species is more deadly than the male. I toyed with the idea. I let it grow on me. Finally it took hold, became decision. Arnold wouldn't give me a chance to change my mind, he kept it at boiling point himself.

"Streak came around in his car, to see if he couldn't win Arnold over by having a man-to-man talk with him alone. I knew he didn't have a chance, I knew what a venomous, diseased mind he was up against. *I* was the one loosened the clamps on that windshield, with a little screwdriver, while they were both inside the house. But it missed fire.

"I tried in one or two other ways. And then suddenly I came back to my senses. I saw what it was I'd been trying to do all those weeks and months. Take away someone's life. Murder. No matter what a fiend he was, no matter how he'd made us suffer, I saw that that was no solution. I'd only have it on my conscience forever after. Dead, he would keep me and Streak apart far more effectively than he had when alive.

"It's ironic, isn't it? When I wanted to kill him, nothing I tried would work. Then suddenly, after I'd stopped trying, he goes off—" she snapped her thumbnail "—like that!"

I said, "D'you realize what you've just been saying? What you've just admitted? That you actually *did* try to murder him several times without succeeding. And now you want me to believe that this last time, that finally did succeed, it wasn't you but an accident!"

"Yes, you've got to—because it's true! I could have denied that I ever had such an idea altogether. But I don't want to mix part truth and part falsehood. What I've told you is *all* truth from beginning to end, and I want you to believe it. I did intend killing him, I did try; then I changed my mind, gave up the idea, and an accident for which I was not responsible took his life.

"All right, now you've heard my side of it, as well as his. If you want me to go with you, I'm ready to go with you. Only think well what you're doing, because once the damage is done, there's no undoing it."

"Suppose I go back to town now without doing anything—for the present. Say just overnight. What will you do?"

"Wait here—hoping, praying a little, maybe—until I hear from you."

"How do I know that?"

"Where can I go? Running away won't help; it'll just fasten guilt on me. It'll just bring on the ignominy *he* wanted Streak and me to suffer, all the faster. If we were going to run away now, we could have run away while he was still alive."

She was right about that, of course. I speared my finger at her. "Then wait here in this house until you hear from me. Consider yourself in the custody of your own conscience. I'm going back to town now, alone. I want to think this whole thing out—by myself, away from here. I can't think clearly when I'm this close to you. You're very beautiful, you know. I'm a human being, I'm capable of making a mistake, and I don't want to make a mistake. As undeniably as you are beautiful, Iveria is just as undeniably dead."

"It's going to be awful," she said, "to have it hang suspended over my head like that. Will it be very long before I know?"

"As soon as I know myself; sometime tomorrow maybe. Don't leave the house. If the doorbell rings, and you see me standing out there—you'll know I've come to take you back to face a charge of murder. If the telephone rings—that means you're in the clear, it's over, you can forget all about it."

Crawley looked in at me at midnight on his way out, said, "What's the matter, haven't you any home?"

I motioned him on his way. "I'm trying to think something out," I said. "I'm going to sit here if it takes all night."

I had the deposition on the table in front of me, and the cigarette case, and the deathbed note he'd left for me. It all balanced so damnably even, his side and hers. Check and double-check. Which was the true one, which the false?

The crux of the whole thing was that final incident. That was where my dilemma lay. If it was murder, Iveria's death demanded reparation. If it was an accident, then it proved him the devil she claimed him to be, for he himself must certainly have known it to be an accident, yet before he died he deliberately phoned me from the hospital and dictated that deathbed message emphasizing that it was murder, in order to fasten the guilt on her inextricably, wreak a lifelong revenge on her in that way after he was gone.

I reviewed the whole case from start to finish. He had walked in to us at headquarters and left an affidavit in my hands telling me he expected his wife to kill him, in the guise of a trivial accident; telling me he would say "This is it" when it happened, if she had. He'd had a trivial accident and he'd said "This is it" before he died. I went out to question her and I found her dancing for joy in the presence of the man she loved. She admitted she had tried to kill Iveria several times in the past. She denied she had tried to kill him this last time. But—*she had tried to bribe me* not to pursue the investigation any further. What was the evidence? A bedside bulb loosened a little in its socket so it wouldn't light, a hassock misplaced from where it belonged.

She had left me, as if overwhelmed by this gossamer evidence, that was no evidence at all. She didn't come back. I sent the maid after her. I went in there and I found the two of them grappling in desperate silence over a gun she had tried to use on herself. As a guilty person who felt that she had been found out might have. Or an innocent person who despaired of ever satisfactorily clearing herself. I calmed her down, listened to her side of the story, and finally left to think it over alone, telling her I would let her know my decision by coming back for her (guilty) or telephoning (exonerated).

And here I was.

And I'd finally reached one. Even though the scales remained as evenly balanced and counterbalanced as ever, to the last hairbreadth milligram. One little grain more had fallen on one side than on the other, I found when I'd concluded my review.

In the cold, early daylight peering into the office I picked up the phone and asked the sleepy headquarters operator to get me the number of the Iveria house up there in the country, where she was waiting to know.

I hadn't heard the maid call out, from that adjoining room, and I had been fully awake. But *he* claimed he had heard his wife cry out in there, and he was supposedly asleep.

No; he had actually been on his way in there at the time, gun in hand, to take *her* life, when a combination of unexpected little mischances turned the tables on him.

I ALWAYS GET THE CUTIES

JOHN D. MACDONALD

Of the many praises that have been heaped on John D. MacDonald, perhaps the most laudatory is the label of "consummate storyteller of our time." He has written (and written well) almost every imaginable type of fiction, from pulp sports yarns to literary exercises for the slicks; from softcover suspense novels to large-scale bestsellers such as Condominium *and* One More Sunday. *And, of course, he is the creator of Travis McGee, whose last few adventures—the most recent of them being* The Lonely Silver Rain *(1985)—have also been bestsellers. A number of his crime stories have featured police officers, never more successfully than in "I Always Get the Cuties"—a Hugoesque tale of a relentless cop named Keegan whose particular meat is "the amateurs who think they can bring off a nice clean safe murder."*

Keegan came into my apartment, frosted with winter, topcoat open, hat jammed on the back of his hard skull, bringing a noisy smell of the dark city night. He stood in front of my birch fire, his great legs planted, clapping and rubbing hard palms in the heat.

He grinned at me and winked one narrow gray eye. "I'm off duty, Doc. I wrapped up a package. A pretty package."

"Will bourbon do, Keegan?"

"If you haven't got any of that brandy left. This is a brandy night."

When I came back with the bottle and the glasses, he had stripped off his topcoat and tossed it on the couch. The crumpled hat was on the floor, near the discarded coat. Keegan had yanked a chair closer to the fire. He sprawled on the end of his spine, thick ankles crossed, the soles of his shoes steaming.

I poured his brandy and mine, and moved my chair and the long coffee table so we could share either end of it. His story was bursting in him. I knew that. I've only had the vaguest hints about his home life. A house crowded with teen-age daughters, cluttered with their swains. Obviously no place to talk of his dark victories. And Keegan is not the sort of man to regale his co-workers with talk of his prowess. So I am, among other things, his sounding board. He bounces successes off the politeness of my listening, growing big in the echo of them.

"Ever try to haggle with a car dealer, Doc?" he asked.

"In a mild way."

"You are a mild guy. I tried once. Know what he told me? He said, 'Lieutenant, you try to make a car deal maybe once every two years. Me, I make ten a day. So what chance have you got?' "

This was a more oblique approach than Keegan generally used. I became attentive.

"It's the same with the cuties, Doc—the amateurs who think they can bring off one nice clean safe murder. Give me a cutie every time. I eat 'em alive. The pros are trouble. The cuties leave holes you can drive diesels through. This one was that woman back in October. At that cabin at Bear Paw Lake. What do you remember about it, Doc?"

I am always forced to summarize. It has got me into the habit of reading the crime news. I never used to.

"As I remember, Keegan, they thought she had been killed by a prowler. Her husband returned from a business trip and found the body. She had been dead approximately two weeks. Because it was the off season, the neighboring camps weren't occupied, and the people in the village thought she had gone back to the city. She had been strangled, I believe."

"Okay. So I'll fill you in on it. Then you'll see the problem I had. The name was Grosswalk. Cynthia and Harold. He met her ten years ago when he was in med. school. He was twenty-four and she was thirty. She was loaded. He married her and he never went back to med. school. He didn't do anything for maybe five, six years. Then he gets a job selling medical supplies, surgical instruments, that kind of stuff. Whenever a wife is dead, Doc, the first thing I do is check on how they were getting along. I guess you know that."

"Your standard procedure," I said.

"Sure, So I check. They got a nice house here in the city. Not many friends. But they got neighbors with ears. There are lots of brawls. I get the idea it is about money. The money is hers—was hers, I should say. I put it up to this Grosswalk. He says okay, so they weren't getting along so good, so what? I'm supposed to be finding out who killed her, sort of coordinating with the State Police, not digging into his home life. I tell him he is a nice suspect. He already knows that. He says he didn't kill her. Then he adds one thing too many. He says he couldn't have killed her. That's all he will say. Playing it cute. You understand. I eat those cuties alive."

He waved his empty glass. I went over and refilled it.

"You see what he was doing to me, Doc. He was leaving it up to me to prove how it was he couldn't have killed her. A reverse twist. That isn't too tough. I get in touch with the sales manager of the company. Like I thought, the salesmen have to make reports. He was making a western swing. It would be no big trick to fly back and sneak into the camp and kill her, take some money and junk to make it look good, and then fly back out there and pick up where he left off. She was killed on maybe the tenth of October, the medical examiner says. Then he finds her on the twenty-fourth. But the sales manager tells me something that needs a lot of checking. He says that this Grosswalk took sick out west on the eighth and went into a hospital, and he was in that hospital from the eighth to the fifteenth, a full seven days. He gave me the name of the hospital. Now you see how the cutie made his mistake. He could have told me that easy enough. No, he has to be cute. I figure that if he's innocent he would have told me. But he's so proud of whatever gimmick he rigged for me that he's got to let me find out the hard way."

"I suppose you went out there," I said.

"It took a lot of talk. They don't like spending money for things like that. They kept telling me I should ask the L.A. cops to check because that's a good force out there. Finally I have to go by bus, or pay the difference. So I go by bus. I found the doctor. Plural— doctors. It is a clinic deal, sort of, that this Grosswalk went to. He gives them his symptoms. They say it looks to them like the edge of a nervous breakdown just beginning to show. With maybe some organic complications. So they run him through the course. Seven days of tests and checks and observations. They tell me he was there, that he didn't leave, that he *couldn't* have left. But naturally I check the hospital. They reserve part of one floor for patients from the clinic. I talked to the head nurse on that floor, and to the nurse that had the most to do with Grosswalk. She showed me the schedule and charts. Every day, every night, they were fooling around with the guy, giving him injections of this and that. He couldn't have got out. The people at the clinic told me the results. He was okay. The rest had helped him a lot. They told him to slow down. They gave him a prescription for a mild sedative. Nothing organically wrong, even though the symptoms seemed to point that way."

"So the trip was wasted?"

"Not entirely. Because on a hunch I ask if he had visitors. They keep a register. A girl came to see him as often as the rules permitted. They said she was pretty. Her name was Mary MacCarney. The address is there. So I go and see her. She lives with her folks. A real tasty kid. Nineteen. Her folks think this Grosswalk is too old for her. She is tall, Irish, all black and white and blue. It was warm and we sat on the porch. I soon find out this Grosswalk has been feeding her a line, telling her that his wife is an incurable invalid not long for this world, that he can't stand hurting her by asking for a divorce, that it is better to wait, and anyway, she says, her parents might approve of a widower, but never a guy who has been divorced. She has heard from Grosswalk that his wife has been murdered by a prowler and he will be out to see her as soon as he can. He has known her for a year. But, of course, I have told him not to leave town. I tell her not to get her hopes too high because it begins to look to me like this Grosswalk has knocked off his wife. Things get pretty hysterical, and her old lady gets in on it, and even driving away in the cab I can hear the old lady yelling at her.

"The first thing I do on getting back is check with the doctor who took care of Mrs. Grosswalk, and he says, as I thought he would, that she was as healthy as a horse. So I go back up to that camp and unlock it again. It is a snug place, Doc. Built so you could spend the winter there if you wanted to. Insulated and sealed, with a big fuel-oil furnace and modern kitchen equipment and so on. It was aired out a lot better than the first time I was in it. Grosswalk stated that he hadn't touched a thing. He said it was unlocked. He saw her and backed right out and went to report it. And the only thing touched had been the body.

"I poked around. This time I took my time. She was a tidy woman. There are twin beds. One is turned down. There is a very fancy nightgown laid out. That is a thing which bothered me. I looked at her other stuff. She has pajamas which are the right thing for October at the lake. They are made from that flannel stuff. There is only one other fancy nightgown, way in the back of a drawer. I have found out here in the city that she is not the type to fool around. So how come a woman who is alone wants to sleep so pretty? Because the husband is coming back from a trip. But he couldn't have come back from the trip. I find another thing. I find deep ruts off in the brush beside the camp. The first time I went there, her car was parked in back. Now it is gone. If the car was run off where those ruts were, anybody coming to the door wouldn't see it. If the door was locked, they wouldn't even knock maybe, knowing she wouldn't be home. That puzzles me. She might do it if she didn't want company. I prowl some more. I look in the deep freeze. It is well stocked. No need to buy stuff for a hell of a while. The refrigerator is the same way. And the electric is still on."

He leaned back and looked at me expectantly.

"Is that all you had to go on?" I asked.

"A murder happens here and the murderer is in Los Angeles at the time. I got him because he tried to be a cutie. Want to take a try, Doc?"

I knew I had to make an attempt. "Some sort of device?"

"To strangle a woman? Mechanical hands? You're getting too fancy, Doc."

"Then he hired somebody to do it?"

"There are guys you can hire, but they like guns. Or a piece of pipe in an alley. I don't know where you'd go to hire a strangler. He did it himself, Doc."

"Frankly, Keegan, I don't see how he could have."

"Well, I'll tell you how I went after it. I went to the medical examiner and we had a little talk. Cop logic, Doc. If the geography is wrong, then maybe you got the wrong idea on timing. But the medico checks it out. He says definitely the woman has been dead twelve days to two weeks when he makes the examination. I ask him how he knows. He says because of the extent of decomposition of the body. I ask him if that is a constant. He says no—you use a formula. A sort of rule-of-thumb formula. I ask him the factors. He says cause of death, temperature, humidity, physical characteristics of the body, how it was clothed, whether or not insects could have got to it, and so on.

"By then I had it, Doc. It was cute. I went back to the camp and looked around. It took me some time to find them. You never find a camp without them. Candles. They were in a drawer in the kitchen. Funny-looking candles, Doc. Melted down, sort of. A flat side against the bottom of the drawer, and all hardened again. Then I had another idea. I checked the stove burners. I found some pieces of burned flaked metal down under the heating elements.

"Then it was easy. I had this Grosswalk brought in again. I let him sit in a cell for four hours and get nervous before I took the rookie cop in. I'd coached that rookie for an hour, so he did it right. I had him dressed in a leather jacket and work pants. I make him repeat his story in front of Grosswalk. 'I bought a chain saw last year,' he says, acting sort of confused, 'and I was going around to the camps where there are people and I was trying to get some work cutting up fireplace wood. So I called on Mrs. Grosswalk. She didn't want any wood, but she was nice about it.' I ask the rookie when that was. He scratches his head and says, 'Sometime around the seventeenth, I think it was.' That's where I had to be careful. I couldn't let him be positive about the date. I say she was supposed to be dead a week by then and was he sure it was her. 'She wasn't dead then. I know her. I'd seen her in the village. A kind of heavy-set woman with blonde hair. It was her all right, Lieutenant.' I asked him was he sure of the date and he said yes, around the seventeenth like he said, but he could check his records and find the exact day.

"I told him to take off. I just watched that cutie and saw him come apart. Then he gave it to me. He killed her on the sixteenth, the day he got out of the hospital. He flew into Omaha. By then I've got the stenographer taking it down. Grosswalk talks, staring at the floor, like he was talking to himself. It was going to be a dry run. He wasn't going to do it if she'd been here in the city or into the village in the previous seven days. But, once she got in the camp, she seldom went out, and the odds were all against any callers. On his previous trip to Omaha he had bought a jalopy that would run. It would make the fifty miles to the lake all right. He took the car off the lot where he'd left it and drove to the lake. She was surprised to see him back ahead of schedule. He explained the company car was being fixed. He questioned her. Finally she said she hadn't seen or talked to a living soul in ten days. Then he knew he was set to take the risk.

"He grabbed her neck and hung on until she was dead. He had his shoulders hunched right up around his ears when he said that. It was evening when he killed her, nearly bedtime. First he closed every window. Then he turned on the furnace as high as it would go. There was plenty of oil in the tank. He left the oven door open and the oven turned as high as it would go. He even built a fire in the fireplace, knowing it would be burned out by morning and there wouldn't be any smoke. He filled the biggest pans of water he could find and left them on the top of the stove. He took the money and some of her jewelry, turned out the lights, and locked the doors. He ran her car off in the brush where nobody would be likely to see it. He said by the time he left the house it was like an oven in there.

"He drove the jalopy back to Omaha, parked it back in the lot, and caught an eleven-fifteen flight to Los Angeles. The next morning he was making calls. And keeping his fingers crossed. He worked his way east. He got to the camp on the twenty-fourth—about ten in the morning. He said he went in and turned things off and opened up every window, and then went out and was sick. He waited nearly an hour before going back in. It was nearly down to normal temperature. He checked the house. He noticed she had turned down both beds before he killed her. He remade his. The water had boiled out of the pans and the bottoms had burned through. He scaled the pans out into the lake. He said he tried not to look at her, but he couldn't help it. He had enough medical background to know that it had worked, and also to fake his own illness in L. A. He went out and was sick again, and then he got her car back where it belonged. He closed most of the windows. He made another inspection trip and then drove into the village. He was a cutie, Doc, and I ate him alive."

There was a long silence. I knew what was expected of me. But I had my usual curious reluctance to please him. He held the glass cradled in his hand, gazing with a half smile into the dying fire. His face looked like stone.

"That was very intelligent, Keegan," I said.

"The pros give you real trouble, Doc. The cuties always leave holes. I couldn't bust geography, so I had to bust time." He yawned massively and stood up. "Read all about it in the morning paper, Doc."

"I'll certainly do that."

I held his coat for him. He's a big man. I had to reach up to get it properly onto his shoulders. He mashed the hat onto his head as I walked to the door with him. He put his big hand on the knob, turned, and smiled down at me without mirth.

"I always get the cuties, Doc. Always."

"You certainly seem to," I said.

"They are my favorite meat."

"So I understand."

He balled one big fist and pumped it lightly against my chin, still grinning at me. "And I'm going to get you too, Doc. You know that. You were cute. You're just taking longer than most. But you know how it's going to come out, don't you?"

I don't answer that anymore. There's nothing to say. There hasn't been anything to say for a long time now.

He left, walking hard into the wild night. I sat and looked into my fire. I could hear the wind. I reached for the bottle. The wind raged over the city, as monstrous and inevitable as Keegan. It seemed as though it was looking for food—the way Keegan is always doing.

But I no longer permit myself the luxury of imagination.

H AS IN HOMICIDE

LAWRENCE TREAT

Lawrence Treat's first novel featuring the talents of homicide cop Mitch Taylor, V as in Victim *(1945), was hailed by critic Anthony Boucher as marking "a fresh, new, realistic approach to police procedure." The novels and stories about Taylor (and his co-workers Jub Freeman and Bill Decker) which followed over the next twenty-five years have borne out Boucher's assessment and firmly established Treat as a pathfinder in the modern, realistic approach to police fiction. "H as in Homicide" is arguably the finest of all of Mitch Taylor's cases, an opinion shared by Treat's peers in the Mystery Writers of America, who awarded it an Edgar as the Best Short Story of 1964.*

She came through the door of the homicide squad's outer office as if it were disgrace to be there, as if she didn't like it, as if she hadn't done anything wrong—and never could or would.

Still, here she was. About twenty-two years old and underweight. Wearing a pink sleeveless dress. She had dark hair pulled back in a bun; her breasts were close together; and her eyes ate you up.

Mitch Taylor had just come back from lunch and was holding down the fort all alone. He nodded at her and said, "Anything I can do?"

"Yes. I—I—" Mitch put her down as a nervous stutterer and waited for her to settle down. "They told me to come here," she said. "I went to the neighborhood police station and they said they couldn't do anything, that I had to come here."

"Yeah," Mitch said. It was the old runaround, and he was willing to bet this was Pulasky's doing, up in the Third Precinct. He never took a complaint unless the rule book said, "You, Pulasky—you got to handle this or you'll lose your pension."

So Mitch said, "Sure. What's the trouble?"

"I don't like to bother you and I hope you don't think I'm silly, but—well, my friend left me. And I don't know where or why."

"Boyfriend?" Mitch said.

She blushed a deep crimson. "Oh, no! A real *friend*. We were traveling together, and she took the car and went, without even leaving me a note. I can't understand it."

"Let's go inside and get the details," Mitch said.

He brought her into the squad room and sat her down at a desk. She looked up shyly, sort of impressed with him. He didn't know why, because he was only an average-looking guy, of medium height, on the cocky side, with stiff, wiry hair and a face nobody remembered, particularly.

He sat down opposite her and took out a pad and pencil. "Your name?" he said.

"Prudence Gilford."

"Address?"

"New York City, but I gave up my apartment there."

"Where I come from too. Quite a ways from home, aren't you?"

"I'm on my way to California—my sister lives out there. I answered an ad in the paper—just a moment, I think I still have it." She fumbled in a big canvas bag, and the strap broke off and the whole business dropped. She picked it up awkwardly, blushing again, but she kept on talking. "Bella Tansey advertised for somebody to share the driving to California. She said she'd pay all expenses. It was a wonderful chance for me. . . . Here, I have it."

She took out the clipping and handed it to Mitch. It was the usual thing: woman companion to share the driving and a phone number.

"So you got in touch?" Mitch prodded.

"Yes. We liked each other immediately and arranged to go the following week."

She was fiddling with the strap, trying to fix it, and she finally fitted the tab over some kind of button. Mitch, watching, wondered how long *that* was going to last.

Meanwhile she was still telling him about Bella Tansey. "We got along so well," Prudence said, "and last night we stopped at a motel—The Happy Inn, it's called—and we went to bed. When I woke up, she was gone."

"Why did you stop there?" Mitch asked sharply.

"We were tired and it had a vacancy sign." She drew in her breath and asked anxiously, "Is there something wrong with it?"

"Not too good a reputation," Mitch said. "Did she take all her things with her? Her overnight stuff, I mean."

"Yes, I think so. Or at least, she took her bag."

Mitch got a description of the car: a dark blue Buick; 1959 or 1960, she wasn't sure; New York plates, but she didn't know the number.

"Okay," Mitch said. "We'll check. We'll send out a flier and have her picked up and find out why she left in such a hurry."

Prudence Gilford's eyes got big. "Yes," she said. "And please, can you help me? I have only five dollars and the motel is expensive. I can't stay there and I don't know where to go."

"Leave it to me," Mitch said. "I'll fix it up at the motel and get you a place in town for a while. You can get some money, can't you?"

"Oh, yes. I'll write my sister for it."

"Better wire," Mitch said. "And will you wait here a couple of minutes? I'll be right back."

"Of course."

Lieutenant Decker had come in and was working on something in his tiny office, which was jammed up with papers and stuff. Mitch reported on the Gilford business and the lieutenant listened.

"Pulasky should have handled it," Mitch said, finishing up. "But what the hell—the kid's left high and dry, so maybe we could give her a little help."

"What do you think's behind this?" Decker asked.

"I don't know," Mitch said. "She's a clinger—scared of everything and leans on people. Maybe the Tansey woman got sick and tired of her, or maybe this is lesbian stuff. Hard to tell."

"Well, go ahead with an S-4 for the Buick. It ought to be on a main highway and within a five-hundred-mile radius. Somebody'll spot it. We'll see what cooks."

Mitch drove Prudence out to the motel and told her to get her things. While she was busy, he went into the office and spoke to Ed Hiller, who ran the joint. Hiller, a tall, stoop-shouldered guy who'd been in and out of jams most of his life, was interested in anything from a nickel up, but chiefly up. He rented cabins by the hour, day, or week, and you could get liquor if you paid the freight; but most of his trouble came from reports of cars that had been left unlocked and rifled. The police had never been able to pin anything on him.

He said, "Hello, Taylor. Anything wrong?"

"Just want to know about a couple of dames that stayed here last night—Bella Tansey and Prudence Gilford. Tansey pulled out during the night."

"Around midnight," Ed said. "She came into the office to make a phone call, and a little later I heard her car pull out."

Time for the missing girl to pack, Mitch decided. So far, everything checked. "Who'd she call?" he asked. "What did she say?"

Hiller shrugged. "I don't listen in," he said. "I saw her open the door and then I heard her go into the phone booth. I mind my own business. You know that."

"Yeah," Mitch said flatly. "You heard the coins drop, didn't you? Local call or long distance?"

Hiller leaned over the counter. "Local," he said softly. "I think."

"Got their registration?" Mitch asked. Hiller nodded and handed Mitch the sheet, which had a record of the New York license plates.

That was about all there was to it. Nobody picked up Bella Tansey and her Buick, Prudence Gilford was socked away in a rooming house in town, and Mitch never expected to see her again.

When he got home that night, Amy kissed him and asked him about things, and then after he'd horsed around with the kids a little, she showed him a letter from her sister. Her sister's husband was on strike, and what the union paid them took care of food and rent and that was about all; but they had to keep up their payments on the car and the new dishwasher, and the TV had broken down again, and could Mitch and Amy help out for a little while—they'd get it back soon.

So after the kids were in bed, Mitch and Amy sat down on the sofa to figure things out, which took about two seconds and came to fifty bucks out of his next paycheck. It was always like that with the two of them: they saw things the same way and never had any arguments. Not many guys were as lucky as Mitch.

The next morning Decker had his usual conference with the homicide squad and went over all the cases they had in the shop. The only thing he said about the Gilford business was the next time

Pulasky tried to sucker them, figure it out so he had to come down here, personally, and then make him sweat.

Mitch drew a couple of minor assault cases to investigate, and he'd finished up with one and was on his way to the other when the call came in on his radio. Go out to French Woods, on East Road. They had a homicide, and it looked like the missing Tansey woman.

He found a couple of police cars and an oil truck and the usual bunch of snoopers who had stopped out of curiosity. There was a kind of rough trail going into the woods. A couple of hundred yards in, the lieutenant and a few of the boys and Jub Freeman, the lab technician, were grouped around a dark blue car. It didn't take any heavy brainwork to decide it was the Tansey Buick.

When Mitch got to the car, he saw Bella Tansey slumped in the front seat with her head resting against the window. The right-hand door was open and so was the glove compartment, and Decker was looking at the stuff he'd found there.

He gave Mitch the main facts. "Truck driver spotted the car, went in to look, and then got in touch with us. We've been here about fifteen minutes, and the medical examiner ought to show up pretty soon. She was strangled—you can see the marks on her neck—and I'll bet a green hat that it happened the night before last, not long after she left the motel."

Mitch surveyed the position of the body with a practiced eye. "She wasn't driving, either. She was pushed in there, after she was dead."

"Check," Decker said. Very carefully, so that he wouldn't spoil any possible fingerprints, he slid the junk he'd been examining onto the front seat. He turned to Jub Freeman, who was delicately holding a handbag by the two ends and scrutinizing it for prints.

"Find anything?" the lieutenant asked.

"Nothing," Jub said. "But the initials on it are B.T.W."

"Bella Tansey What?" the lieutenant said. He didn't laugh and neither did anybody else. He stooped to put his hands on the doorsill, leaned forward, and stared at the body. Mitch, standing behind him, peered over his head.

Bella had been around thirty and she'd been made for men. She was wearing a blue dress with a thing that Amy called a bolero top, and, except where the skirt had pulled up maybe from moving the body, her clothes were not disturbed. The door of the glove com-

partment and parts of the dashboard were splotched with fingerprint powder.

Mitch pulled back and waited. After about a minute the lieutenant stood up.

"Doesn't look as if there was a sex angle," Decker said. "And
this stuff"—he kicked at the dry leaves that covered the earth—
"doesn't take footprints. If we're lucky, we'll find somebody who
saw the killer somewhere around here." He made a smacking sound
with his thin, elastic lips and watched Jub.

Jub had taken off his coat and dumped the contents of the
pocketbook onto it. Mitch spotted nothing unusual—just the junk
women usually carried; but he didn't see any money. Jub was
holding the purse and rummaging inside it.

"Empty?" the lieutenant asked sharply.

Jub nodded. "Except for one nickel. She must have had money,
so whoever went through this missed up on five cents."

"Couldn't be Ed Hiller, then," Mitch said, and the gang laughed.

"Let's say the motive was robbery," Decker said. "We got something of a head start on this, but brother, it's a bad one. Why does
a woman on her way to California make a phone call and then
sneak off in the middle of the night? Leaving her girlfriend in the
lurch, too. Doesn't sound like robbery now, does it?"

"Sounds like a guy," Mitch said. "She had a late date, and the
guy robbed her, instead of —"

"We'll talk to Ed Hiller about that later," the lieutenant said.
"Taylor, you better get going on this. Call New York and get a line
on her. Her friends, her background. If she was married. How much
money she might have had with her. Her bank might help on that."

"Right," Mitch said.

"And then get hold of the Gilford dame and pump her," Decker
said.

Mitch nodded. He glanced into the back of the car and saw the
small overnight bag. "That," he said pointing. "She packed, so she
didn't expect to go back to the motel. But she didn't put her bag in
the trunk compartment, so she must have expected to check in
somewhere else, and pretty soon."

"She'd want to sleep somewhere, wouldn't she?" Decker asked.

"That packing and unpacking doesn't make sense," Mitch said.

Decker grunted. "Homicides never do," he said grimly.

Mitch drove back to headquarters thinking about that overnight bag, and it kept bothering him. He didn't know exactly why, but it was the sort of thing you kept in the back of your mind until something happened or you found something else, and then everything clicked and you got a pattern.

But what with organizing the questions to ask New York he couldn't do much doping out right now. Besides, there was a lot more information to come.

He got New York on the phone and they said they'd move on it right away; so he hung up and went to see Prudence. He was lucky to find her in.

She was shocked at the news, but she had nothing much to contribute. "We didn't know each other very long," she said, "and I was asleep when she left. I was so tired. We'd been driving all day, and I'd done most of it."

"Did she mention knowing anybody around—anybody in town?" Mitch asked. Prudence shook her head, but he put her through the wringer anyhow—it was easy for people to hear things and then forget them. You had to jog their memories a little. And besides, how could he be sure she was telling all she knew?

He felt sorry for her, though—she looked kind of thin and played out, as if she hadn't been eating much. So he said, "That five bucks of yours isn't going to last too long, and if you need some dough—"

"Oh, thanks!" she said, sort of glowing and making him feel that Mitch Taylor, he was okay. "Oh, thanks! It's perfectly wonderful of you, but I have enough for a while, and I'm sure my sister will send me the money I wired her for."

By that afternoon, most of the basic information was in. Locally, the medical examiner said that Bella Tansey had been strangled with a towel or a handkerchief; he placed the time as not long after she'd left the motel. The lieutenant had questioned Ed Hiller without being able to get anything "hot." Hiller insisted he hadn't left the motel, but his statement depended only on his own word.

Jub had used a vacuum cleaner on the car and examined the findings with a microscope, and he'd shot enough pictures to fill a couple of albums.

"They stopped at a United Motel the first night," he recapitulated, "and they had dinner at a Howard Johnson place. They ate sandwiches in the car, probably for lunch, and they bought gas in Pennsylvania and Indiana, and the car ate up oil. There was a gray kitten on the rear seat some time or other. They both drove. Bella Tansey had ear trouble, and she bought her clothes at Saks Fifth Avenue. I can tell you a lot more about her, but I'm damned if I've uncovered anything that will help on the homicide. No trace in that car of anybody except the two women."

The New York police, however, came up with a bombshell. Bella Tansey had drawn eighteen hundred dollars from her bank, in cash, and she'd been married to Clyde Warhouse and they'd been divorced two years ago. She'd used her maiden name—Tansey.

"Warhouse!" the lieutenant said.

Everybody knew that name. He ran a column in the local paper— he called it "Culture Corner"—and he covered art galleries, visiting orchestras, and egghead lectures. Whenever he had nothing else to write about, he complained how archaic the civic architecture was.

"That's why she had the W on her bag," Mitch said. "Bella Tansey Warhouse. And Ed Hiller didn't lie about the phone call. She made it, all right—to her ex-husband."

Decker nodded. "Let's say she hotfooted it out to see him. Let's say that she still had a yen for him and they scrapped, that he got mad and lost his head and strangled her. But why would he take her dough? She must've had around seventeen hundred with her. Why would he rob her?"

"Why not?" Mitch said. "It was there, wasn't it?"

"Let's think about this," Decker said. "Prudence says Bella unpacked. Did Bella start to go to bed, or what?"

"Prudence doesn't know," Mitch said. "I went into that for all it was worth, and Prudence *assumes* Bella unpacked—she can't actually remember. Says she was bushed and went right to sleep. Didn't even wash her face."

"Well," Decker said, "I guess Warhouse is wondering when we'll get around to him. I'll check on him while you go up there." The lieutenant's jaw set firmly. "Bring him in."

Mitch rolled his shoulders, tugged on the lapels of his jacket, and went out. The first time you hit your suspect, it could make or break the case.

Clyde Warhouse lived in a red brick house with tall white columns on the front. Mitch found him at home, in his study. He was a little guy with big teeth, and he didn't really smile; he just pulled his lips back, and you could take it any way you pleased.

Warhouse came right to the point. "You're here about my former wife," he said. "I just heard about it on the radio, and I wish I could give you some information, but I can't. It's certainly not the end I wished for her."

"What kind of end were you hoping for?" Mitch asked.

"None." The Warhouse lips curled back, telling you how smart he was. "And certainly not one in this town."

"Let's not kid around," Mitch said. "You're coming back with me. You know that, don't you?"

The guy almost went down with the first punch. "You mean— you mean I'm being arrested?"

"What do *you* think?" Mitch said. "We know she phoned you and you met her. We know you saw her."

"But I didn't see her," Warhouse said. "She never showed up." Mitch didn't even blink.

"How long did you wait?" he asked.

"Almost an hour. Maybe more."

"Where?"

"On the corner of Whitman and Cooper." Warhouse gasped, then put his head in his hands and said, "Oh, God!" And that was all Mitch could get out of him until they had him in the squad room, with Decker leading off on the interrogation.

The guy didn't back down from that first admission. He knew he'd been tricked, but he stuck to his guns and wouldn't give another inch. He said Bella had called him around midnight and said she must see him. He hadn't known she was in town, didn't want to see her, had no interest in her, but he couldn't turn her down. So he went, and he waited. And waited and waited. And then went home.

They kept hammering away at him. First Mitch and Decker, then Bankhart and Balenky, then Mitch and Decker again.

In between they consulted Jub. He'd been examining Warhouse's car for soil that might match samples from French Woods for evidence of a struggle, of Bella's presence—of anything at all. The examination drew a blank. Warhouse grinned his toothy grin and kept saying no. And late that night they gave up on him, brought him across the courtyard to the city jail, and left him there for the night. He needed sleep—and so did the homicide squad.

At the conference the next morning, Decker was grim. "We have an ex-wife calling her ex-husband at midnight and making an appointment; we have his statement that he went and she never showed up; and we have a homicide and that's all."

"The dough," Bankhart said.

Decker nodded. "When we find that seventeen hundred, then we might have a case. We'll get warrants and we'll look for it, but let's assume we draw another blank. Then what?"

"Let's have another session with Ed Hiller," Mitch said.

They had it, and they had a longer one with Warhouse, and they were still nowhere. They'd gone into the Warhouse background thoroughly. He earned good money, paid his bills promptly, and got along well with his second wife. He liked women, they went for him, and he was a humdinger with them, although he was not involved in any scandal. But in Mitch's book, he'd humdinged once too often. Still, you had to prove it.

For a while they concentrated on The Happy Inn. But the motel guests either couldn't be found, because they'd registered under fake names with fake license numbers, or else they said they'd been asleep and had no idea what was going on outside.

The usual tips came in—crank stuff that had to be followed up. The killer had been seen, somebody had heard Bella scream for help, somebody else had had a vision. Warhouse had been spotted waiting on the corner, which proved nothing except he'd arrived there first. Every tip checked out either as useless or a phony. The missing seventeen hundred dollars didn't show up. Decker ran out of jokes, and Mitch came home tired and irritable.

The case was at full stop.

Then Decker had this wild idea, and he told it to Jub and Mitch. "My wife says I woke up last night and asked for a drink of water, and I don't even remember it."

"So you were thirsty," Mitch remarked.

"Don't you get it?" Decker exclaimed. "People wake up, then go back to sleep, and in the morning they don't even know they were awake. Well, we know Bella packed her bag, and she was in that motel room with Prudence and must have made some noise and possibly even talked. I'll bet a pair of pink panties that Prudence woke up and then forgot all about it. She has a clue buried deep in her mind."

"Granted," Jub said, "but how are you going to dig it up?"

"I'll hypnotize her," Decker said, with fire in his eyes. "I'll ask a psychiatrist to get her to free-associate. Taylor, ask her to come in tomorrow morning, when my mind is fresh. And hers, too."

Mitch dropped in on Prudence and gave her the message, but the way he saw things, the lieutenant was sure reaching for it—far out. Mitch told Amy about this screwy idea of Decker's, but all she said was that tomorrow was payday and not to forget to send the fifty dollars to her sister.

That was why Mitch wasn't around when Prudence showed up. He took his money over to the post office and there, on account he liked to jaw a little, make friends, set up contacts—you never knew when you might need them—he got to gabbing with the postal clerk.

His name was Cornell and he was tired. Mitch figured the guy was born that way. Besides, there was something about a post office that dragged at you. No fun in it, nothing ever happened. All the stamps were the same (or looked the same) and all the clerks were the same (or looked the same) and if anything unusual came up, you checked it in the regulations and did what the rules said, exactly. And if the rules didn't tell you, then the thing couldn't be done, so you sent the customer away and went back to selling stamps.

Which people either wanted or they didn't. There were no sales, no bargains. A damaged stamp was never marked down—it was worth what it said on its face or nothing. There was nothing in between.

Still, the post office was a hell of a lot better than what Decker was doing over at the homicide squad, so Mitch handed in his fifty bucks for the money order and said, "It's not much dough, I guess. What's the most you ever handled?"

The clerk came alive. "Ten thousand dollars. Six years ago."

"The hell with six years ago. Say this week."

"Oh. That dame with seventeen hundred dollars. That was the biggest."

Click.

Mitch said cautiously, "You mean Prudence Gilford?"

"No. Patsy Grant."

"P.G.—same thing," Mitch said with certainty. "Same girl. And I'll bet she sent the dough to herself care of general delivery, somewhere in California."

Cornell looked as if he thought Mitch were some kind of magician. "That's right," he said. "How did you know?"

"Me?" Mitch said, seeing that it all fitted like a glove. Prudence—or whatever her name was—had strangled Bella for the dough, then packed Bella's bag, dragged her out to the car, driven it to the woods, and left it there. And probably walked all the way back. That's why Prudence had been so tired.

"Me?" Mitch said again, riding on a cloud. "I know those things. That's what makes me a cop. Ideas—I got bushels of 'em." He thought of how the lieutenant would go bug-eyed. Mitch Taylor, Homicide Expert.

He walked over to the phone booth, gave his shield number to the operator so he could make the call free and save himself a dime, and got through to the homicide squad.

Decker answered. "Taylor?" he said. "Come on back. The Gilford dame just confessed."

"She—*what?*"

"Yeah, yeah, confessed. While she was in here, the strap on her bag broke and she dropped it. Everything fell out—including seventeen money-order receipts for a hundred bucks apiece. We had her cold and she confessed. She knew all about Warhouse and planned it so we'd nail him."

There was a buzz on the wire and Lieutenant Decker's voice went fuzzy.

"Taylor," he said after a couple of seconds. "Can you hear me? Are you listening?"

"Sure," Mitch said. "But what for?"

And he hung up.

Yeah, Mitch Taylor, Homicide Expert.

NIGHT WORK

WILLIAM CAMPBELL GAULT

William Campbell Gault sold his first short story to a pulp magazine in 1936; nearly half a century later he is still writing fiction of the same high quality that has marked his long and prolific career, as such recent Walker mysteries as Death in Donegal Bay *and* Dead Seed *attest. In his fifty-year career he has published more than three hundred short stories and novelettes—mystery, fantasy, science fiction, sports—and some sixty novels, half of which are mystery/suspense and half of which are juvenile sports books. "Night Work," about a young patrolman on a personal quest for justice, is typical of Gault's crime fiction: sensitive, insightful, well-written, and peopled with believable characters and honest human emotion.*

He'd been on the force a year, now, and was doing all right. There'd been some doubt about him, at headquarters, but he'd scored high in his examination and there'd been a recommendation from a quarter the chief didn't like to ignore. He was young. And you shouldn't hold a young man's past against him.

So Joe Leeds, at twenty-three, was working for a little under three hundred a month, cost of living bonus, and all. He'd made ten times that in one night, over the felt, when he was twenty-one. But he didn't regret his decision to give up gambling and join the police force.

He liked his job. He patrolled the area between Hampton and Wright, between Adams and Chestnut. A residential area, almost suburban, and he was well liked in the neighborhood. It was good, the citizens said, to see a smiling cop for a change.

He liked the kids too, at the Wright Street School. Sassy, a lot of them, and they gave him a bad time occasionally. But they got along and when Joe stopped smiling and raised his voice they knew it was time to quit the nonsense. With the possible exception of Tommy Hart.

When the kids waited beside Joe at the Wright Street crossing for traffic to change, Tommy always had some fresh remarks to make.

"Let's go, let's go!" Tommy would call loudly. "How about stopping that traffic, Joe? Our lunch is getting cold. We haven't got all day." Then he'd dash ahead of the other kids, before Joe gave the word to go.

When traffic was finally stopped and the other kids trooped across obediently, Tommy would already be on the playground, throwing a football or a baseball or a snowball, as the season warranted.

Tommy's father had told Joe, "If Tommy gives you any trouble, take him across your knee. There are times when nothing else works with Tommy."

Joe Leeds decided that would be the last resort. Joe had a lot of regard for Tommy, despite the size of his mouth. He knew there'd be some way to get to the youngster, make a buddy of him.

He gave Tommy a long and serious talking to one afternoon and it seemed to score. Tommy took it quietly, with understanding in his blue eyes, and Tommy called him "Officer Leeds" when they parted. Things were going to be all right, Joe decided.

But the next morning, when he held the kids up for a line of cars, Tommy was the same as usual.

"All right, all right," Tommy called, "you want us to be late for school, Joe?"

Joe ignored him, decided to try another line of attack.

"Let's go, let's go," Tommy called. "We haven't got all day."

Joe said, "I'll see you after school, Tommy. We're going home to talk to your dad."

"He doesn't get home until six," Tommy said, grinning at him.

"All right. I'll be over after supper, then," Joe said. He stopped the traffic, and filed them across. . . .

At noon Tommy wasn't in the crowd of kids waiting at the curb. But as Joe waved them across the street, he saw Tommy coming slowly out of the school entrance.

Joe could see that the boy was worried as he came along the walk.

When he stopped in front of Joe, he looked up anxiously, said, "Can we make a deal, Joe?"

"Maybe," Joe said, his face expressionless.

"You don't come over after supper, and I'll stop acting up. How's that?"

"Sounds all right," Joe agreed. "You'll never say, 'Let's go, let's go' again? You'll never give me any backtalk?"

"Never," Tommy said.

Joe grinned at him. "Okay, Tommy, it's a deal. Now, scoot across!"

There was no traffic but Tommy looked both ways before he scooted.

He was halfway across when the Cadillac came gunning out of Adams, ignoring the stop sign, its tires screaming, its big motor roaring. Joe thought it was going to tip over; it curved so abruptly as it turned into Wright. He was hoping it would tip over because Tommy was in its path if it didn't.

Tommy froze there in the middle of the street, paralyzed by fright, unable to scream or run. Then the big car hit him.

There was a sickening thud as Tommy hurtled through the air. The car didn't stop, didn't even slow its pace. It was still accelerating as it disappeared around the corner a block up. Joe had caught the first two digits of its license plate only, for he tried to get a good look at the man behind the wheel also. But he got only a glimpse of a crouched, hatted figure and not even that much of the figure in the rear seat.

The car had hit Tommy hard, thrown him against the curb. Tommy Hart would never bother Joe again.

The chief said, "I can't see how anybody could assume you were negligent, Joe. Traffic was clear on Wright and the car should have stopped at the arterial. Your report's clear and absolves you completely."

"The kids are my responsibility," Joe said stubbornly. "And Tommy was a kind of special responsibility. I'm sure it was murder, sir."

"Manslaughter," the chief said. "Murder needs a motive, Joe. We've got the boys working on it. When we make the arrest, we'll throw the book at the driver. But that's not your province. You handle your beat and we'll handle the rest."

"But—"

The chief raised his hand. "That's an order, Joe. I respect your feeling about this, but that's an order."

They found there was no local Cadillac with a license number starting with 1-5. But they checked the stolen car list and discovered a set of missing plates with those first two digits. They'd been stolen from a car parked in dead storage at a west side garage.

It was out of Joe's province, as the chief had said, but Joe made a note of the garage's address.

That afternoon Les Gargan was found dead in his eight-room house on Adams. Gargan's wife had been away from home for a few days, and she'd found the body when she returned. There was a bullet hole through Les, and they dug the bullet out of the woodwork in the room where he lay.

That was two blocks from the corner of Wright and Adams. Joe had known Les well, had once won over two thousand dollars from him in one night of stud. Joe had liked Les, and he went to see his widow the night after the funeral.

She was a beautiful girl. June Wilson was her name when Les married her out of a featured spot in Tony Valentine's Revue. Tony was noted for the lovelies he picked.

She didn't seem too broken up over Gargan's death, or perhaps she was exercising admirable control. Control was one thing Tony insisted upon in his girls.

She told Joe, "Les and I weren't getting along too well. But it was a horrible shock to find him like that." She shuddered. Then she said, "Drink, Joe?"

"Scotch would be all right, with water," he said.

She mixed it and handed it to him. "You're looking fit."

It was after hours and he wasn't wearing the uniform. He was wearing a two-hundred-dollar suit and a twenty-dollar tie.

"I'm outdoors a lot," he said. "You know about any trouble Les was having?"

She was measuring out her own Scotch, and Joe judged it to be a triple jolt. Her hand was steady. "Trouble? Les was the kind of boy who made it a point to avoid trouble as much as possible." She took a sip of her drink, met Joe's gaze candidly.

"He was," Joe agreed. "Les never liked trouble. He must have left you pretty well fixed, June."

She smiled at him. "You're on the nosy side tonight, aren't you, Joe?"

"Sorry," he said. "I kind of liked Les. You were out of town when it happened, weren't you?"

She gazed at him for seconds without speaking. Then she said, "Look, Joe, I'm glad to see you. Or was. But you're making a noise like a cop. And I just happened to remember a silly rumor I heard some time ago."

"Rumor?"

"Mmmm-hmmm. Somebody said you'd joined the force."

"So? You've nothing to fear from the law, have you?"

"Not when a cop comes to me openly. You came as a friend, Joe."

"All right, now I'm coming as a cop. And a friend of that kid who was killed. And I'd like to know about Les's enemies."

She met his gaze evenly, her face suddenly hard. "He didn't have any."

"He must have had at least one," Joe said. He rose. "But I'm not here to heckle you. I expected your cooperation."

She looked thoughtful, appeared about to say something. Then her face resumed its hardness and she said, "Drop in any time, Joe." She walked to the door with him. "That is—as a friend."

At the door Joe told her, "It's always the smart ones who make the really dumb moves. You've come a long way from the chorus, June, just by using your head."

"And keeping my nose clean," she said. "Good-night, Joe."

He went down to his car, and she still stood on the porch, watching him. He had a hunch she could have helped him.

But she said nothing as he got into the car and drove off.

He went directly to the west side garage where the plates had been stolen. It was a long, one-story building on Hanover, with a set of pumps on the curb and fronted with plate-glass windows.

Joe had his badge with him, and he flashed it for the benefit of the lone night attendant, a youth of about twenty.

"I'd like to check your customer list," Joe told him.

"We haven't got any list," the boy said. "We've got a record of the people who park here, though, if that's any help."

"That'll do. And a list of your employees, including any who quit in the last month."

The youth looked at him suspiciously. "The police department's got all that."

Joe got tough. "Have they? Didn't the badge look official to you? You want another look at it?"

The youth said, "The records are in the office. Over here."

Joe followed him to a glassed-in corner of the garage. He sat at the desk while the attendant brought the books over, and the time cards.

There were no names in the books that rang any bells with him. Nor in the time cards. But it didn't seem logical that a stranger could come into an open garage like this and steal a set of plates.

He left the garage and drove downtown to Tony Valentine's theatre-restaurant on Fortieth Street, a better-than-average night spot with a huge neon heart above the entrance, over the name *Valentine's*.

Tony was in his office. He waved Joe to a chair and said, "It's been a long time, Joe." He was a short, stocky man with a square face.

"What do you know about June Gargan?" Joe asked.

"Good shape, good voice, lot of sex appeal. Kind of smart, too, for a dame. Knows her way around."

"How long did she work for you?"

"About a year in the chorus, then I featured her for a couple months. Then Les took her out of circulation."

"Any boyfriends?"

Tony shrugged, studied Joe. "What is this? Is it about the murder, Joe? You digging into that?"

"Some. Les was a friend of mine."

"I read the papers," Tony said. "I saw your name in the papers, Joe, when that kid was hit. You're a cop now, I see."

"That's right," Joe nodded.

"Patrolman," Tony said. "So, maybe this is all on your own. You couldn't have been promoted to the plainclothes squad so fast, not in this town, Joe."

"On my own," Joe agreed. "You want to help me, Tony?"

"If I can. But I've already told the law all I know about June

Gargan. About Les, I knew nothing excepting that he was a gambler. I didn't tell them that. They knew it. Everybody knew Les."

"Everybody," Joe said. "But how many people didn't like him, that's what I'm trying to find out."

"Some of the boys he beat at cards, maybe. Outside of that, I couldn't even guess, Joe. And a guess wouldn't do you any good."

By the deliberate blankness of Tony's face, Joe knew there'd be no more information dispensed even if Tony had it.

There were men in the department trained for this sort of work, and they were working on this case. He was no detective; he'd thought because he knew the principals in the case he might have an advantage over the homicide men. But he was on the other side of the fence from the principals now that he was a cop. He couldn't expect any cooperation from the old gang.

He should go home and go to bed, a cocky, boyish voice kept saying, "Let's go, let's go, Joe!" over and over in his head.

He drove down Fortieth, cut over to the avenue and down to Forty-Sixth. On Forty-Sixth, three numbers from the corner, was the *Domino.* It was a three-story building, narrow and old-fashioned. The first floor held a dimly lighted bar and a row of booths along one wall.

Joe nodded to the bartender, who pressed a buzzer that opened a gate separating the bar from the rear of the floor. Joe went through the gate. There was a self-service elevator, but it was old and slow, so Joe walked up to the second floor.

There were two tickers going, and the pair of men at the blackboard covering all the racetracks were the same pair who'd always been there. Art Needles still sat behind the three-sided counter, his back to the wall, writing out the tickets.

There were a couple of dozen horse-players in the room, sharing the despondent shabbiness of the breed. All their lives they wait for the killing. Percentages mean nothing to them, Joe thought.

Art said, "Long time no see, Joe. What's on your mind?"

"Game upstairs?"

Art was casual. "Why?"

"Thought I'd drop a couple of dollars."

"On the cops now, aren't you?"

Joe nodded.

"Can't figure it," Art went on. "A smart operator like you."

"I can't, myself," Joe said, grinning. "But I had saved a pretty good pile, and I wanted to be a solid citizen. Didn't you ever get the feeling, Art, that you were in the wrong business?"

"Once in a while," Art admitted. "But that bartender downstairs made a mistake, letting you come up here."

"This is as far as I go, Art?"

"I didn't say that." Art spoke carefully. "I'm not forgetting the loans you made me when I was in trouble, Joe. But I want to know it—and straight. Are you going upstairs as a cop, or a poker player?"

"I'm going up as a friend of Les Gargan's," Joe said, "and as a friend of that kid who was killed. If the chief knew I was here, I'd get fired."

Art looked at him for seconds before saying, "Okay, Joe. You know where the door is. Good luck."

Joe knew where the door was, and he heard it buzz as he approached it. It was to the left of the gent's washroom door, and the catch was controlled from Art's corner of the room.

He went up another flight of steps and into a single, large room on the floor above. There were five tables of poker, four of them with house dealers and limited. The fifth table had no house dealer, no limit, and was rented by the evening to any party of freewheelers who applied and were considered eligible.

The same old gang was there. The furrier, Nick Klatt, and the publisher, Allan Gillespie; Leo Boone, the fight promoter, and Jud Kelland, who did nothing besides gamble that Joe knew of. The other two Joe knew only slightly, but they all gave him the big hello.

"Hear you're an honest man, now," Leo Boone joked. "Here to pinch the game, Joe?" He was a big man, about fifty and strikingly handsome. He had three loves in life: the fight game, poker, and his daughter, a beautiful girl of twenty. He also had a fatal weakness for a poker player—he never wanted to go home wondering.

"I'm here for revenge," Joe said. "Last time I tangled with you pirates I bled."

"It's too long ago for me to remember," Klatt said. "But there's always room for one more fish."

Joe sat down. A waiter came, and he ordered a Scotch and water. Leo Boone was banking.

Joe wrote out a check for two thousand and Boone passed him

his chips. As he did so he asked, "Anything you can tell us about Les Gargan, Joe?"

"Nothing official," Joe said. "I'm just a guy walking a beat. You fellows could probably tell me more than I know."

"A man named Trescott, from homicide, came to see me about it today," Boone said. "Seems to think I'd have some reason—" He broke off, picked up his cards.

None of the others pressed Boone for more details, but Joe said, "Reason to kill him, Leo?"

Boone looked steadily at Joe. "That's right. He was making a play—I mean, he was seeing too much of Helen."

Helen was his daughter. Joe knew now why the others hadn't pressed him for details. He said no more about it.

He played a close game that night, varying little more than a hundred each way, and went home early, before the game broke up.

He'd learned only that Les had been making a play for Helen Boone, something the department knew or they wouldn't have called on Leo. He'd spent above five hours and learned nothing. He'd spent five hours and caused some old friends annoyance.

But he wasn't going to quit, he told himself.

His precinct captain had other ideas about that. He called Joe into his office next morning. "Got a call from headquarters last night, Joe. You nosing in on this Gargan case?"

"I saw some of the people involved," Joe admitted.

"Well, they put in a complaint and homicide is burning. What got into you?"

"I knew Gargan pretty well," Joe said, "and I saw that car hit Tommy Hart. I thought I could do some good."

"Homicide's sensitive," Captain Nard said. "I'm not going to discipline you for this because your intentions were good. But from now on stick to your beat."

Joe thought of several things to say, and said none of them. What he said finally was, "Yes, sir." Then he left, feeling properly humiliated, and went over to the school to handle the morning traffic.

As he worked he thought of all the people he'd seen last night. Then he thought of Tommy Hart and knew he couldn't give up the hunt, futile though it had been so far.

The children were quiet this morning; they'd been orderly and subdued since the accident. He got them across the street and waved the traffic on. One of the cars in the row that passed was an Olds convertible, and it pulled over to the curb after passing the intersection.

June Gargan was behind the wheel. She kept the motor running. "You look fine in your uniform, Joe," she called.

He said, "Thanks." He walked over and stood beside the car.

"You're not angry with me, Joe?"

"Why should I be?"

"Oh, I was sort of snippy last night." She smiled. "Drop in tonight, Joe. I want to talk to you."

He looked at her steadily, "About Les?"

She nodded. Then the Olds moved on.

Just before noon he saw the latest edition of the *Courier* in Wrede's drugstore. There was nothing new on the murder, though the paper hinted that many leads were being investigated and the police were optimistic.

In the afternoon a department car cruised by, and he saw it turn up Adams, going toward the Gargan house.

All afternoon Joe kept trying for one elusive bit of knowledge that might give him a clue. But nothing came to him. He was leaving the precinct station, going home, when he was accosted from a car for the second time that day.

Helen Boone sat behind the wheel. Joe didn't know if it was her youth or her beauty which was so appealing. She had black hair, dark eyes and a thin, well-modeled face.

She opened the car door. "Want a ride, Joe?"

"If you're going my way."

"I'm going your way. I came back to pick you up."

Joe got in and the car moved out into the traffic. "They think it's Dad, don't they?" she said.

"I don't know what they think," Joe said.

"One thing Dad didn't tell them, Joe, is that he lost a lot of money to Les about a week ago. He was trying to—break him, I think."

"Because of you?" Joe asked.

"I suppose so. Les wanted to marry me, Joe. He was going to

divorce June if I'd marry him." A pause. "That's something else
the police *don't* know."

"I'm one of the police," Joe reminded her.

"To me," she said, "you're a friend."

Joe thought about it for a minute. "Don't you think the police
should know these things?"

"They won't unless you tell them. I'll never tell them."

"How much did your dad lose?"

"Nearly eighty thousand dollars. He paid off the next day—*in
cash.*"

Eighty thousand in cash or any other way was a lot of money to
lose in a poker game, even among players of the Boone and Gargan
level. For that kind of money a lot of men would commit murder.

But not, Joe was sure, a man like Leo Boone. Though, for his
daughter . . .

Joe said, "I'll bet Les never declared that money, and didn't
intend to, in his income tax. I wonder where it is, now?"

Helen shrugged. "He wasn't going to tell June about it. He
wanted it for—for us. In case I decided—" She stopped.

"To marry him?"

She nodded. "He was very insistent, Joe. But I wasn't sure I loved
him; I don't believe I did. He was attentive, and—" Again she
paused.

Joe said, "Les was a lot like your dad, though it isn't anything I'd
say to your dad."

The car stopped in front of his apartment building. Joe looked at
Helen. "Why did you tell me all this? What did you think *I* could
do?"

"Nothing, I suppose. I wanted to tell somebody, and I've always
thought a lot of you, Joe, admired you."

"Maybe," he said jestingly, "that's why you couldn't make up
your mind about Les."

She flushed, then looked at him squarely. "Maybe it is. I hoped
you could help me."

"I'm going to do what I can," he told her. "And against orders.
But I don't know that I'll have any success. Don't worry about your
dad, Helen. He can take care of himself, and we know he's in the
clear, don't we?"

"I should know it," she said. "But he—he hated Les so."

Leeds got out of the car, turned to face her. "Chin up, kid. Something will crack, soon. And your dad will be all right."

But he wasn't as convinced as he tried to sound. Eighty thousand dollars was a lot of money. . . .

He ate in the apartment, that evening, a well-balanced blend of fried eggs and corn flakes. He read the evening paper, which revealed nothing new on the double killing. Then he went over to the garage on Hanover, before going to see June.

The same youth was inside, but Joe didn't go in. He sat in his car and studied the front of the garage. Then his glance wandered to the big apartment building next door, and, suddenly something clicked in his memory.

It had been some time ago, when June and Les were first married, but he remembered it clearly. The apartment in this building had been June's; she and Les shared it for only a short while before moving to Adams.

He drove out to the Gargan home, thinking about those early days of Les and June's marriage, trying to recall anything that might fit into the picture now.

June opened the door before he had a chance to ring the bell. She was wearing a chiffon negligee, and it didn't do her figure any harm. For some reason Joe felt suddenly uncomfortable. Something was wrong with the picture. . . .

They went into the living room and she poured Joe's Scotch and water without asking what he'd have. She sat on the davenport beside him as she handed him the drink.

"I've been thinking about Les," she said. "Les and Helen Boone." She looked down at her drink. "And Leo Boone."

Joe ignored that, asked, "Did you put in a complaint about me last night, to the homicide department?"

Her surprise was honest. "Me? Of course not. What ever gave you that idea?"

"Some one did. But go on—about the Boones."

"I think Les wanted to marry Helen. And I heard rumors that Leo Boone was out to get Les."

"He was," Joe said. "He was out to break him, take all his money.

That's why Les won all that money from him. Leo had the wrong attitude for a poker game."

"Money?" June said, but her surprise was forced now, as phony as both her eyebrows, Joe knew it immediately.

"Have you got it, June?" he said.

Her face hardened. Joe wondered how often Les had seen that expression. He said, "The eighty thousand, June. Have you got it?"

The drink was trembling in her hand. She set the glass on the table. "Who's been telling you ridiculous stories?"

Joe said, "I just remembered tonight that you and Les used to live on Hanover, right next to that garage where the plates were stolen. I was only there once. You didn't live there long. It was your place, wasn't it, that apartment? It was yours before you were married to Les."

She nodded stiffly. "So—?"

"Who was paying the rent?" Joe asked softly. "My guess would be Tony Valentine. You certainly couldn't have paid it out of your salary. Tony was featuring you about then, and Tony didn't give you star billing because of your singing talent. You're a lousy singer, June."

She was facing him squarely now, and her face was very hard. But she didn't say anything.

"Tony probably parked his car in that garage. Maybe he still does. Maybe Tony took those plates—or did he pay one of the employees to steal them for him?"

"I don't know what you're talking about," she said harshly.

Joe said, "I'm just trying to put a case together, June. Les wanted a divorce. Maybe he'd found out you still see Tony. You might not get alimony in that case. As his widow, though, you'd get everything—*including eighty thousand of taxfree money.*"

"I was out of town when Les was killed," she said.

"Sure. So you'd be in the clear. But Tony had your key, didn't he? Tony killed Les. Has Tony got the eighty grand?"

"You can ask him," she said, her face rigid. "Or you can take your story to your *superiors.*" Her laugh was bitter. "Flatfoot!"

Joe rose. "I intend to," he said. "And something else. I've finally placed the guy I saw in the back seat of the Cadillac that hit the kid. It was Tony Valentine. He was fleeing the scene of the crime—your house, where he'd just killed Les."

She leaped to her feet. "You're lying!" she screamed.

He was, but she couldn't be sure of it. He said, "That's what I'm going to tell the chief. Tonight." He headed toward the door.

"Wait," she said.

He turned back to see her standing rigidly in the center of the living room. And from the dimness of the dining room behind her, he saw a shadow move.

He hadn't brought his badge tonight, but he'd brought his gun. He hit the floor as he dug for it. But there was no shot from the dining room. Tony Valentine walked out of the shadows, a gun in his hand. He stopped about twelve feet away, stood looking down at Joe.

Joe was on one knee now, his gun levelled at Tony.

Tony said, "What's your angle, kid? For your kind of wages you wouldn't be sticking your neck out this far. You want in?"

Joe shook his head. "It's something you wouldn't understand, Tony. Drop your gun and come along with me."

Tony's laugh was short and cynical. "This is a single-shot gun, Joe, with a silencer. A single shot is all I need. I never miss."

"That wasn't the kind of gun that killed Les," Joe said. His eyes never left the pistol that was directed in a line with his eyes.

"No," Tony said, "it wasn't. That was—"

Joe stopped listening. He had seen the trigger finger tighten, and he dropped prone and his police Positive began to bark.

He saw Tony begin to crumple and heard the noise at the door before the lights went out and the sparks cascaded through his brain.

The man, who sat beside the davenport on which he lay, Joe recognized as Lieutenant Trescott from homicide. The lieutenant smiled as Joe gingerly touched the bandage on his head.

"We got here just in time, Leeds. That tigress was about to crown you with some pottery. I thought you were told to lay off this case?"

Joe said nothing.

"Got a guy down at headquarters," the lieutenant went on, "who used to work in that garage. He answers the description you gave us. If you can identify him we'll clean up the rest of it." He coughed. "With your help, of course. Think you're able to navigate now?"

Joe nodded. "What are we waiting for. Let's go. If he's the driver,

I'll know him." As he rose carefully to his feet the sound of a shrill, boyish voice came to him: "Let's go! Let's go, Joe!"

THE DROWNED MEN'S INN

GEORGES SIMENON

For more than fifty years, Simenon's novels and stories about Inspector Maigret of the Paris police have been applauded by readers and critics in every corner of the globe. (The first Maigret novel, The Strange Case of Peter the Lett, *appeared in 1933.) It is impossible to gauge, as film director Federico Fellini has said, "how many dreary hours of waiting, disturbing breakups, lonely evenings, stretches of convalescence the world over have been, at least for the moment, effaced and as it were healed by immersion in a Simenon [story]." Maigret is at his best in "The Drowned Men's Inn," an eerie tale in which he must solve "the foulest, most stupid and revolting crime" at a country inn on the banks of the Loing.*

I

"**W**ill you really not take shelter?" the captain of the gendarmes urged Maigret, with a certain embarrassment.

And Maigret, his hands in his overcoat pockets, the brim of his bowler hat full of water which spilled over at his least movement, Maigret at his moodiest, massive and motionless, growled between teeth still clenched round the stem of his pipe.

"No!"

It's a remarkable fact that particularly tiresome cases, the ones which are the most difficult to disentangle and which end up more or less unpleasantly, are always those in which one has become involved rather stupidly through chance, or simply through lack of the courage to say no while there was still time.

Maigret was, once again, in this situation. He had come to Nemours the previous evening, on a matter of minor importance that had to be settled with Captain Pillement of the gendarmerie.

Captain Pillement was a charming, cultured, and athletic man, who had been trained at the artillery school in Saumur. He had insisted on doing Maigret the honors of his table and his cellar, and then, as it was pouring with rain, had invited him to spend the night in the guest room.

Autumn was at its worst and, for the past fortnight, rain and fog had prevailed, while the Loing in full spate carried along branches of trees in its muddy waters.

"This was bound to happen," sighed Maigret when, at six in the morning, while it was still dark, he heard the telephone bell ring.

A few moments later Captain Pillement was at his door, saying softly, "Are you asleep, Superintendent?"

"No, I'm not asleep!"

"Would you like to come along with me to a place fifteen kilometers away? A curious accident has occurred there during the night. . . ."

Maigret had gone there with him, of course—to the banks of the Loing, where the highway follows the course of the river, between Nemours and Montargis. The landscape was of a sort to put one off early rising for good. A cold, lowering sky. Heavy, slanting rain. The river a dirty brown, and beyond it the line of poplars that edged the canal.

There was no village. There was a single inn, the Auberge des Pêcheurs, seven hundred meters away, and Maigret already knew that it was known locally as *L'Auberge aux Noyés,* the Drowned Men's Inn.

As for the people who had been drowned there on this occasion, nothing was known about them yet. The crane was at work, creaking away, and a diver had gone down; there were two men in seamen's oilskins working his pump. Cars had drawn up, five or six of them at the roadside. Others, coming from both directions, slowed down and sometimes halted to see what was happening; then they went on their way.

There were uniformed gendarmes, there were ambulances summoned during the night whose services would obviously not be needed now.

It was just a matter of waiting until the car which was down there, in mid-stream under the swiftly flowing water, could be firmly fastened to the crane and hoisted out of the river.

A ten-ton lorry, one of those stinking monsters that travel by day and by night along main roads, was drawn up just before the bend in the road.

Nobody knew exactly what had happened. The night before, this lorry, which travelled regularly between Paris and Lyon, had driven along this road shortly after eight o'clock. At the turning, it had run into a stationary car with all its lights switched off, and the car had been sent hurtling into the Loing.

The driver, Joseph Lecoin, had thought he heard cries and the skipper of the barge *Belle-Thérèse,* which was moored in the canal less than a hundred meters away, asserted that he too had heard someone shouting for help.

The two men had met on the river bank and had searched, after a fashion, with the aid of a lantern. Then the lorry driver had gone on his way as far as Montargis, where he had informed the gendarmerie.

The spot where this accident had occurred being within the jurisdiction of Nemours, the gendarmerie of that town had duly been informed, but since nothing could be attempted before day-break it was not until six A.M. that the lieutenant had woken his captain.

The scene was a depressing one. Everybody was cold and stood with hunched shoulders glancing at the muddy water, without even very much anxiety.

The innkeeper was there, sheltering under a huge umbrella, and discussing the matter knowledgeably.

"Unless the bodies are wedged in the car, they won't be recovered for a long time, for all the weirs are down, and they'll float as far as the Seine unless they get caught in tree-roots."

"They're surely not in the car," retorted the lorry driver, "because it was an open car!"

"That's odd!"

"Why?"

"Because yesterday a young couple in an open car came to stay the night and had lunch at the inn. They were to come back tonight but I haven't seen them again."

Maigret was not really listening to this chatter, but he heard it and recorded it involuntarily.

Finally the diver emerged, and the others quickly unfastened his big brass helmet.

"You can get going," he announced. "I've hooked on the pulley-block."

Motorists were hooting on the road, puzzled by the sight of this gathering. Heads appeared at car windows.

The crane, which had been brought from Montargis, was making an intolerable din, and at last the upper part of a gray car was brought up out of the water, followed by the wheels. . . .

Maigret's feet were wet and the bottom of his trousers muddy. He would have liked a cup of hot coffee, but he did not want to leave the place to go as far as the inn, and the captain of the gendarmerie did not venture to distract his attention.

"Careful, boys! . . . Keep it clear on the left . . ."

The front of the car showed clear traces of the collision, thus proving that, as the lorry driver had already said, the roadster had been facing towards Paris at the time of the crash.

"Up she goes! . . . One . . . Two . . . Up she goes!"

At last the car stood on the bank. It looked strange with its twisted wheels, its mudguards crumpled like paper, its seats already covered with mud and rubbish.

The lieutenant of gendarmerie noted the registration number, while the captain searched the dashboard for the plate bearing the owner's name. It was inscribed: R. Daubois, 135 Avenue des Ternes, Paris.

"I'll call Paris, shall I, Superintendent?"

Maigret seemed to be saying, "Do as you please, it's no concern of mine!"

This was a job for the gendarmerie, and not for the Superintendent of the Police Judiciaire. A sergeant on a motorcycle dashed off to call Paris. Everybody, including a dozen curious onlookers who had got out of passing cars, surrounded the wreck that had been brought up out of the water, and some of them automatically felt the coachwork or leaned forward to look inside.

It was one of the crowd, in fact, who out of curiosity turned the handle of the luggage compartment. The car was so battered that it opened unexpectedly, and the man uttered a cry and started back, while his neighbors pressed forward to look.

Maigret went up with the rest, frowned, and for the first time that morning spoke instead of merely grunting.

"Now then, back, everyone! . . . Don't touch anything!"

He, too, had seen. He had seen a human figure curiously doubled up, crammed into the back of the luggage compartment as though some effort had been required to close the lid. A mass of platinum blonde hair showed that the bundle was the body of a woman.

"Captain! Clear the ground, will you? There's something new, something rather unpleasant . . ."

And an unpleasant task in prospect! To begin with, the dripping corpse had to be extracted from the car. . . .

"Don't you smell something?"

"Yes . . ."

"Don't you think that . . ."

And they had the proof of it a quarter of an hour later. One of the motorists who had stopped to look happened to be a doctor. He examined the corpse on the bank beside the road, and the curious crowd of onlookers, including children, had to be kept back.

"She has been dead at least three days."

Someone pulled Maigret by the sleeve. It was Justin Rozier, the innkeeper from the Auberge aux Noyés.

"I recognize the car," he declared, deliberately assuming an air of mystery. "It belonged to my young couple!"

"Have you got their names?"

"They filled in a form."

The doctor spoke again. "Do you realize that this woman has been murdered?"

"With what?"

"A razor. She's had her throat cut."

And the rain still poured down on the car and on the corpse and on all the black figures moving to and fro in the grayness.

The motorcycle reappeared, and the sergeant jumped down.

"The car doesn't belong to Monsieur Daubois any longer; I spoke to him personally on the phone. He sold it last week to a garage owner at the Porte Maillot."

"What does the garage owner say?"

"I called him too. The garage sold the car again three days ago to a young man who paid cash down and therefore left no name."

"But I tell you, I've got the name!" broke in the innkeeper, impatiently, obviously feeling that he was not getting enough attention. "Just come up to my place and . . ."

Meanwhile a redheaded fellow had come on the scene, a journalist from the one local paper of Montargis who was also correspondent of a big Paris daily. Heaven knows how he carried out his inquiry, for Maigret sent him packing and so did Captain Pillement, which however did not prevent him, almost immediately afterwards, from spending over a quarter of an hour in the telephone booth.

An hour later, the policeman responsible for keeping inquisitive people from invading the inn was besieged by reporters armed with their press cards. Photographers were there too, climbing on to tables and chairs and taking pictures which had nothing to do with the tragedy.

As for Maigret, he was on the phone to Paris, getting the answer to his request.

"The Criminal Investigation Department agrees. Since you're there, carry on with the inquiry unofficially. You'll be sent an inspector from the Rue des Saussaies later in the day . . ."

It was a curious affair, and the inn was a curious place, oddly situated at a sudden bend in the road. Hadn't Maigret just been told that this was the third car in the last five years to have fallen into the Loing at just this spot?

The other two cases had been less mysterious: cars being driven at top speed which had not anticipated the turning and, unable to change course, had plunged into the river. In one of them a family of five had been trapped. In the other there had only been one victim.

The place had nonetheless earned its nickname, particularly as one Whitsunday a young woman had deliberately drowned herself there for personal motives while her husband was fishing a hundred meters further on.

The Auberge aux Noyés! A glance at the telephone booth, which journalists were occupying one after the other, told one that before the day was up it would be famous.

. . . *The Crime at Drowning Corner . . . The Mystery of the Auberge aux Noyés . . . The Body in the Car . . . The Puzzle of the Gray Car . . .*

Maigret, calm and stolid, went on smoking his pipe, devoured a huge ham sandwich with a glass of beer, and observed without the least curiosity the traditional agitation which invariably complicates the task of the police.

In all this crowd, two people alone interested him: the skipper of the *Belle-Thérèse* and the driver of the lorry.

The skipper had come to ask him humbly:

"You know we get a bonus for speed . . . I should have left this morning . . . So if I might possibly . . ."

"Where are you going to unload?"

"Quai des Tournelles in Paris . . . Another day on the canal, then nearly a day on the Seine. We'll be there by evening the day after tomorrow . . ."

Maigret got him to repeat his statement:

"We'd finished supper and my wife had gone to bed already. I was going to bed myself when I heard a queer noise . . . From inside the boat you can't quite make out what's happening. I stuck my head through the hatch . . . I thought I heard a voice calling for help . . ."

"What sort of voice?"

"Oh, a voice . . . The rain was rattling down on the iron roof . . . A voice that sounded far away . . ."

"A man's voice or a woman's?"

"More like a man's!"

"How long after the first noise?"

"Not quite immediately, because I'd been taking my shoes off and I had time to put on my slippers . . ."

"What did you do next?"

"I couldn't go out there in slippers. I went downstairs again; I put on my leather jacket and my rubber boots. I said to my wife, who wasn't asleep yet, 'Maybe somebody's drowning . . .' "

Maigret pressed him. "Why did you think it was somebody drowning?"

"Because, along the river and the canal, if we hear somebody calling for help, it generally means that! With my boathook, I've saved half a dozen of them."

"So you made for the river?"

"I was practically there, you see, because at that point there's less than twenty meters between the canal and the Loing. I saw the lights of a lorry. Then I noticed a big fellow walking about . . ."

"The lorry driver . . . was that who it was?"

"Yes. He told me he'd run into a car, and it had rolled into the river. I went to fetch my torch."

"And all this took a certain time?"

"Yes, in fact it did!"

"What was the lorry driver doing meanwhile?"

"I don't know . . . I suppose he was trying to make out something in the darkness."

"Did you go up to his lorry?"

"I may have done . . . I don't remember. I was chiefly trying to see if a body could have come to the surface . . ."

"So you don't know if the driver was alone in his lorry?"

"I suppose he was. If anyone else had been there they'd have come to help us."

"When you realized there was nothing to be done, what did the driver say to you?"

"That he'd go and inform the gendarmerie."

"He didn't specify where?"

"No . . . I don't think so . . ."

"You never thought of pointing out that he could telephone from the inn, which is only seven hundred meters away?"

"I thought of that afterwards, when I saw that he'd driven off . . ."

The driver was of Herculean build. He had rung up his employers to warn them that he had been detained by the police following an accident, and he was waiting quite patiently to see what would happen, being treated to drinks by the journalists in return for endlessly retailing his story.

Maigret took him aside into a small private dining room with a couch in it, which clearly suggested that the inn with the ominous name was welcoming to loving couples.

"I thought lorry drivers usually travelled in pairs, especially on long journeys?"

"Yes, we mostly do! My mate hurt his hand a week ago, and he's on sick leave, so I travel on my own."

"What time did you leave Paris?"

"At two o'clock. I've got a mixed load, and I couldn't go fast on these slippery roads."

"I suppose you stopped for dinner at a regular drivers' pull-up?"

"You're right there! We have our own places, and we meet there at more or less the same time. I stopped right after Nemours at Mère Catherine's, where the food's first-class."

"How many lorries were parked there?"

"Four. Two removal vans from Morin's, a petrol tanker and an express delivery van."

"Did you eat with the other drivers?"

"With three of them. The others were at the next table."

"In what order did you leave?"

"I don't know about the others. I left last because I was putting through a phone call to Paris."

"Whom were you calling?"

"My boss, to have some piston-rings ready for me at Moulins. I'd noticed that the engine wasn't running smoothly and that the third cylinder . . ."

"All right! How far away from your mates were you?"

"I left ten minutes after the last of them, one of the removal vans. As I was going faster, he must have been four or five kilometers ahead of me . . ."

"And you didn't see the roadster until you ran into it?"

"When it was a few meters away, too late to avoid a crash."

"There were no lights on?"

"None at all!"

"And you saw nobody?"

"I can't say. It was raining. My windscreen wiper isn't too good. All I know is that, when the car was in the water, I fancied I saw someone in the darkness, trying to swim. Then I heard a sort of cry for help . . ."

"One more question: just now, in the box under your seat, I noticed an electric torch, in good working order. Why didn't you pick it up?"

"I don't know . . . I was panicking . . . I was afraid my truck might skid into the river too . . ."

"When you passed the inn, wasn't it lit up?"

"It may have been!"

"Do you often take this road?"

"Twice a week."

"Didn't it occur to you to telephone from the inn?"

"No! I remembered Montargis wasn't far off, so I went there . . ."

"While you were looking around, could anybody have hidden in your truck?"

"I don't think so."

"Why not?"

"Because they'd have had to unfasten the ropes of the tarpaulin."

"Thank you. You'll stay here, of course, in case I need you."

"If I can be of any use to you!"

His only concern was to eat and drink his fill, and Maigret saw him go off to the kitchen to arrange for his midday meal.

The cooking was done by Madame Rozier, a lean, sallow woman who was finding it hard to cope with the sudden rush of customers. Added to which, the journalists would not even let her get to the telephone to order supplies from the town.

A young barmaid, Lili, over-pert for her age, was joking with everybody as she served apéritifs, and the landlord, at the bar, had not a moment's breathing-space.

It was the off-season; whereas in summer the inn could count on tourists, lovers, and fishermen, its autumn customers generally consisted only of a few sportsmen from Paris who hired a shoot in the neighborhood and ordered their meals for a set day.

Rozier had stated to Maigret, "The day before yesterday, in the evening, a young couple turned up in a gray car, the one that's been fished out of the river. I assumed they must be a honeymoon couple. Here's the form they filled in for me."

The writing on the form was spiky and irregular. It read:

"Jean Vertbois, twenty years of age, advertising agent, 18 Rue des Acacias, Paris."

He was described as coming from Paris and going to Nice.

Finally, when he had been asked to fill in a form for his companion, he had scrawled across his own: *"And Madame."*

The information had already been telephoned through to Paris, and an inquiry was in progress in the Rue des Acacias, in the seventeenth arrondissement, not far from the garage where the car had been purchased.

"A very pretty young lady, seventeen or eighteen," the landlord answered Maigret's question. "The chick, I called her privately! She

was wearing a dress that was too thin for the time of year and a
sports coat . . ."

"Did they have luggage?"

"One suitcase, it's still up there . . ."

The suitcase contained only a man's clothes and underwear,
which suggested that the mysterious girl had left home unexpectedly.

"Did they seem nervous?"

"Not particularly . . . To tell you the truth they were chiefly
thinking about making love, and they spent most of yesterday in
their bedroom . . . They had their lunch taken up there, and Lili
observed that it was an awkward business serving people who took
so little trouble to hide their feelings . . . You see what I mean?"

"They didn't tell you why, if they were on their way to Nice, they
stopped less than a hundred kilometers from Paris?"

"I fancy they'd have stopped anywhere, provided they could
have a bedroom . . ."

"And the car?"

"It was in the garage. You've seen it. A classy car, but fairly old,
the sort people buy who haven't a great deal of money. It looks rich
and it costs less than a mass-produced car."

"You never tried to open the luggage compartment out of
curiosity?"

"I'd never have taken such a liberty."

Maigret shrugged his shoulders, for the fellow had nothing worth-
while to tell him, and he knew how inquisitive that type of landlord is.

"In short, the couple was expected back to sleep in the hotel?"

"To sleep and to dine. We waited until ten o'clock to clear away."

"At what time was the car taken out of the garage?"

"Let's see . . . It was dark already . . . About half-past four . . . I
assumed that, after spending so long shut up in their bedroom, the
young people had felt like going off for a jaunt to Montargis or
elsewhere. The suitcase was still there, so I wasn't worried about
the bill."

"You knew nothing about the accident?"

"Nothing until the gendarmes turned up about eleven at night."

"And you immediately thought it must be something to do with
your guests?"

"I was afraid of it. I had noticed how clumsily the young man had backed out of the garage. He was obviously an inexperienced driver. Now we know about the sharp bend by the river."

"You noticed nothing suspicious in these people's conversation?"

"I didn't listen to their conversation."

In brief, the situation was as follows:

On Monday, about five P.M., a certain Jean Vertbois, aged twenty, an advertising agent, resident at 18 Rue des Acacias, Paris, had bought from a garage near his home a luxurious but old-fashioned car, for which he had paid with five thousand-franc notes. (The garage owner, Maigret had just been informed, had the impression that there was still a thick wad of notes in his customer's wallet. Vertbois had not tried to bargain with him, but had mentioned that he would have the identity plate changed next day. He had been alone when he visited the garage.)

Nothing was as yet known about Tuesday's happenings.

On Wednesday evening the same Vertbois, with his car, had arrived at the Auberge aux Noyés, less than a hundred kilometers from Paris, accompanied by a very young girl whom the landlord, presumably an experienced judge, had taken for a girl of good social standing.

On Thursday the couple had gone out in their car as though for a pleasure trip in the neighborhood, and a few hours later the car, with all its lights out, was run into by a lorry at seven hundred meters from the inn, and both the lorry driver and the skipper of a barge had apparently heard cries for help in the darkness.

Of Jean Vertbois and the girl there was no trace. The whole police force of the district had been searching since early morning. They had drawn blank at railway stations; and nobody corresponding to the description of the missing couple had been seen at any farm or inn, or on any of the roads.

On the other hand, in the luggage compartment of the car, the body of a woman had been found, aged between forty-five and fifty, well-groomed and smartly dressed.

And the pathologist confirmed the observation made by the first doctor, namely that the woman had been slashed to death with a razor on the previous Monday!

With less certainty, the pathologist had suggested that the body had been somewhat clumsily packed into the luggage compartment of the car only a few hours after death.

The conclusion was that there was already a corpse in the car when the couple drove up to the inn!

Was Vertbois aware of this? And was his young companion?

What was their car doing at eight in the evening, all lights out, on the edge of the road?

Had there been a breakdown, which an inexperienced driver could not deal with?

Who had been in the car at the time?

And who had called out in the darkness?

The captain of gendarmerie, being the soul of tact, had not wanted to disturb Maigret in his inquiry, but was meanwhile endeavoring, with his men, to collect as much evidence as possible.

Ten flat-bottomed boats went to and fro along the Loing, which was being searched with hooks. Some men were splashing about on the river banks, others busied themselves around the weirs.

The journalists considered the inn as conquered territory and established themselves there, filling every room in the place with their din.

The *Belle-Thérèse* had set off towards the Quai des Tournelles with her cargo of tiles, and the truck driver, quite indifferent to all this excitement, was philosophically enjoying an unexpected holiday with pay.

The rotary presses of newspapers had begun to print their headlines, the most sensational being in the heaviest type, such as one reporter's effort:

Teen-age Lovers Carry Corpse in Back of Car

then, in italics:

The muddy waters of the Loing engulf the guilty couple and their victim.

This was the gloomy period of the inquiry, during which Maigret, on edge, spoke to nobody, growled, drank beer, and smoked pipes, while he prowled about like a caged bear; it was the uncertain period, in which all the data that have been collected seem to contradict one another, and when one searches in vain amid a jumble of futile information for a guiding thread, in constant fear of picking the wrong one which will lead nowhere.

The crowning misfortune was that the inn was poorly heated, and

with central heating at that, which the superintendent particularly
loathed. Furthermore, the cooking was poor and the sauces were
diluted in order to cope with the increased demand.

"You'll forgive me for what I'm going to say to you, Superintendent . . ."

Captain Pillement, a sly smile on his lips, sat down at last in front
of an excessively ungracious Maigret.

"I know you're annoyed with me. But I myself am delighted to
have kept you here, for I'm beginning to think that this road
accident which started off in so commonplace a fashion is gradually
going to turn into one of the most mysterious cases imaginable."

Maigret merely went on helping himself to potato salad, sardines,
and beetroot, the inevitable hors d'oeuvres served in bad inns.

"When we know the identity of the pretty girl who was so much
in love . . ."

A big, mud-splashed car, driven by a chauffeur in uniform, drew
up in front of the door, and a gray-haired man got out, instinctively
recoiling before the relentless assault of the photographers.

"Look at this!" murmured Maigret. "I bet that's her father!"

II

The superintendent had not been mistaken, but if he apprehended
a painful scene it was spared him, thanks to the remarkable dignity
of the lawyer Monsieur La Pommeraye. After dismissing the journalists with a wave of the hand, like one used to displaying his
authority, he had followed Maigret into the little private dining
room and introduced himself.

"Germain La Pommeraye, notary at Versailles."

His profession, and the royal town where he practiced it, were
perfectly in keeping with his tall, elegant figure, his pale complex-
ion, and the features which barely quivered as he inquired, with
his eyes fixed on the floor, "Have you found her?"

"I shall be obliged," Maigret sighed, "to ask you a certain number
of questions for which I apologize."

The notary waved his hand as though to say: "Carry on! I know
what you're going to ask . . ."

"Can you tell me, first, what made you think your daughter might
be involved in this affair?"

"You'll understand. My daughter Viviane is seventeen and looks twenty. I said *is* although I suppose by now I should perhaps have said *was*. She's a creature of impulse, like her mother. And, rightly or wrongly, particularly since I became a widower, I have always been unwilling to thwart her instincts. I don't know where she made the acquaintance of this Jean Vertbois, but I think I recall that it was at the swimming pool, or in a sports club whose grounds are in the neighborhood of the Bois de Boulogne."

"Do you know Jean Vertbois personally?"

"I met him once. My daughter, as I said, is impulsive. One evening she suddenly announced to me, 'Daddy, I'm going to get married!' "

Maigret rose, suddenly opened the door, glanced with contempt at the journalist who had his ear pressed to it.

"Go on, monsieur!"

"At first I took the thing as a joke. Then, seeing that it was a serious matter, I asked to see her suitor. That was how Jean Vertbois turned up at Versailles one afternoon. One detail displeased me from the start; he drove up in a fast sports car borrowed from a friend. Do you see what I mean? Young men have every right to be ambitious, but I object when at the age of twenty they indulge their taste for luxury at little expense to themselves, particularly for a luxury which is in rather bad taste . . ."

"In short, the interview was scarcely a friendly one?"

"It was definitely stormy. I asked the young man how he expected to support a wife, and he replied with disconcerting frankness that pending an improvement in his financial situation my daughter's dowry would at all events prevent her from starving. As you see, the very type of shameless little opportunist in words as well as in attitude! So much so that I wondered for a moment if this shamelessness could not perhaps be a pose concealing a certain timidity.

"Vertbois held forth to me at length on the way parents assume rights, and on the reactionary ideas of certain bourgeois of whom I was obviously considered the perfect representative.

"After an hour I flung him out."

"How long ago was this?" asked Maigret.

"Barely a week. When I saw my daughter afterwards she declared that she would marry Vertbois and nobody else, that I didn't know him, that I had misjudged him, and so forth. And she actually threatened to run away with him if I would not agree to their marriage."

"You stood firm?"

"Unfortunately I believed it was an empty threat. I counted on the lapse of time to settle things. And now, since yesterday afternoon, Viviane has disappeared. I went round that evening to the Rue des Acacias, where Vertbois lives, but I was told he had gone off on a journey. I questioned the concierge and I ascertained that he had been accompanied by a very young girl, who must have been Viviane. That's why, when I read in the midday papers the account of last night's happenings . . ."

He retained his quiet dignity. Yet there were beads of sweat on his forehead as, with averted eyes, he said, "One thing I beg of you, Superintendent: be frank! I'm still tough enough to take a direct blow, but I shouldn't find it easy to stand up to a long period of alternating hope and despair. In your opinion, is my daughter still alive?"

There was a long pause before Maigret replied.

"Let me first of all ask you one final question. You seem to know your daughter well. It looks as if her love for Vertbois was a wholehearted romantic passion. Do you think your daughter, if she learned that Vertbois was a murderer, would have become his accomplice out of love? Don't be in a hurry to reply. Suppose your daughter, on arriving at her lover's—which he was, in the fullest sense of the word, I'm afraid—learned that in order to be able to escape with her and find the money necessary for this elopement he had been driven to kill someone . . ."

The two men fell silent. At last Monsieur La Pommeraye sighed.

"I don't know . . . However, I can tell you one thing, Superintendent, something that nobody else knows. I told you just now I was a widower. That is true. My wife died three years ago in South America, where she had gone to live with a coffee planter eight years previously. Now when she left me she took a hundred thousand francs out of the safe in my office. Viviane is like her mother . . ."

He was startled to hear Maigret say with a sigh, "I hope so!"

"What do you mean?"

"Because if Jean Vertbois has nothing to fear from his companion, he has no reason to get rid of her. If, on the other hand, when your daughter discovered the body in the boot she displayed indignation and uttered threats . . ."

"I follow your argument, but I don't understand the sequence of events as described in the newspapers. When the collision took place, the car was not empty, since the lorry driver and the bargee both heard cries. Vertbois and Viviane had no reason to separate. So it's likely . . ."

"The men have been dredging the river all day, so far without results. May I ask you to come with me for a moment into the room the couple occupied in this inn?"

It was a commonplace room with a floral-patterned wallpaper, a brass bedstead, a mahogany wardrobe. On the dressing table stood a few toilet articles, a razor, a shaving brush, and two toothbrushes, one of them new.

"You see," Maigret observed, "the man had his personal belongings. But the couple must have stopped somewhere on the way to buy a toothbrush for the girl, and those travelling slippers that I see beside the bed. But I should have liked to find some proof that it really was your daughter who . . ."

"Here's the proof!" the father said sadly, pointing to a piece of jewelry gleaming on the mat. "Viviane always wore these earrings, which belonged to her mother. One of them fastened badly, and she kept losing it and finding it again as though by miracle. This is it! Now do you still believe I've any hope of finding my daughter alive?"

Maigret dared not answer by saying that in that case Mademoiselle Viviane La Pommeraye would probably be charged with complicity in a murder!

After much pressure, the notary had been persuaded to return to Versailles, and under the unceasing rain the Auberge aux Noyés had come to look more and more like an army headquarters.

Journalists, tired of standing about in the rain watching the water-men exploring the river, had resigned themselves to a game of *belote*. The captain of gendarmerie had put his car at Maigret's disposal, but the superintendent made no use of it, and his haphazard activities were not such as to inspire confidence in anyone ignorant of his methods.

So, when they saw him go into the telephone booth, the reporters imagined they were about to learn something fresh, and, with professional indiscretion, they unhesitatingly surrounded the door.

But it was to the Paris Observatory that Maigret had been telephoning, asking first for the latest weather forecast, and insisting on certain details.

"You say there was no moon yesterday at about eight P.M.? Will it be so again tonight? It rises at ten minutes past midnight? Thank you . . ."

As he left the telephone booth he seemed really satisfied with himself. He even took a mischievous pleasure in saying to the journalists, "Good news, gentlemen; we shall have torrential rain for three more days."

After which he was seen holding a lengthy conversation with Captain Pillement, who then disappeared and was not seen again that day.

There was some hard drinking going on. Someone had discovered a bottle of Vouvray, and everybody wanted some of it; Lili, moving from one table to another, encountered roving hands which she did not repulse too sharply.

Darkness, falling at half-past four, put an end to investigations in the Loing and it was becoming unlikely that the body or bodies would be recovered, since by this time they would have been carried downstream as far as the Seine.

To clear the road, a breakdown truck had come to fetch the car that had been fished out of the river, and had taken it to Montargis, where it was impounded by the police.

It was six o'clock when a reporter called out to the innkeeper, "What are you giving us for dinner tonight?"

And a voice was heard replying, "Nothing!"

Nobody was more surprised than the innkeeper, who looked round to see who had dared to speak in his place and particularly in a way so damaging to his business. It was Maigret, who stepped forward calmly.

"I am going to ask you, gentlemen, not to dine here tonight. I don't forbid you to come back about ten o'clock if you feel like it, and even to sleep at the inn. But between seven and nine I am anxious for the place to be occupied only by those people who were here last night . . ."

"A reconstruction?" some smart-aleck interrupted.

"Not even that! I warn you straight away that it's no use hiding in the neighborhood, for you would see nothing. On the other hand, if you behave well, you'll probably have a fine scoop for tomorrow's issue . . ."

"At what time?"

"Let's say before eleven . . . I know a place at Montargis where you can get a first-class meal: the Hôtel de la Cloche . . . Go there, all of you. Tell the proprietor that I sent you, and you'll be very well looked after. When I come to join you . . ."

"You're not dining with us?"

"I'm already engaged. But I shan't be late . . . Now, you can take it or leave it, and if anyone wants to play it smart I can guarantee he won't get the slightest bit of information. Well, gentlemen, goodbye and good eating!"

When they had left, he breathed more freely, and cast a mischievous glance at the landlord, who was furious.

"Come, come! You make your money from selling drinks and not from serving meals. Now they've been drinking ever since this morning . . ."

"They'd have gone on!"

"Listen to me! It's essential that between seven and ten everyone should be in the same place as yesterday, and that the same lights should be on."

"That's easy enough."

There was still somebody there who seemed to have been forgotten. Joseph Lecoin, the lorry driver. He stared at Maigret in astonishment and finally spoke up.

"What about me?"

"You're going to drive me to Nemours."

"In the lorry?"

"Well, why not? Failing a ritzy limousine . . ."

And so Superintendent Maigret left the Auberge aux Noyés on the seat of a ten-ton lorry which kept up an infernal racket.

III

"Where shall I drop you?"

They had driven in silence, in the darkness, in the rain, meeting cars that dipped their headlights, and the windscreen wiper kept up a regular humming like a great bumblebee.

"You're not going to drop me anywhere, old man!"

The driver looked at his companion in astonishment, thinking he must be joking.

"So what? Are we going back to Paris?"

"No! Let me just look at the time . . ."

He had to strike a light to see his watch, the hands of which stood at half-past seven.

"Good, we've got time. Stop at the first pub you see . . ."

And Maigret turned up his coat collar as they crossed the pavement; then he stood with his elbows propped in easygoing fashion on the bar-counter of a small tavern, while Lecoin, by his side, wondered at this sudden change of attitude.

Not that the superintendent had become at all threatening, or showed the least trace of ill-humor; on the contrary, he was calm, and from time to time there was even a twinkle in his eyes. He was full of self-confidence, and if he had been asked he would readily have replied, "Life's good!"

He savored his apéritif, looked at his watch again, paid for the drinks and announced, "Off we go!"

"Where are we going?"

"First to have dinner at Mère Catherine's, as you did last night. You see! It's raining just as hard; it's just the same time of night . . ."

There were only three lorries outside the inn, which was unprepossessing in appearance but in which lorry drivers knew they could enjoy a well-cooked meal. The proprietress served it herself, assisted by her fourteen-year-old daughter.

"Hello, you back again?" she greeted Lecoin with some surprise.

He shook hands with his fellow-drivers and sat down in a corner with the superintendent.

"Suppose we ordered the same thing that you had yesterday?" suggested Maigret.

"Here there aren't umpteen dishes to choose from. You have to take what's on the list . . . Look, it's *fricandeau* of veal with sorrel . . ."

"One of my favorite dishes . . ."

Had not the last few minutes revealed a certain alteration in the attitude of the big lorry driver? His mood seemed less forthright.

He kept glancing stealthily at his companion, wondering no doubt what the policeman was getting at.

"Come on, Catherine! We haven't got time to waste . . ."

"You always say that, and then you spend a quarter of an hour over your coffee . . ."

The *fricandeau* was perfect, the coffee more like real coffee than what is usually served in bistros. From time to time Maigret pulled out his watch and seemed to await the departure of the other drivers with some impatience.

They got up at last, after a round of old *marc,* and soon afterwards the purr of their engines was heard.

"*Marc* for us too," ordered Maigret. To Lecoin he said, "That's how it was yesterday, wasn't it?"

"Yes, indeed. Just about this time I was going off, I'd had my phone call . . ."

"Let's go!"

"Back there?"

"Do just what you did yesterday . . . Do you mind?"

"No, why should I mind? Since I've got nothing to hide . . ."

Just at that moment Catherine came up and asked the driver, "Did you give my message to Benoît?"

"Yes, it's all settled!"

Once back in the lorry, Maigret asked, "Who is Benoît?"

"He keeps a petrol pump at Montargis. He's a pal of mine. I always stop there to fill up. Old Catherine wants to have a pump fixed up at her place, and I was to tell Benoît . . ."

"It's raining hard, isn't it!"

"Even a bit harder than yesterday . . . Just think! When one has to travel all night in such muck . . ."

"We're not going too fast?"

"Same as yesterday . . ."

Maigret lit his pipe.

"We chaps always get the blame," Lecoin was muttering, "because we keep to the middle of the road or don't pull over fast enough. But if people who drive small cars had to cope with monsters like ours . . ."

He let out a sudden oath and braked so violently that Maigret was almost thrown head first into the windscreen.

"Good Lord!" cried Joseph Lecoin. And he looked at his companion with a frown, muttering, "Was it you who put it there?"

For there was, in fact, a car standing exactly where Jean Vertbois's car had been hit the day before. A gray car, too! and its lights were off, and the rain was falling, and the night was dark!

And yet the lorry had stopped more than three meters away from the car!

For a moment the lorry driver's face had betrayed incipient anger, but he merely growled, "You might have warned me . . . Suppose I hadn't seen it in time . . ."

"And yet we were busy talking . . ."

"What about it?"

"Yesterday you were by yourself. You had nothing to distract your attention . . ."

And Lecoin asked, with a shrug, "What do you want now?"

"We're going to get down . . . This way . . . Wait a minute . . . I want to try an experiment. Shout for help . . ."

"Me?"

"Since the people who were shouting yesterday aren't there, someone has to take their place."

And Lecoin shouted unwillingly, scenting a snare.

His most anxious moment came when he heard footsteps and saw a figure moving in the darkness.

"Come here!" Maigret called out to the newcomer.

This was the skipper of the *Belle-Thérèse*, whom the superintendent had summoned through the gendarmerie without telling anyone.

"Well?"

"It's not easy to say definitely . . . I think it was about the same . . ."

"What's that?" growled Lecoin.

"I don't know who shouted, but I'm saying it was more or less the same sound as yesterday."

This time the big fellow was on the point of losing his temper and hitting out at the skipper, who was unaware of the part he was playing in this performance.

"Get back into the lorry!"

Someone else now came up, someone who had hitherto not stirred: it was Captain Pillement.

"It's going all right!" Maigret told him in a low voice. "We shall see what happens next . . ."

And he went back to sit beside Lecoin, who was making no further effort to seem pleasant.

"What am I to do now?"

"What you did yesterday!"

"Go to Montargis?"

"Just as you did yesterday!"

"All right! I don't know what idea you've got in your head, but if you think I've anything to do with this affair . . ."

They were already passing the inn, where four windows were lit up, on one of which the telephone number was inscribed in enamel letters.

"So you never thought of stopping to telephone?"

"I've already told you so . . ."

"Carry on!"

Silence; Maigret smoked his pipe in his dark corner, beside the sullen man with his occasional abrupt movements.

They reached Montargis, and suddenly the superintendent remarked, "You've gone past it . . ."

"What?"

"The gendarmerie . . ."

"That was your fault, making all this fuss . . ."

He started to back the lorry, for the gendarmerie station was only fifty meters away.

"No, no, carry on!" Maigret protested.

"Carry on what?"

"Doing just what you did yesterday . . ."

"But I went . . ."

"You didn't go straight to the gendarmerie. The proof is that the times don't fit . . . Where is Benoît's filling station?"

"At the second turning."

"Let's go there!"

"What for?"

"Nothing. Do what I tell you."

It was a very ordinary filling station, in front of a house with a bicycle shop below. The shop was not lit up, but through the windows one could see at the back of it a kitchen in which shadowy figures were moving.

The lorry had scarcely stopped when a man emerged from the kitchen, having obviously heard the engine and the grinding of the brakes.

"How many liters?" he asked without glancing at the lorry. Then, a minute later, he recognized it, and looked up at Lecoin, asking, "What are you doing here? I thought . . ."

"Give me fifty liters!"

Maigret sat still in his corner, unseen by the mechanic. Benoît, thinking himself alone with his friend, might perhaps have talked, but Lecoin, sensing the danger, remarked hastily, "Is that all you want, then, Monsieur le commissaire?"

"Oh, is there somebody with you?"

"Someone from the police who's doing what he calls a reconstruction. I don't understand a thing about it. It's always people like us that get pestered, while . . ."

Maigret had jumped out of the lorry and gone into the shop, to the great surprise of its owner. He had caught sight of the man's wife in the room at the back.

"Lecoin wants to know how things are going . . ." he remarked on the off-chance.

She looked at him suspiciously and leaned forward to peer through the window.

"Is Lecoin there?" she asked.

"He's filling up."

"He's not got into any trouble?"

Anxiously, puzzled by the intrusion of this bowler-hatted man, she went to the door.

It was difficult, in the bad light, to make out people's faces.

"Say, Paul . . ." she said to her husband, who was encumbered with his petrol hose. "Is Lecoin there?"

Maigret, taking advantage of the shelter of the shop, quietly filled his pipe and lighted it, thus casting a momentary gleam on the nickel handlebars of the cycles.

"Are you coming in, Paul?"

Then the superintendent clearly heard one of the two men asking the other, "What'll we do?"

By way of precaution he seized his revolver and kept it in his pocket, ready to fire through his coat if necessary. The street was deserted and dark, and Lecoin was big enough to fell an adversary with one blow of his fist.

"What would *you* do?"

The woman was still standing in the doorway, her shoulders hunched against the cold. Joseph Lecoin climbed down heavily from his seat and took a couple of steps undecidedly along the pavement.

"Suppose we go and discuss things inside?" Maigret said calmly.

Benoît hung up his petrol hose. Lecoin, who seemed still undecided, was screwing up the stopper of his tank.

Finally he said gruffly, walking towards the door of the shop, "After all, this hadn't been foreseen in the arrangement. After you, Superintendent . . ."

IV

It was a typical working-class home, with its carved oak sideboard, a check oilcloth on the table and some horrible pink and mauve fairground trophies by way of vases.

"Sit down," the woman muttered as she mechanically wiped the table in front of Maigret.

Benoît fetched a bottle from the sideboard and filled four small glasses in silence, while Lecoin slumped down astride a chair and leaned his elbows on the back of it.

"Did you suspect something?" he said sharply, looking Maigret straight in the eyes.

"For two reasons: first because the only shouts heard were in a man's voice, which was rather strange, considering that a girl was present and that if she'd been drowning she was a good enough swimmer to stay on the surface long enough to call for help . . . Next, after an accident of this sort, why should anyone drive twenty kilometers to warn the police when there's a telephone close by. The inn windows were lighted up. It was impossible not to think of . . ."

"Sure," admitted Lecoin. "It was he who insisted . . ."

"He'd got into the lorry, obviously?"

It was too late to retreat. In any case the two men had resigned themselves and the woman, meanwhile, seemed relieved. It was she who advised them, "Better tell the whole story. It's not worth it, for two wretched thousand-franc notes . . ."

"Joseph'll tell," put in her husband.

And Lecoin, after swallowing the contents of his glass, explained, "Let's say that it happened just like this evening. You were quite right. In spite of the rain and my bad wiper I've got good enough eyes and good enough brakes not to run into a stationary car. So I drew up a meter and a half away. I thought someone must have had a breakdown and I got off the lorry to lend a hand. That was when I saw a young man who seemed very excited and who asked me if I wanted to earn two thousand francs . . ."

"By helping him push the car into the water?" interrupted Maigret.

"At a pinch he could have pushed it by hand. That's what he was trying to do when I turned up. But what he chiefly wanted was to be taken off somewhere without anyone knowing. I really think that if he'd been by himself I'd not have agreed. But there was the girl . . ."

"She was still alive?"

"Yes indeed! To persuade me, he explained that people were trying to stop them getting married, that they were in love, that they wanted to fake a suicide so that nobody would try to find them and separate them . . . I don't much like that sort of game, but if you'd seen her, the kid, in the rain . . . So, after all, I helped them shove the car into the Loing. The young people hid in my lorry. They asked me to shout for help, to make things more convincing, and I shouted . . . So that it would seem as if they'd both got drowned . . . Afterwards I merely had to drive them to Montargis . . ."

"For that matter I noticed on the way that the young man was no fool. He knew he couldn't stop at a hotel. He didn't want to take the train either. He asked me if I didn't know someone who for another two thousand francs would keep them a few days until the inquiry was over. I thought of Benoît . . ."

The woman asserted, "We believed that they were runaway lovers, too . . . So as our brother-in-law, who's away with the army, has a room here . . ."

"Are they still in the house?"

"*She* isn't . . ."

"What?" And Maigret looked around anxiously.

"In the afternoon," the motor mechanic began, "when I saw the newspaper, I went upstairs and I asked if the story about the corpse

was true. The girl tore the paper from my hands, glanced through it
and suddenly, taking advantage of the door being open, she dashed
out . . ."

"Without her coat?"

"Without a coat or a hat . . ."

"And the young man?"

"He swore he couldn't understand, that he had only just bought
the car and hadn't thought of opening the luggage compartment . . ."

"Has your house any other door besides this one?"

At that very moment, as Benoît shook his head in reply, a crash
was heard in the street. Maigret ran out on to the pavement and
saw there a prostrate figure, a young man trying excitedly to get up
and run away, although he had broken his leg jumping down from
the upstairs window.

It was a dramatic and yet a pitiful sight, for Vertbois was mad
with rage and would not yet admit himself defeated.

"If you come near I shall fire . . ."

Maigret, however, pounced on him, and the young man did not
fire, from fear or through failure of nerve.

"Quiet, now . . ."

The young man was inveighing against the lorry driver, the
garage mechanic and his wife, accusing them of having betrayed
him.

He was the typical young delinquent, the sort Maigret knew only
too well from dozens of specimens, devious, resentful, ready to go
to any lengths to satisfy his greed for money and pleasure.

"Where is Viviane?" Maigret asked, as he put the handcuffs on.

"I don't know."

"So you'd managed to convince her that you pushed the car into
the river with the sole object of faking a suicide pact?"

"She stuck to me like a leech . . ."

"And it's tiresome, isn't it, to be landed with a corpse you can't
get rid of?"

It had been the foulest, most stupid and revolting crime, the sort
moreover which never pays!

Jean Vertbois, seeing that his marriage plans had fallen through
and that the La Pommeraye fortune would never come his way,
even if he abducted Viviane, had turned to a middle-aged woman
who had been his mistress for a long time and got her to visit his

apartment; he had murdered her and stolen her money, with part of which he had bought a cheap car, planning to dispose of the body in some lonely spot.

And then Viviane had turned up, with her young, whole-hearted passion, determined to run away from home and throw in her lot with her lover's.

She would not leave him for a moment! The hours sped by as they drove along, carrying the corpse with them.

Viviane believed she was enjoying a honeymoon, whereas she was deeply involved in a horrible drama!

While she embraced the man she loved, he was thinking only of the sinister load of which he must get rid at all costs!

It was then that, in desperation, he was invented this fake suicide, which the chance advent of a lorry had assisted and yet complicated.

"The news you promised us, Superintendent?"

The journalists had enjoyed a regular feast at La Cloche and their mood reflected this.

"The murderer of Marthe Dorval is in hospital . . ."

"Marthe Dorval?"

"A former light opera singer, who had some money put aside, and who was the mistress of Jean Vertbois . . ."

"He's in the hospital?"

"At Montargis, with broken leg. I give you permission to go and take his picture and ask him all the questions you like . . ."

"But the girl?"

Maigret hung his head. About her he knew nothing, and there was always the fear that she might have taken some desperate action.

It was after midnight, and the superintendent was with Captain Pillement in the latter's house at Nemours, discussing events, when the telephone rang.

The captain, who answered it, displayed surprise and delight, and asked a few questions. "You're certain of the address? Listen! To make quite sure, bring me the taxi driver here . . . Even if he's tipsy . . ."

And he explained to Maigret:

"My men have just discovered a taxi driver at Montargis who, some time during the day, took on a girl who was bareheaded and wore no coat. She had him drive her into the country, near Bourges, to a lonely manor house. On the way, as the driver was getting worried about his fare seeing that she wasn't even carrying a handbag, she repeatedly told him, 'My aunt will pay.' "

For Viviane La Pommeraye, panting and exhausted, had taken refuge with one of her aunts, with whom, ever since childhood, she had gone to spend her holidays.

CAPTAIN HEIMRICH STUMBLES

FRANCES AND RICHARD LOCKRIDGE

Frances and Richard Lockridge are best known as the creators of that quintessential husband-and-wife sleuthing team, Pam and Jerry North. But they were also the parents of a number of other enduring series characters, most notably Captain Merton Heimrich of the New York State Police. Captain Heimrich appears in a number of the Mr. and Mrs. North books, and as solo detective in more than a score of novels authored by the Lockridges collaboratively and by Richard Lockridge alone after Frances's death in 1963. In "Captain Heimrich Stumbles," the likeable policeman demonstrates that a member of his breed "needs to have a smattering of many kinds of knowledge; he needs such a smattering to detect patterns . . ."

The widow of Paul Winters stood just inside the door of Captain M. L. Heimrich's office in the Troop K barracks at Hawthorne at a little after two o'clock on a Saturday afternoon late in March. She was a slight woman, with a feather of gray in her dark hair. Her eyes were very wide, very shocked. Heimrich wished he could help her, but had no certainty that he could—or that anybody could.

Paul Winters had died violently some four hours earlier. But Heimrich's concern is with homicide, and Winters had died in an automobile accident—an accident that had involved only him. It was simple, uncomplicated; already, the troopers assigned to the case had it wrapped up and filed away. It had nothing to do with the Bureau of Criminal Investigation, New York State Police, and hence nothing to do with Captain M. L. Heimrich.

So there was nothing he could do to help the woman whose dark

eyes were so wide, so fixed—the woman who looked so much as if
she had been cruelly, physically and, above all, unexpectedly struck
in the face.

Ten minutes before she came into his office, Heimrich had been
sitting at his desk, involved in other matters. The telephone had
rung, and he had picked it up and said, "Heimrich." He listened,
then said, "What's the name again?" since he had not heard the
name before. He listened further. Finally he said, "Why, if it's
accidental?" But then, after a moment more, he murmured, "All
right. That's what we're here for. But let me have the report first.
Then the lady."

The report came. He looked at it. A man—name of Winters,
Paul—had lost control of his car on a friend's driveway. The car
had pitched down a steep slope, hit a low retaining wall, landed
upside down in ten feet of water. Tossed in the car, Winters had
struck his head on something—the sharp corner of an opened
ashtray probably—and so had been unconscious when he drowned.
But he would not have been able to escape, in any case, since both
doors had jammed when the car crashed.

Winters, presumably, had lost control of his car—as many others
had that morning—because he was driving through a blinding
snowstorm. Heimrich looked up from the accident report and out
of his office window. Snow was still falling, although not so heavily
now.

It had been very bad that morning, when Heimrich had driven
cautiously down to Hawthorne from Van Brunt Center. "Hazard-
ous driving conditions," his car radio told him, needlessly. It was
no great consolation to learn, at the same time, that in Manhattan
it was merely raining. It had been merely raining when Paul Winters set out that morning from Manhattan, where he lived, to visit
a Mr. Bertram Smith, his partner in business (importing), who had
recently bought a riverside house near North Salem.

It was Smith who had reported the accident to the police. The
accident had occurred on the steep, twisting driveway down to
Smith's house. Winters's car had skidded off into Smith's small
lake, made by damming a little river, and it was there that Paul
Winters had died.

So—a fatal accident. An accident properly investigated, duly reported on. But Paul Winters's widow insisted on seeing Captain Heimrich.

Heimrich lifted his telephone again and said, "All right. Ask Mrs. Winters to come in, please." Then he stood up, a large and solid man, with very blue eyes in a square face.

Somebody in the anteroom opened the door for Mrs. Paul Winters and she stepped into Heimrich's office and somebody closed the door behind her. She was crying and did not seem to know that she was crying. When she spoke, her voice was very low—so low that Heimrich had to strain to hear her words.

"I had to see someone," she said. "Someone who—who could tell me. Who *would* tell me. I'd—something I heard about you made me think you would. I don't remember who said—" She stopped speaking. Then she whispered, "I can't seem to stop crying." It was as if she spoke to herself.

Heimrich went around the desk and did not touch the slender woman, but he spoke very gently and got her to sit in a wooden chair across from his desk; he did not look at, but saw, her hands twisting a handkerchief. Then Heimrich went back to his own chair and held out a pack of cigarettes toward her. She did not seem to see it.

"Captain Heimrich," she said, "I have to know. Paul—my husband wanted to die, didn't he? I mean—he killed himself. Isn't that true? You don't want to tell me and I—I understand that. You think it wouldn't do any good, wouldn't make any difference. The others—they're just trying to be kind. That's it, isn't it?"

"Killed himself?" Heimrich repeated. "Why do you say that, Mrs. Winters?"

"Then he did," she said and covered her face with frail hands as her whole body shook. She spoke in so low a tone that, with her hands muffling the sound, Heimrich could not be wholly sure what she said. But then he was sure. "It's my fault," she said, behind the screening hands. "My fault. My—"

"Mrs. Winters," Heimrich said. "Listen to me. There's nothing—nothing at all—to suggest your husband killed himself. Everything to show it was an accident. There were many traffic accidents this morning."

She took her hands down from her face. Her eyes still had the startled look, the look of shocked surprise.

"Mrs. Winters," Heimrich said, speaking very slowly, "I want you to listen to me. There is nothing—*nothing at all*—to suggest that this was anything but an accident. The troopers who went there are good men, trained men. If there had been anything suspicious—"

He stopped. She did not seem to be listening.

"You don't understand," she said, and it was clear she had not been listening to Heimrich, but only to her own thoughts. She spoke toward him, not to him. "It was up to me to see—see that he didn't die. The doctor said that. As good as said that. A few months. That was what the doctor said. A few months—six months perhaps—and Paul would be himself again. He said it was almost always like that when—when the case was simple. As he said Paul's was. What I had to do was see that he didn't die."

She put her hands over her face again and Heimrich waited. "Didn't kill himself," she said. " 'It's up to his friends'—that's what the doctor said. 'Most of all, of course, it's up to you.' To me. *Me.*"

Again her body began to shake. There was nothing Heimrich could do about that. He waited, and gradually she grew quieter. She took her hands away from her face and looked at him. Her eyes had not changed. "I have to know whether I failed," she said. "Whether I have to live with that. I—*I have to know.*"

A policeman needs to have smattering of many kinds of knowledge; he needs such a smattering to detect patterns.

"Your husband had been in a depression?" Heimrich said. "Had been seeing a psychiatrist?"

She nodded. She was crying again, and paid no attention to the tears on her face.

"And had thoughts of suicide?" Heimrich said, although the answer to that was clear enough. "Had got better under treatment as—I mean, the doctor called it a simple depression?" She nodded her head again. "As usually happens," Heimrich added, "given time."

"And," she said, "protection. Protection from—himself. Do you understand now?"

Heimrich did. A man, almost himself again, not quite himself again, entrusted to tenderness and—watchfulness. The swings between depression and elation shortened, the periods of equilibrium, of normality, growing longer. But—the moments of mind's darkness still occurring. In which—She was, of course, quite right. She might have failed. Failure might have been inevitable, guiltless.

He looked at the slender woman. It would do no good to tell her that.

Because Paul Winters might well have taken this way to kill himself when darkness settled on his mind. There was no point in denying that to the shaken woman. She would have to live with that—live, at the best, with the possibility of that; with a question which could not, Heimrich supposed, ever be answered. At least, he saw no way to answer it.

But she waited—waited for an answer.

"Mr. Winters had been ill for some time?" Heimrich asked, not seeing that the answer to that would lead to any other answer.

He had been. For about a year he had been under psychiatric treatment in a private hospital. Two weeks ago he had been discharged as much improved, ready to try for the adjustment which he would have to make. But released with a proviso—always with a proviso.

"He seemed quite himself," his widow said and now—although Heimrich thought the effort was great for her—she spoke steadily. "Until yesterday."

The day before he had gone to his business office for the first time. And when he came home, she thought he was upset. He denied it, laughing at her gently, saying she must quit worrying about him. He admitted he was a little tired. That was all. Taking hold again after so long a time away was, naturally, tiring. That was all.

"The doctor," she said, "told me not to be—to be *too* protective. Not to let him feel that I didn't trust him or was worrying about him too much."

Winters had told his wife that he was driving up the next morning to see Bert. If he could find Bert's new house. "Bertram Smith," she said. "His partner." Heimrich nodded. "He said something about there being a business point or two he wanted to clear up with Bert. I tried to talk him out of it, but he laughed at me. Said he'd already made the date with Bert and—"

Unexpectedly she broke down and her body shook again.

"I had an appointment," she said. "An appointment to have my hair done. *To have my hair done.* So—I let him go alone. For nothing more than that! To have my—" Once more she covered her face with her hands. She moved her head slowly from side to side. Heimrich could only wait. There wasn't anything to say. She steadied herself again, and again it was painful to watch the effort.

"You see now," she said. "I have to know. You do see that? If—if Paul killed himself, if I failed him, I have to know. *One way or the other.* You can live with a thing you know—some way you can—" She paused. "But I have to know."

And saying that, she laid the problem in Heimrich's hands, laid the impossible in his hands. Because there was no way, there never would be any way, of knowing. Accident or intention? The result was the same, and the answer was lost forever in a mind snapped off.

"I'll do what I can," Heimrich heard himself say. "I can't promise anything."

She would wait for him—wait there. No matter how long it would take. "I've nothing else to do," she said. "Nothing to do anywhere."

Heimrich drove north and east. The plows had not yet got to the township road which he turned into beyond North Salem, and when he turned from that onto the private road which served three widely separated houses—one of them Bertram Smith's—the surface was a churned-up mess. Churned up, Heimrich supposed, by policemen who had been there before him—been there when there was possibly something to find out.

The private road, narrow and twisting, had been staked—staked for winter guidance in snow, and left staked into late March, with a pessimism that events had fully justified. The stakes were driven on either side of the road, at intervals of twenty feet or so, and marked the road's course. A little-travelled road can disappear in heavy snow.

The road dead-ended in turn-around beyond a sign which just protruded above the snow and was lettered "Bertram Smith." Heimrich stopped his car in the turn-around and walked back.

Winters could not, Heimrich thought, looking down the driveway, merely have missed the turn. The driveway was staked as the road had been—round, green stakes, dahlia stakes, driven in on both sides and about twenty feet apart. Even driving through heavily falling snow, as Winters had been, he could hardly have failed to see the guiding stakes.

So—he had skidded off the roadway.

Or—he had deliberately turned off it, seeking death.

The drive was rutted. Police cars had crept up and down it; an ambulance had gone down empty and climbed back, not empty.

Heimrich walked down in the ruts to the twist in the drive. He did not expect to find anything the troopers had missed—he did not expect to find anything at all. Even if the car had skidded, even if it had left skid marks, nothing would be proved. A car turned sharply on a slippery surface is likely to skid.

The marks the car had made in snow and earth went straight down to the river. The marks would tell him nothing; they had already told nothing to the troopers, beyond what was obvious. Nevertheless, as he started down the slope toward the battered car—hauled out of the water now, a wreck by the water's edge—Heimrich did not walk in the tracks, but through unmarked snow beside them. If there *was* anything to be discovered, there was no use in trampling it out.

Halfway down, shuffling carefully through the snow, Heimrich stumbled. He flailed the air, seeking balance, not finding it on the slope. Captain Heimrich fell—not quite flat on his face, since he broke his fall with outstretched hands, but flat enough. He swore, got up, brushed himself off. Of all the awkward damn things to do. . . .

He went back to see what he had stumbled over. He squatted down and brushed the snow aside. He had stumbled over the broken end of a green stake which protruded three or four inches from the ground into which—*into which it had been driven.*

Heimrich then sat back on his heels and stared at nothing. After a time he said, just audibly, that he would be damned.

He rose and walked on, very slowly, down the slope, his eyes on the ground. He found what he was looking for—a place where the snow had been disturbed. He squatted again and, carefully, brushed the snow aside. Again he found what he was looking for—a neat, round hole through turf, into clayish earth. This stake had come out clean when it was pulled out, had not broken off as the other stake—the other lying stake—had broken. There would be more holes, without doubt, where the other stakes had been pulled from clinging earth. But they could be looked for later.

Heimrich went back to the drive and began to walk down it toward the house—toward the house and a man who had known Paul Winters was driving up that morning and had wanted Winters dead; toward, it was almost inevitable, a man named Bertram Smith, since who else could have switched the stakes in Smith's front yard and not been caught at it? Switched them to guide a car off an unfamiliar road and to almost certain death. Switched them to kill. Hence, a murderer and one who, murder achieved, had merely to pull up the lying stakes and put them back where they should be—where they must be found later, along the driveway's true edges, telling the truth again.

And by then, a murderer in a hurry—in such a hurry that he had broken one of the stakes he wrenched at and had to leave the three- or four-inch stump in the ground—had broken it off so that enough remained above ground to make a policeman, seeking something else, stumble on murder. He would have needed to hurry. The crash of the car against the retaining wall might well have been heard, so the accident had to be reported quickly. There had been also, of course, the need to cover footmarks he had left in the snow as he went from stake to stake, pulling them out. A broom would start that and the thickly falling snow would finish it. Still, there had been a need to work fast—too fast, as it had turned out.

What Paul Winters, on his first visit to his business office in a year, had discovered was anybody's guess. Certainly something Smith could not let go further. Theft of some kind probably. They would have to find out.

There was much that remained to be found out, to be organized, to be proved. There might be difficulties: Smith was clearly an ingenious man—a most ingenious man. But now that they knew what had happened, now that they knew what to look for. . . .

Heimrich stopped going down the drive, stood for a moment, then turned back. Smith, in his house or not, would keep a few minutes longer.

Heimrich went back to his car and used the two-way radio to call the barracks. He could do nothing for Paul Winters now, except catch his murderer. But he might, with what he had to tell his wife, help an anguished woman go on living, help her pick up the pieces—he could, at any rate, free her from the agony of guilt.

Which was not much; which was something. . . .

BY CHILD UNDONE

JACK RITCHIE

*Jack Ritchie published several hundred short stories between
1953 and his death in 1983, almost all of which are cleverly
plotted, economically written, and beautifully crafted. In an
introduction to Ritchie's only book,* A New Leaf and Other
Stories *(1971), Donald E. Westlake wrote: "Jack Ritchie happens to be a brilliant man in the wrong pew, a miniaturist in
an age of elephantiasis. He knows . . . that a short story needs
emphasis on both words—it should be a* story, *full and round
and plotted and peopled and with a satisfactory finish, and it
should also be* short.*" "By Child Undone" succeeds on both
counts; it also has an ingenious plot (even by Ritchie's stan-
dards) that features some unusual police work from a very
unusual source. . . .*

It was well past midnight when Henry Wilson returned home after
a late show. As he inserted the key into the lock of his apartment
door, he was shot once through the back and died almost immediately.

George Clinton died the next night in an equally direct fashion.

Our police department receives a number of letters every day—
some offering information or seeking it, others obscene, some
threatening, some rambling tirades. A great many of them, to be
truthful, we drop into the wastebasket. We simply do not have the
personnel or the budget to follow through on everything that comes
through the mail. There are some messages, however, which do
command our attention.

This was one. The envelope and note paper were of an ordinary
type which can be purchased at any of a thousand stationery
departments. The message was typewritten, without salutation, and
unsigned. It had been received by the commissioner's office earlier
in the day and forwarded to my department for action. It read:

On the supposition that any organization as large as yours might inadvertently overlook the matter, I suggest that you compare the bullets which killed Henry Wilson and George Clinton.

I believe you will find that they were fired from the same gun.

I looked up at Detective Sergeant Harrison. "Well?"

He nodded. "It checks out. The same gun."

"I presume you had the lab go over this letter for fingerprints?"

"Sure, but nothing. Just Millie's prints. The commissioner didn't touch it."

Millie Tyler is the commissioner's secretary. She opens and prereads his official mail, so when it becomes necessary to forward a letter from his office to the fingerprint department, Millie's prints invariably appear on the paper. The technicians in the laboratory claim to be able to recognize them on sight, and we grant them that.

I drummed my fingers lightly on the desk. "If the writer of this note knew that the bullets came from the same gun, the question is obvious. Why?"

"I have a sneaking suspicion."

"So have I, especially since he took the pains not to forward his fingerprints. Did Clinton and Wilson know each other?"

"As far as we've been able to find out, they never even saw each other in their lives. There's just one thing common to the both of them. They were members of the American Legion."

I looked out of the window.

Harrison cleared his throat. "I'm sure we'll come up with something more than that, sir."

As long as we were stuck at that point, I asked, "Did they both belong to the same post?"

"No. They lived on opposite sides of the city."

"But at least they attended the same war?"

"No. Clinton was a World War II vet and Wilson a Korean vet."

I picked up the report on the first victim, Henry Wilson.

Henry Wilson had been a bachelor, thirty-eight; bookkeeper with a construction firm, steady worker. Not particularly extrovert in conversation, but he did belong to four weekly bowling leagues.

Saved his money, but wasn't fanatic about it, worth around six thousand in a savings account. Had twenty thousand in insurance, ten of which was G.I. and the other ten with a private firm. The beneficiaries were half a dozen charitable organizations.

"Was he a nut on charities?"

"No," Harrison said. "According to the people who knew him, Wilson took out the insurance policies early in his life because they were good buys. Low rates, you know. He figured that, if he got married, he could always change the beneficiaries."

"But evidently he didn't. Any matrimonial prospects or rejects?"

"None that we've run across so far. I guess he preferred bowling."

I turned to the file on George Clinton.

Age, forty-six; veteran of Second World War; vice-president of Madison Avenue advertising agency. Divorced in 1963; wife and two teen-aged daughters promptly returned to the state of Washington, where his wife's parents still lived.

Clinton drank heavily, but evidently kept it under control during working hours. Had a trigger temper. According to an associate, Clinton engaged in a fistfight with a customer at a downtown bar three days before he was shot.

He lived alone, his body found in apartment near door. Neighbor says he heard something that *might* have been a shot at one in the morning, but wasn't sure enough to bother the police.

"What about this fistfight thing?" I asked.

"We're looking for him. The bartender says he drops in occasionally, but he doesn't know the guy's name or anything about him. You know how it is in those crowded downtown bars. The faces get familiar, but there's nothing worth remembering except a man's favorite drink."

I put Clinton's file in the Out tray. "So we're left riding two tiny parallels. Both victims belonged to the American Legion, and they lived alone."

"And they were both men."

"Thank you," I said.

"Well, that could be important, you know."

Late that afternoon, Sergeant Harrison came back to my office. "The bartender just called and said that the customer who had the fight with Clinton is in the place right now working on a whiskey sour."

"Has it occurred to you to pick him up?"

"I already sent somebody," Harrison said. "They'll bring him in."

I told my secretary, Sue Adams, where I'd be, and we took the elevator down to the interrogation rooms.

Fifteen minutes later, two detectives brought in a man in his early thirties. He was neatly dressed, though at the moment he was perspiring and his hair was a bit disturbed and moist. He informed us that he was the junior partner of Polk and Polk, Certified Public Accountants.

"Honest," he said, "I never even saw this Clinton before."

"Then what was the argument about?" I asked.

"There was no argument. I mean, no talk at all. I guess he had a lot of drinks in him and he bumped into me on his way to the cigarette machine or something. I said, 'Watch it,' and the next thing I knew, he swung at me and it went like that."

"You didn't know who he was?"

"I swear. Not until one of those detectives told me."

"Where were you at one A.M. Tuesday?"

"At home. In bed asleep. My wife will vouch for that. She's a light sleeper and very jealous. I couldn't go anywhere without her knowing."

When I got to the office Thursday after lunch, Sue Adams informed me that the commissioner had received another letter and that it now lay on the desk in my office.

I unfolded the notepaper carefully, anchored it open with a ruler, and read:

Reading the newspapers, I see that you have definitely established that one gun killed both Clinton and Wilson.

Good for you.

The revolver belongs to me and I intend to use it again.

I sent for Sergeant Harrison. He read the message and pursed his lips. "It's not signed."

I studied him.

He flushed. "I wasn't expecting him to sign his real name, but you sort of expect to see something like 'The Avenger.' "

"How do we know it's a 'he'?"

"We don't," Harrison admitted, "but somehow I just can't picture a woman writing notes like this. I guess I'm an incurable romantic."

"Take this letter to the lab and see if there are any fingerprints besides Millie's."

There were none.

The third man to die was William A. Wheeler, musician and music teacher.

I was routed from my bed at three in the morning—and so was Harrison, for that matter—by the call from headquarters. Half an hour later, I joined Harrison and we stared down at the pajama-clad body of William A. Wheeler.

"According to the reconstruction," Harrison said, "the buzzer got him out of bed at two in the morning. Wheeler left the chain on the door when he opened it, but that didn't help any. As soon as it was open a few inches, the murderer fired."

The photographer finished and two ambulance attendants put Wheeler's body on a stretcher and covered it.

Harrison continued. "The man in the next apartment was hunched over hot milk trying to beat insomnia and heard the shot. He didn't jump up right away, but thought it over before he decided that it just might have been a shot, though it wasn't anywhere near as loud as the ones on television. So he peeked down the hall and there he saw Wheeler's hand sticking out of the partly opened door. Didn't see any signs of the killer though, and he phoned the police right away."

I looked about the apartment. It was rather cluttered. I noticed some small trophies on one of the shelves of a bookcase and examined them. They had been earned by Wheeler while a member of the swimming team at Jefferson High in 1946 and 1947.

"What do we know about Wheeler?" I asked.

"Nothing yet," Harrison said, "except that he's thirty-six."

At ten-thirty that morning Millie Tyler, the commissioner's secretary, brought an unopened envelope to my office. "This came in the commissioner's mail and it looks like another one of those letters. I'm almost beginning to recognize the style of typing."

I opened the envelope, carefully extracted the note, and read:

I trust that by the time you receive this you will have found the body of Wheeler.

Are you perhaps thinking that I detest the human race so much that I kill indiscriminately?

You are only half-right.

I do not kill indiscriminately.

I wondered about the swift mail service until I studied the envelope again. The letter was postmarked at eight the previous evening, six hours before Wheeler had been killed.

I sent the letter on to the lab and it was returned to me just before Harrison came into my office.

Harrison read it and shook his head. "He's crazy."

"We all are," I said, "only at different times."

"And confident. I mean, mailing the letter six hours before he kills the man. Any fingerprints?"

"None at all. Not even Millie's."

Harrison opened his notebook. "About William A. Wheeler: He played the clarinet, gave class lessons under the city's musical development program and took private pupils on the side. One of the rooms of his apartment is soundproofed."

"What about friends, acquaintances and so forth?"

"The normal number. We're checking them out. Wheeler had two brothers, one's a dentist and the other operates a drugstore. Wheeler spent two years in the army during the Korean War with various post and regimental bands, including overseas."

"I suppose he was a member of the American Legion?"

"No. Veterans of Foreign Wars. But that's still a service organization. He was a swimmer in high school. Got some trophies."

I worried my pipe. "What the devil connects Wilson, Clinton and Wheeler? Do we have anything that goes across the board? No matter how trivial?"

Harrison ticked off a series. "They were all men, they lived alone in apartments, they were single or divorced, they were all former servicemen and members of a veterans' organization, they were killed in the early hours of the morning, they all had brown hair and they all could swim. I checked up on that last thing after I saw Wheeler's trophies."

I closed my eyes. "You forgot that all of them inhaled and exhaled from time to time, and they were notorious for having their features fixed at the front of their heads."

Harrison was mildly reproving. "You told me you wanted anything connecting them, no matter how small it was."

I conceded. "Did Wheeler carry insurance?"

"Ten thousand, G.I. insurance; one thousand allocated for burial
expenses, and nine thousand to his mother. She's widowed, on
social security, and lives in an apartment over her son Albert's
drugstore. You don't suppose she killed him for the policy?"

"Of course not."

Harrison was faintly dubious. "How can you be so positive about
that? I know it's unnatural, but mothers do sometimes murder their
children."

"But not after they've grown up."

He rubbed his jaw. "You know, I never realized that before.
Makes you stop and think," and he stopped and thought a while.

The next morning Sue Adams greeted me as I came to work.
"This time the letter's addressed directly to you instead of the
commissioner. I opened it along with your other mail. It's on your
desk now."

In my office I examined the envelope for a moment. It had been
mailed early yesterday evening.

Dear Captain Hayes,

I address you directly since the papers mention that you are
in immediate charge of this case. I assume that you have
found victim number four?

I feel a great deal like that race driver who knows that taking
a curve at 75 miles an hour will result in catastrophe. And yet
he attempts to round it at 74 miles an hour . . . and then 74.5
. . . and then 74.6. To come ever closer without disaster
becomes the joy of the game.

How many dare I kill before you learn to anticipate me?
Perhaps I will kill one too many.

I got Sue Adams on the intercom. She gets to work a half hour
before I do and is usually briefed on the night's happenings.

"Sue, why didn't you tell me that they found number four?"

"I don't think they have," she said. "At least, I haven't heard
anything. There were two homicides last night, but they were
husband-and-wife affairs, one a hammer job and the other a knife.
Not what we're looking for, is it, Captain?"

When I returned from lunch at one, Sue had been fretting impatiently. "They found number four, I think. Harrison left fifteen minutes ago and he's probably there by now." She handed me a slip of paper with an address on it.

When my driver left me off, I walked up to a small cottage set back on the lot in a tree-shaded, older part of the city.

"His name's Fairbanks," Harrison said. "Charles W. Fairbanks, but the neighbors called him Charley. Age, seventy-two, widower, no children. Retired and living alone on social security and a pension."

I looked down at the body on the kitchen floor. Charley Fairbanks had been shot through the right temple.

Harrison continued. "The doctor estimates that he died between one and three A.M., give or take. Anyway, nobody in the neighborhood remembers hearing the shot. At that time of night everybody's usually asleep. I guess that's why the murderer chooses that time to strike."

"Brilliant deduction."

"It looks like Fairbanks was sitting here at the kitchen table having a cup of coffee."

"Between one and three in the morning?"

"He lived alone so he made his own hours. When he felt like drinking a cup of coffee, he drank it. Anyway, the murderer stood right outside and fired through the window screen beside him."

"Who found his body?"

"His niece. I talked to her a little. Being that Fairbanks lived alone and because of his age, she phones him every day at about noon. This noon he didn't answer so she came over to see if anything was wrong."

"What about insurance?"

"Only a two-thousand-dollar policy and the niece is his beneficiary, but it's understood that she pays his funeral expenses. Also he owns this cottage and that goes to her, too." After a few moments of silence, Harrison sighed. "Fairbanks couldn't swim a damn stroke."

I looked at Harrison.

He cleared his throat. "I mean that there goes another one of the connecting links. About all the victims being able to swim, you know? And not only that, what hair Fairbanks had was gray and before that red. So that also shoots our theory about them all having brown hair."

I looked out of the window. "Stop using the word 'our.' "

Harrison was not yet defeated. "But at least he spent two weeks in an army camp outside of Lincoln, Nebraska, and then World War I ended. Been a loyal member of the American Legion since it was founded in 1919."

Harrison nodded to himself. "So we still got this: They were all men, they lived alone, they were all former servicemen and members of a veterans' organization."

I took a deep breath. "Are you really happy with that?"

Victim number five met his death between two and three A.M. the next morning. We were able to pinpoint the time of death because he had been a night watchman and was required to punch the clock hourly. When he failed to do so at three, the Merchant Police responded automatically and found his body lying inside the heavy wire fence enclosing the Humphrey Tool and Die Company.

At nine that morning I had the personal effects of the victim on my desk. I read the information on his driver's license. "Richard M. Johnson. Born 1912. That makes him fifty-four."

Harrison seemed shaken at the report we'd just gotten from the lab. "But Johnson can't be number five. It doesn't fit our pattern."

"But the bullet does," I said. "It came from the same gun that killed the others."

"Johnson was never in the army, the navy, the marines, or even the coast guard," Harrison said a bit plaintively. "Double hernia and classified 4-F. And he didn't live alone, either. He had a wife and two grown children who boarded with him."

I put my hand on his shoulder. "That happens sometimes. Did you really have your heart set on those veterans' organizations?"

He nodded. "Now the only thing tying the victims together is the fact that they were men and there are millions of those." He frowned thoughtfully. "They weren't murdered in alphabetical order, were they?"

I am ashamed to admit that I had momentarily considered that, too. "No," I said testily, "they weren't."

Harrison rubbed his jaw. "I don't think the murderer's insane at all."

"Why not?"

"Well . . . I know it's insane to kill people in that chain letter style, but that's not really his *type* of insanity. He just wants us to *think* that there's a mad killer running around loose. He's got an understandable motive for killing at least *one* of his victims, but he prefers to have us running around looking for a mass murderer instead of examining each case individually and coming up with an answer that would hurt him."

There are times when I have the feeling that I underestimate the intelligence of some of my associates. Not often, but it is there.

"All right," I said, "and which one of the victims is his real prey?"

"I don't know," Harrison said. "Maybe he hasn't even gotten around to him yet."

At ten that evening I was in my office. I was tired and hungry and wanted to go home to a hot bath, but the fact that someone else would be dead by tomorrow morning kept me going over and over everything we had on the murders.

The door to my office clicked open and Sergeant Harrison and his somewhat owlish ten-year-old son, William, entered. They both seemed rather formally dressed and Harrison explained: "Just got through with the Father and Son Banquet at the Y.M.C.A. Thought I'd drop in and see if there was anything new?"

"There isn't," I said and stared morosely at the sheet of paper on my desk.

1. Henry Wilson
2. George Clinton
3. William A. Wheeler
4. Charles W. Fairbanks
5. Richard M. Johnson

I became aware of Harrison's son at my elbow. "Well," I said somewhat irritably, "do they mean very much of anything to you?"

He pushed his glasses back up the bridge of his nose. "Sure, Captain Hayes. They were all vice-presidents of the United States."

I regarded him stonily for nearly twenty seconds and then went to the nearest set of encyclopedias.

William was correct.

I immediately recalled all off-duty detectives, sat down at the city directory, and began assigning stake-outs.

One of them—outside the mansion of the very rich Mr. William A. King—apprehended King's nephew and only heir as the young man prepared to put a bullet through his sleeping uncle's skull.

Mr. King's namesake had served as vice-president under Franklin Pierce.

I held a small coffee-and-cake celebration in my office.

"I think it's a little unfair of the murderer," Sue Adams said. "Who in the world is expected to remember vice-presidents? Now, if they had been the names of our presidents, I would have gotten suspicious right away. Everybody knows our presidents."

Sergeant Benjamin Harrison cut a piece of chocolate cake and handed it to his son, William Henry Harrison. "At first I thought the murderer might be that certified public accountant with Polk and Polk."

Millie Tyler put sugar into her coffee. "You mean the one who slugged it out with the vice-president with the advertising firm on Madison Avenue? Well, frankly, at the time I thought it might be his wife, but then she had this alibi about being in the state of Washington."

Sue Adams had a one-track mind. "If he'd just mentioned somebody like Jefferson or Lincoln."

I rubbed my jaw thoughtfully and tried to think back. Now that she mentioned it, it seemed to me that . . .

The commissioner opened the office door. "We're making out a citation for you, Captain. I keep forgetting your first name."

"Rutherford," I said. "Rutherford B. Hayes."

THE KING IN PAWN

MICHAEL GILBERT

Michael Gilbert's stories about Patrick Petrella, currently Detective Chief Inspector of the South London Division of the Metropolitan Police, have been widely praised as a British equivalent of Ed McBain's 87th Precinct series. Petrella's rise from constable to chief inspector, chronicled throughout the series, is just one of its many strong points; others include expert writing, a nice leavening of humor, a sharp sense of realism, a vivid evocation of south London and other locales, and an intangible that Ellery Queen has called "substance and style . . . woven into a tapestry of fascinating shapes and colors, of subtle and ingenious designs." In "The King in Pawn," Petrella goes up against the King of Receivers ("fences," in American parlance, those who buy and sell stolen merchandise), with very satisfying results.

The Queen's own Royal South London Rifles has its depot in Southwark High Street and has long recruited both its regular and territorial regiments from the tough boys who live thereabouts. How Detective Inspector Petrella became an honorary member of this excellent regiment and a welcome guest at its functions is a story which has never been fully or truthfully told before.

It started on a blustery evening in March. It had been a tiresome day. There had been a case of shoplifting, rendered more unpleasant than usual by the fact that children had been trained to do the stealing; there had been three larcenies from parked cars, a case of organized pocket-picking in a bus queue, and—that the measure should be pressed down and overflowing—a little matter of defalcation from the police canteen at Gabriel Street Station itself.

"Is everyone incurably dishonest?" said Petrella to Superintendent Benjamin.

"Lucky the canteen job wasn't one of our boys," said Benjamin. "I never trusted that civilian caterer."

"Most of the people we've had in today didn't need the money—not really need it. Those dreadful women, smoking like chimneys, dressed up to the nines, training their *own* kids to lift stuff—"

"Opportunity," said Benjamin, "makes crime. Cut down the opportunities, you'll cut down the crime. You know who I'd like to put inside, Patrick? Receivers. Shut one of them up and you stop a hundred crimes that haven't yet been committed."

Petrella had heard all this before, and knew it to be true. But it had been too hard a day for easy optimism.

"Receivers are like the Hydra," he said. "Cut off one head and a hundred more spring up."

"Little men," said Benjamin. "You're talking about little men. People who'll hide a carton of stolen cigarettes in the washtub and sweat every time the doorbell rings. I'm not talking about little men, Patrick. I'm talking about the two or three who matter. You know you did your best job the first month you were here? When you ran in old Bonny. Pick up the King of Receivers and you can claim your pension."

Pick up the King, thought Petrella, as he left Gabriel Street that evening. He had one more call to make, in the Pardoe Street area, and then he was going home. Pick up the King. It sounded easy, when you said it. And someday, no doubt, somebody would do it. Even the smartest criminals made a mistake in the end.

But the King of Receivers had had a very long run. His name had been spoken in South London for twenty years or more. It had been whispered among informers—the little, spreading grass roots of the underworld.

The King was older than the oldest detective in X Division. He dealt in jewelry, in precious stones and metals of all sorts. So much was known. A man who pulled a job of this sort had only to wait for a telephone call. Sooner or later it would come: be at a certain place at a certain time. The place was somewhere, anywhere, in South London. The time was after dark. A car would draw up, a gloved hand hold out a packet of bank notes. The same hand would receive the parcel of stolen goods. Then the car would drive off. It was as simple as that.

There was no pause to check the jewelry, no time to count the notes. Both sides trusted the other because, in the long run, it paid them to do so. Just once, soon after the war ended, "Big" Lewis had the idea of substituting a packet of inferior stones for the diamonds he had lifted from Curliers. He had hidden the real diamonds at home, under a loose tile in the kitchen, with an eye to disposing of them subsequently at even greater profit. When he got home he found three plainclothesmen waiting for him. They knew about the loose tile, too. The King of Fences was quick.

It was from Big Lewis, who realized that he had been shopped, that the police had got most of their information about the King. It amounted to precious little. It was clearly a waste of time trying to trace him through the cars he used, for these would be "borrowed" from a car park and returned without the owners ever being aware of the use to which their property had been put. It was a method which left remarkably few loose ends.

The name itself might have some significance. In the curiously warped humor of the underworld, names might have two or even three meanings. (Had there not been another famous receiver known as Mr. Eleven, who turned out to be a middle-aged man also known as Johnny Cricket?)

Petrella had his own ideas about the King. He thought maybe they were dealing with a dynasty—not one King, but a line of Kings. The stock in trade of such a man was knowledge: knowing who would be likely to pull certain jobs, knowing the disgruntled deckhands and too clever airline operatives who carry the stuff out of the country, knowing the buyers in Paris and Amsterdam, knowing how to get the money back to England. When the reigning King had made his pile, what was to prevent him from disposing of his know-how to a carefully chosen successor?

"A Hydra," said Petrella. "A dynasty of Hydras."

It was at this point in his reflections that a heavy brass ashtray came sailing through a window close to his right cheek, covered him with splintered glass, ricocheted from a lamp-post, and came to rest in the gutter with a sullen clang.

Petrella shook the glass carefully out of his raincoat while he considered the matter.

The window through which the ashtray had come belonged, he saw, to the private bar of a small public house, The Kentish Giant. He was aware of raised voices and stamping feet within. There came another crash, then a progression of crashes, as though a child was dragging the cloth off a dinner table set for twelve.

He opened the door of the pub and looked inside.

The fight was almost over. In the middle of the room a subsiding group was composed of a stout man in shirt sleeves, a youth in an apron, a man in a blue suit, and a man in denim overalls. All of them were holding onto portions of a fifth man, a large man with a red face, a shock of close-cropped hair, and a pugnacious expression.

The large man heaved, like a balloon at its guide ropes. But his captors held firm. A steady flow of obscenity issued from all five— it rose, mingled, and ascended with the dust of their struggling.

Petrella stepped cautiously past the overturned table and through the litter of broken glasses on the floor.

"Lay off, now," said the stout man in shirt sleeves. "Lay off, do you hear, or we'll do you proper."

The red-faced man said an unprintable word and stamped on the stout man's toe. The group swayed dangerously.

"Stop it," ordered Petrella.

The note of authority was unmistakable. Petrella added, formally, "I'm a detective inspector, and I shall have to take you—" he addressed the red-faced man "—into custody for occasioning a breach of the peace."

"You take him right away," agreed the man in shirt sleeves. "Come in here, busting up my place, eh?"

"That's right," said the youth. It seemed to be the general opinion.

Petrella said, "Come with me."

The man, now unconstrained, swayed on his feet and blinked at him.

"Right away," said Petrella. He stepped up close, seized the man's forearm just above the elbow, and started to push. Surprisingly the man did not resist. There was no reason for him to do so. By any computation he was stronger and bigger than Petrella. But the fight seemed to be out of him. All the same, Petrella was relieved to meet a pair of policemen at the first corner.

He went with them to Southwark Police Station and saw to the formalities. The red-faced man, who gave his name as Albert Porter, was taken to a cell, and Petrella went home.

Before he went into Court next morning, he found time for a word with the landlord of The Kentish Giant.

"Albert's all right," said the landlord. "Generally he's quite all right. I've known him for years. So have the boys. Don't know what came over him last night."

The landlord's son said, "Before he started busting the place up, he was raving about that business of his, you know, the garage."

"I heard he'd been led up the old garden path," said the landlord. "Something he put his money into when he came out of the army. Maybe that's what set him off. Yes, I expect that was it. Funny thing, I've known it happen before. Like Jock Andrews. Lost his wife, brooded over it. Came in about a month later, had a couple of pints—not more than a couple of pints—and started breaking up the place."

Petrella steered the conversation back to Albert Porter.

"He was in the South Londons," said the landlord's son. "Company sergeant major. *My* sergeant major."

His voice had the disillusion of youth. Petrella sympathized with him. A tragedy in the Greek fashion—the godlike figure of the parade ground and the barrack hut reduced to a red-faced, brawling public nuisance.

"He had his troubles," said the landlord, "like I said. Came out two years ago, when they were thinning 'em out and paying 'em off. Officers and N.C.O.'s. Albert collected what was coming to him and put it in a garage. Diddun turn out so well."

"I see," said Petrella. It seemed to him a remote reason for going berserk in a friendly public house. "You'll probably both have to give evidence."

"Wooden want to do that," said the landlord.

Fortunately there was no need for anyone to give evidence. Albert Porter, revived by his night in the cell and spruced up in a way known only to ex-sergeant majors, stood four-square in the box and pleaded guilty. Petrella told his story, leaning heavily on the side of mitigation, and the prisoner was bound over.

Petrella caught up with him as he was leaving the court and said, "Come and have a cup of tea. I want to hear about your garage trouble."

Porter looked at Petrella doubtfully, grunted, and said, "I've told so many people about it, another can't hurt, I suppose."

"I'll pay for the tea," said Petrella. "You do the talking."

It was a sad story, but not a new one. Ex-Sergeant Major Porter, with two thousand pounds burning a hole in his pocket, had met Mr. Morris, a perfectly respectable citizen. At fifty yards on a foggy night he was still a respectable citizen, a pillar of an unspecified church, a member of the local chamber of commerce. The source of Mr. Morris's wealth and respectability was the Roundabout Garage.

"The Roundabout," said Petrella. "Yes, of course I know it. Corner of Buckingham Road. I've often stopped there for a couple of gallons myself."

"It's a fine business," said Porter. "No fooling, a lovely business. Big repair shed. Lot of concessions for brand goods. Steady oil and petrol sales. Old Morris said he was aiming to get out gradually. Offered me a quarter share for two thousand pounds, *and* a job. I've done a lot of work on engines—I started in the R.E.M.E. It seemed to be just the job."

"So you paid down your money," said Petrella, "without getting a lawyer or an expert to check the proposition first, and you discovered the snag when it was too late to do anything about it. Right?"

Mr. Porter nodded glumly.

"What *was* the snag?"

"It's going to be pulled down, condemned. Road widening."

"I see. All the same—" Petrella considered. "If the local authorities acquire the site and pull down the garage, they'll have to pay compensation. Good compensation. You'll get a quarter of that."

"Not me. The bank's got a mortgage on the place. For more than the compensation."

"What about all the gear?"

"The pumps and stuff belong to the oil company. They've got a mortgage on the place, too. There's an awful lot of other stuff, but I doubt it'll fetch a thousand pounds at knockdown prices."

"I see," said Petrella again.

"The site's the real value of the place—the site and the connection. Once they've gone, there's nothing left. I paid two thousand pounds for nothing. That's the short and the long of it, and there's nothing anyone can do about it."

"Maybe. Maybe not," said Petrella.

He spent half an hour that afternoon with a dry but helpful little man in the office of the local planning authority, who unrolled the planning map and confirmed that the Roundabout Garage was, indeed, due to disappear.

"The real trouble," the little man said, "is Palace Crescent. It's residential and packed with private cars. That means there's a constant flow of traffic where we least want it—here." He put his thumb down, a modern Roman Emperor, condemning a full arena. "Where it runs out into the main road. And the garage is right on the corner, the corner site."

"That's right," said Petrella. "That's what makes it such a marvelous place for a garage."

"It'll be a year or more before we get going on that bit. And when we do acquire it, your friend will get compensation."

"Nothing like enough, I'm afraid," said Petrella.

He said it absentmindedly. For an idea had come to him. A wild, splendid, mad idea. An idea of curious ramifications and infinite possibilities; and he wanted time to ponder on it. He made some excuse, got out of the Council offices, and walked back in the direction of the Roundabout Garage.

A café across the street offered a handy observation point. He took a cup of tea across to a table by the window. Business at the garage was brisk. In the first half hour he counted twenty cars in and out. The petrol pumps, which Albert was serving, stood in a forecourt, at the point of the angle made by the two roads. Behind them stood the garage itself, with a main drive-in for cars and a glass door on the right, leading to an office. Behind the garage were the repair shops. The whole thing was one of those confused, casual, but workable jumbles, calculated to infuriate any rightminded planner.

At the end of the half hour Petrella's patience was rewarded. The office door opened and Mr. Morris came out. Petrella felt sure that it was Mr. Morris—a man of about sixty-five, stocky, bright-eyed, rosy-cheeked, sporting a short but aggressive white beard. He stood for a moment, eyeing the hurrying traffic, as his Norse ancestor might have stood at the prow of his longboat, surveying potential victims.

He said something to Albert. They still seemed to be on friendly terms. Petrella was surprised at this, but reflected that in Albert's place he would probably have acted the same. The closer he stuck to the garage, the closer he stayed by his own two thousand pounds.

It was at this point that Petrella's original idea became greatly enlarged. It ceased to be nebulous, and became concrete. He paid his bill and went back to Gabriel Street.

"Go to a lawyer?" said Albert. "Throw good money after bad? I ought to have gone to one to start with, there I agree with you. But it can't do any good now. Morris hasn't broken any law that I know of."

"Try it," urged Petrella.

"Don't know any lawyers."

"I know lots of them," said Petrella. He considered the solicitors with whom he had had dealings and selected Mr. Trask as most appropriate to this problem. "And what's more I'll come with you."

"You think it'll do any good?"

"I've got an idea. Until we've talked it over with someone who knows the ropes, I can't tell if it's a good one or not."

"Might as well try it," said Albert.

Mr. Trask had an office near the Oval Cricket ground. He was big, heavy, full-jowled, and had hair so strong and black that he never looked properly shaved. He called Petrella by his first name, greeted Albert kindly, listened to his story, and perused the contents of the envelope of papers that Albert had brought along with him.

"He certainly did the thing in style," said Mr. Trask. "That's old Morris who owns the Roundabout, isn't it? Chap with a beard. Looks like a regular old pirate."

"All I can say is, it looked all right at the time," said Albert.

"Nice little business, I should have said. What's the catch? Oh, planning trouble."

Petrella explained about the planning trouble. Mr. Trask listened carefully, but continued reading the papers at the same time, a facility that busy lawyers seem to be able to acquire.

"Hullo," he said. "What's this? You didn't tell me he'd given you a debenture on the place."

Albert took the proffered document cautiously and said, "That's right. A debenture. A sort of mortgage, isn't it?"

"Yes and no," said Mr. Trask. "It's a mortgage to the extent that it gives you a charge on the place. Well, that's not much good because the bank and the petrol company have got charges in front of you, if you follow me?"

"In a way," said Mr. Porter.

"But it gives you other remedies, as well. For instance, this entitles you to six per cent on your money payable monthly. Have you had that?"

"What I get from Morris is my wages. Twelve pounds a week, and he takes the P.A.Y.E. off himself, before he pays 'em."

"In that case," said Mr. Trask, folding his massive black hands on the desk, "your debenture interest is clearly in arrears. You should appoint a receiver at once."

The word hung in the dusty office.

"A receiver?" said Petrella.

"Not the sort of receiver you're thinking of. I mean a legal receiver. Any debenture holder or mortgagee has that remedy."

"What does a receiver do?"

"He takes charge," said Mr. Trask briskly. "His authority will be supported, if necessary, by the court. He receives all rents, controls the bank account, runs the business, makes an inventory of the stock, arranges for periodical checks and audits."

"Can he exclude the proprietor?"

"If it was the proprietor who granted the debenture, certainly. It might be his duty to exclude him. Prevent him tampering with assets, you see."

"Do you—" As Petrella spoke he was conscious of a fierce and unhallowed joy as his idea began to fulfill itself. "Do you know any receivers?"

"Oh, dozens of 'em. Accountants mostly. I think Bowles would be the right man for you here."

"How do we appoint him?"

"Just sign a document I'll draw up for you. What's today? Friday. I'll get Bowles on the telephone. Give him a day to get organized. I suggest he goes in on Monday."

"Mr. Morris is rather an explosive personality," said Petrella. "He might try to make things a bit hot for Mr. Bowles."

"Bowles is quite capable of looking after himself," said Mr. Trask.

On Monday morning, as was his custom, Mr. Morris arrived at the Roundabout Garage at nine o'clock sharp. Petrella had been at his observation post in the café for half an hour. He wanted to see the curtain go up.

The first big moment arrived when Mr. Morris found that the office door was not only locked but apparently bolted, too. He walked round and put his nose up against the window—from which a light was showing. Then he rapped on the window and shouted something through it.

Petrella paid his bill, crossed the street higher up, and drifted back toward the garage. As he reached the corner, the door was opened and a tall, thin man, wearing steel spectacles, peered out.

"Are you Mr. Morris?" the man inquired.

"That's right. I am," said Mr. Morris. "And who the flaming something-or-other are you?"

"My name," said the tall man severely, "is Bowles. I am a receiver, placed in possession of the premises by your debenture-holder, Mr. Porter. This is a copy of the instrument appointing me. The original has been filed with the Registrar of Companies."

Mr. Morris made a monosyllabic and, on the whole, improbable suggestion about the Registrar of Companies.

"If you have any proper communication to make," said Mr. Bowles, "I suggest you make it in writing." He started to close the door again, but Mr. Morris got his foot into it.

"You let me in," he said, "or I'll call a policeman. Keeping a man out of his own office!"

"There is a policeman on the corner," said Mr. Bowles. "In fact, I fancy he is coming this way now."

Petrella withdrew discreetly. He was inclined to agree with Mr. Trask that Bowles could look after himself.

So began the siege of the Roundabout. It lasted, in all, for three days. Petrella saw some of it and heard the rest from Albert, who continued to serve oil and petrol to customers unconscious of the drama that was being played around them.

The policeman had apparently decided in favor of Mr. Bowles. Mr. Morris had withdrawn, no doubt to consult his own solicitor. Not finding much comfort in the law, he had decided on a dawn attack, and had arrived, on Tuesday morning, at eight o'clock. Anticipating this, Mr. Bowles had arrived at half-past seven.

In the lunch interval Mr. Morris had sought out Albert.

"Really very nice to me, too," said Albert. "Stood me my lunch, and all. Of course, I told him it wasn't in my hands, really. He ought to approach me through my solicitors. Then he said some things about solicitors. Would have done you good to hear him."

"Keep it up," said Petrella. He thought for a moment, then added, "I'll tell you what. Suggest to Bowles that he ought to start making an inventory. All the old stuff in the repair shops and the store."

"It'd take him a month of Sundays."

"I don't think he'll actually have to do it. But let Mr. Morris hear about it. Tell him that Bowles has been asking you for the keys of the different lockers and boxes. Tell him that if he doesn't get them, he's going to start breaking them open. I think that will do the trick."

On Wednesday, in the early afternoon, Albert telephoned Petrella.

"Worked a treat," he said. "He's going to pay up."

"I thought he might," said Petrella.

"Interest and everything. As long as I get Bowles out by tea time."

"Fine," said Petrella. "Of course, it won't do him much good. Because if you withdraw your receiver and take your money, the bank or the petrol company could put him in again."

"I think he knows that," said Albert. "He's been to his lawyer, too. He doesn't seem to care. What he said was, as long as Bowles is out by tea time, I can have my money, all of it."

"And what does Bowles say?"

"As soon as Morris has paid me, he's got to go. Of course, as you say, he might be put back again by one of the others, but it would take a bit of time."

"All right," said Petrella. "That's fine." And he meant it.

He went round to Division and had a word with Superintendent Benjamin.

"It's still a long shot," said Petrella. "But the odds are shortening."

"Four cars," said Benjamin. "No, make it five. We don't want any slip-up now. One crew to block each of the roads, and one in reserve."

"We could observe from the café," said Petrella. "The proprietor's got an upstairs room he'd let us use. And a telephone—"

Much electricity was consumed that night at the Roundabout

Garage. From their vantage point across the way, Benjamin and Petrella could follow Mr. Morris's progress, by the switching on and off of lights, from front office to back office, from back office to store room, from store room to the repair shops and the garage.

"Having a regular spring cleaning," said Benjamin. "How long's he going to be?"

"He'll be out before daylight," said Petrella.

The superintendent acknowledged this with a grin which had very little humor in it. At five different points in the streets outside the garage, police cars stood, parked inconspicuously, one man dozing at the wheel, one in the back, one alert for the signal.

It was close to two o'clock in the morning when Petrella said, "I think he's coming now, sir."

The big garage doors creaked open. The lights inside were all out now. The length of Buckingham Road lay empty under its glaring orange lamps.

For a moment Mr. Morris stood there, as Petrella had seen him stand once before, head forward, white beard jutting. Then he disappeared. Sidelights came on. A big old-fashioned car nosed out into the forecourt. As Mr. Morris climbed out and went to shut the garage doors behind him, Superintendent Benjamin was talking on the telephone.

"Blue four-door saloon," he said. "Coming now."

Then things started to happen.

The big car turned right out of the garage. Mr. Morris saw the police car draw out to block the road, slammed his own car into reverse, turned in a savage half-circle, and started up one of the side streets. He spotted the second car too late. As Petrella ran out of the café he heard the scream of brakes and the noise of impact.

Mr. Morris was still fighting—screaming a high, thin scream and fighting like a lunatic with two of the patrol-car men. The sergeant stood by, a dripping crimson handkerchief to his face.

"Steady," said Petrella. "Steady. He's an old man."

"Old man, my foot," said the sergeant. "Went for my eyes."

"We want him in one piece," said Petrella.

The screaming had stopped now. Mr. Morris was lying on his back on the pavement, bubbling gently and dribbling into his beard. Petrella thought that the bubbling and dribbling were worse than the screaming.

Three evenings later, in the detective room at Gabriel Street, Superintendent Benjamin straightened his back and said, "That's the lot. All identified. Do you know he had the bits and pieces of more than twenty different jewel robberies in that car?"

"Hidden," said Petrella, "in more than twenty ingenious places round that garage. It took him eight hours to get them all out—and *he* knew where to look!"

"It's magnificent," said Benjamin. He was not a man given to enthusiasm, and when he used a word like magnificent it sounded like an accolade. "There's no doubt about it. We've got our hands on the King at last. We've been so busy the last three days I haven't had time to ask how you spotted him."

"Part hunch," said Petrella. "A garage owner and second-hand car man seemed just right. Plenty of excuse to keep ready money about, plenty of hiding places. And you have to know something about cars if you're going to knock them off. But really it was the joke."

"Joke?"

"You know what they're like round here—names usually have more than one meaning. Puns and jokes, you know. A man living at the corner of Buckingham Road and Palace Crescent—what else *could* they call him?" He looked at his watch and said, "I've got to run. A date with the sergeants and warrant officers of the South Londons. We're celebrating Albert's return to solvency."

CAPTAIN LEOPOLD
GOES TO THE DOGS

EDWARD D. HOCH

*Edward D. Hoch is crime fiction's premier short story writer.
(He is also that* rara avis, *a writer who makes his living entirely
from short fiction.) He has published close to seven hundred
stories since his first professional sale in 1955, and he has
appeared in every issue of* Ellery Queen's Mystery Magazine
*for more than a dozen years. He also has to his credit well over
one hundred anthology appearances, including a score of selec-
tions for* Best Detective Stories of the Year *and* Year's Best
Mystery & Suspense Stories *(which he now edits for Walker &
Company). Of the many series characters he has created, the
most enduring is Captain Leopold, who has appeared in seventy-
five short stories and one collection,* Leopold's Way *(1985), at
the time of this writing. "In the best Leopold tales," critic
Francis M. Nevins, Jr. has written, "Hoch buries unexpected
nuances of character and emotion and meaning beneath the
surface of his deceptively simple style." "Captain Leopold Goes
to the Dogs" is such a story.*

Eddie Sargasso was a gambler.

In his younger days he'd been known to bet on everything from
the fall of a card to the virtue of a woman. Now that he'd passed
forty he was more likely to limit his wagers to recognized sporting
events and games of chance, but he was still always on the lookout
for an angle. He'd been in on the recent jai alai fixes until a grand
jury investigation broke the scandal wide open. Now it was greyhound racing which took his fancy.

Eddie Sargasso was fortunate to live in one of the few northeast-
ern states where dog racing was legal. If he'd resided elsewhere it
wouldn't have stopped him from betting, but it would have kept

129

him from arranging to meet Aaron Flake—by convenient accident—in the Sportsman's Lounge one Sunday evening in July.

Flake was a little man with thin blond hair and glasses that were too big for his face. He was sitting at the bar, nursing a gin and tonic, when Eddie slipped onto the stool next to him. "Hey, aren't you Aaron Flake, the guy from the dog track?"

The man smiled thinly. "I'm a licensed hare controller, if that's what you mean. You may have seen me at the track."

"Damn right," Eddie said, building it up. "You were pointed out to me as knowing more about greyhound racing than anyone in the state."

"After working at something for sixteen years I suppose it's natural that you learn some facts about it."

Eddie Sargasso whistled. "Sixteen years! It hasn't even been legal that long, has it?"

"I worked the Florida tracks before I came north. New England was a whole new territory for me and I figured to get in on the ground floor."

"You got a family here?"

Aaron Flake shook his head and took another sip of his drink. "Wife and kids stayed in Florida. They liked the sun. I'm divorced now."

"I do a little betting on the dogs," Eddie admitted.

"That's what we race 'em for."

"I like them better than horses because they're harder to fix, you know? You bet on a greyhound and you know it's going to be a good honest race."

"Well, there are ways of fixing them. Tampering with the dogs. I read a story once about dog racing in England, and they had a dozen ways of making the dogs run faster, or slower, or whatever they wanted. We check 'em pretty careful over here, though."

Eddie signaled the bartender for two more drinks, and Flake offered no objection. It was a Sunday, after all, and he didn't have to work again till Monday night. "You control the mechanical rabbit, don't you?" Eddie asked, pretending an ignorance of the sport's basics. "How does that work?"

"I usually call it an artificial hare rather than a mechanical rabbit. There's nothing mechanical about it, really. It's a stuffed animal strapped to a device that moves around the track. It's powered by an electric motor, and my job is to maintain just the correct speed for the hare. If it's too slow the lead dog might catch it, and if it's too fast and gets too far ahead of the dogs they lose interest. Judges have been known to declare a no-race if that happens."

"How many dogs are there?"

"We race eight at a time in this state. Some places race nine."

"You can keep them all in view during the race?"

"Sure, it's not hard. I'm in a little booth overlooking the track."

"Which post position is best?"

"Number eight trap is on the outside of the oval, nearest the hare. That dog has to run a few more feet than the number one dog on the inside—but it's not enough to speak of. They usually bunch together after the start anyway. I wait till the hare's about twelve yards in front before I open the traps, and I try to maintain that distance. We have an electric-eye camera at the finish line to record the winner."

"Sure sounds exciting. I've only been a couple of times, but I think I'll drive out again tomorrow night."

Aaron Flake finished his drink. "You'll enjoy it," he said, sliding off the barstool. "See you around."

Flake had left suddenly, but that didn't bother Eddie Sargasso too much. At least he'd made contact, and with any luck he'd fare better than Marie did. Eddie and his wife lived in an expensive colonial house at the edge of the city, not far from the dog track, and driving home that evening he went over the possibilities in his mind. Somehow he needed an edge on the race fixing so he could get his cut of it and still avoid problems with the law. He had a lengthy arrest record over the years, and he knew there were some cops in the city just waiting for a misstep to nail him.

"How'd you make out?" Marie asked as he entered the family room, where she was watching television.

"Pretty good for the first meeting. If anyone knows when the fix is on it must be Flake. Watching the races that carefully every night he has to see something."

"I hope you do better than me. I couldn't get to first base with him. He never even phoned me!"

He bent over and kissed her. "Don't let it bother you. I guess he doesn't go much for the ladies. I thought you could talk to him about Florida but it didn't work out."

"Are we going to the track tomorrow night?"

"Sure. I told him I'd probably be there. We can use the old system till we latch onto something better."

Monday was a warm night and that brought out a good crowd. Marie wore her white pants suit, and Eddie had on his lucky brown jacket. He studied the dogs through binoculars, watching them break from their numbered traps to pursue the motorized rabbit.

After the third race he ran into Donald Wayne of the state betting commission. "Eddie! They haven't barred you from the track yet, I see."

"Come on, Donald. I'm a solid citizen."

"Sure, I know. Do you still make bets on things like whether the next girl into a bar will be wearing slacks or a skirt?"

"That was in my younger days, and I lost too much money. Now I try to bet only on sure things."

"I know. That's why we hate to see you at the dog tracks. We've had enough trouble with jai alai in this state."

"Would you be suspicious of a poker game at my place on Friday night?"

"That's more like it! Close up, I can keep my eyes on you."

Eddie chuckled and patted him on the shoulder. "Make it eight o'clock. I'll see who else I can round up."

It had been more than a year since the weekly poker games with Wayne and a few others. Eddie stopped asking him when Wayne was appointed to the state betting commission, fearing it might somehow compromise his friend's position. But if Wayne didn't mind coming, why should Eddie?

He made a bet on the fourth race, buying his ticket from one of the totalizator operators in their distinctive dark red jackets. Then he stood for a time watching the odds change right up to post time. It was much like horse racing in that respect. There was always big money bet in the closing minute, and late changes to lower odds often indicated inside information on a winner. Often when Eddie saw that happening he sent Marie out to stand in line at one group of windows while he went to a different selling location. When the odds changed on the totalizator screen they'd each buy a hundred-dollar ticket on the horse whose odds showed a sudden last-minute drop.

He went back to his seat in time to see the greyhound wearing the bright blue racing jacket numbered six cross the finish line first. "There was last-minute betting on him," Eddie told his wife. "The smart boys are at it again."

"You want me to get in line for the next race?"

"I think so. Until we get more friendly with Mr. Flake that's the only move we've got." He passed her a hundred-dollar bill. "Watch the odds and be close enough so you can make a last-minute bet just before the machines lock."

"You don't have to tell me. I've done it a thousand times."

He watched her head for the downstairs bank of selling windows and he went back to the windows nearest their seats. As he stood watching the totalizator board, another familiar figure passed into his line of vision. It was Sam Barth, one of the track stewards. "Sam!" Eddie called out.

"How's it going? Where's your lovely wife?"

"Downstairs, Sam. How about a poker game Friday night? Donald's coming over."

"Wayne? That's great! I think I can make it, but not till I get out of here at eleven. That okay?"

"Fine. Come when you can, Sam."

He watched the slender man walk away, wondering vaguely if a track steward could be in on any fixing. Stranger things had happened.

He got into the shorter of the two lines then, hoping he was timing it right. "Hi, Eddie. How they running?"

He turned at the sound of the woman's voice and saw Joyce Train, a woman he'd known quite well in his younger days. "Joyce! Good to see you! How's the family?"

"Who knows?" She smiled and winked. "I'm back to work."

"You are? Since when?"

"The spring. I couldn't take being a housewife."

Eddie chewed at his lower lip. "I'll keep it in mind. I might have something for you."

"I'm at the old place if you need to reach me."

"Fine." She still had a great figure, and she knew how to show it off, wearing a dark brown jumpsuit with some frills at the neck and cuffs. A few years ago she'd quit the call-girl business to get married, but hardly anyone had thought it would last. Apparently it hadn't.

Thinking about her, Eddie wondered if he might try introducing her to Aaron Flake.

The totalizator screen was changing. He memorized the current odds and watched them shift. Minor changes, mostly, at one minute to post time.

Except—

Dog number four dropped from eight-to-one to seven-to-two. That meant a big last-minute bet. He hoped Marie had caught it at the other windows.

"One hundred on number four," he told the ticket seller when he reached the window a few seconds later. He was just walking away when he heard the snap of the machines locking as the starter signaled the release of the hare. Then there was a roar from the crowd as the eight greyhounds burst from their numbered traps.

He made it back to his seat in time to see them rounding the first curve of the oval track. The dogs were closing in on the electric rabbit, and the lead one looked to be almost within striking distance. He'd never seen them that close before. Maybe Flake—

The dogs were onto the rabbit, straining at their muzzles and sending up growls of frustration. Instantly the steward and judges were on the track, signaling it was a no-race. The message flashed on the tote board that all bets were off.

Eddie Sargasso couldn't figure it out. He met Marie by the steps and she was as baffled as he was. "What happened?" she asked.

"I don't know, but it'll probably cost Flake his job. We'll have to start all over with someone else."

They pushed their way through the crowd of disgruntled spectators, watching the trainers and track officials trying to bring some order from the confusion on the track. The dogs were growling and fighting among themselves, separating only reluctantly as the trainers pulled them apart.

The control booth for the hare was some distance away, near the starting gate, and by the time Eddie and Marie reached it he saw Donald Wayne coming out. His face was white as Eddie asked him, "What in hell happened?"

Wayne stared at him blankly, then seemed to recognize him and said, "Murder—that's what! Somebody stabbed Aaron Flake!"

Captain Leopold was not a gambler.

He'd been to the dog track once in his life, with Lieutenant Fletcher and his wife shortly after it opened. That night he'd managed to lose twelve dollars, enough to convince him he was no luckier with dogs than with horses. Now, as he pulled up to the main entrance with Fletcher at his side and the siren wailing, he wondered if he'd be any luckier this night.

"We should have gone home early," Fletcher decided, looking at the crowd of people. "Let the night shift handle it."

"Come on. Maybe it's an easy one—some drunk who's waiting to confess."

"Sure, Captain." Fletcher liked to use the title when he was being sarcastic. Most of the time they were good friends, and Leopold had been out to dinner at Fletcher's house twice so far during the summer. With Connie Trent away on vacation they'd been spending more hours together in the office too.

"This way, Captain," a voice called to him as they entered the stands. Leopold recognized Sam Barth, one of the track stewards whom he knew slightly. Barth stood at the top of a short flight of steps, wearing a dark red blazer like all the track personnel.

"What happened here?" Leopold asked. "The report said a homicide."

"That's it. Our hare operator, Aaron Flake, was stabbed in the back. It happened right during the race, and the dogs caught up with the hare!" That seemed to bother him more than the murder.

"All right, show us the way."

Leopold and Fletcher followed him to a little wooden booth overlooking the dog track. A husky man in a rumpled brown suit was there to greet them. "This is Donald Wayne of the state betting commission. He found the body," Barth said.

Leopold shook hands with Wayne and waited while the man opened the door of the control booth. Then he took a deep breath. The man they identified as Aaron Flake was slumped over in his chair, head down on the desk in front of him. Something—Leopold saw it was the evening's racing program—was pinned to his back with a bone-handled hunting knife.

"All right, Fletcher, get the photographer and the lab boys up here." Leopold glanced at the desk on which the body was slumped, and saw another racing program, an ashtray with one cigarette butt, some pencils, and a blank pad of paper. A pair of binoculars was mounted on a stand in front of the dead man's head.

He turned and looked at the door of the booth, observing a simple hook-and-eye latch. "Did he keep this door latched?"

Donald Wayne nodded. "It's something of an art, keeping that hare just the right distance ahead of the dogs. Flake didn't want anyone walking in during a race and ruining his concentration, so he kept the latch on. The door was unlocked when I found him, though."

"So he admitted his killer. It was someone he knew."

"Looks like it," Wayne agreed. "But that doesn't limit it very much. We have over fifty track employees, plus the owners and trainers of each dog. There are stewards, judges, a starter, a time-keeper, even a veterinary surgeon. Flake knew them all. Plus he might have admitted any one of the spectators that he knew."

"Make up a list of track employees for me," Leopold suggested. "And try to indicate where each one would have been during the race."

Sam Barth, the track steward, was standing outside the little booth. "I can probably do that better than Donald. I work with them. He was just a visitor tonight."

"How's that?" Leopold asked the stocky man.

"Well, I'm on the betting commission, and I figure I should go around to the tracks once a week or so. We don't have thorough-bred racing in this state, but between the greyhounds and jai alai it keeps me busy."

"You were standing near this booth when it happened?"

"Not too far away," he told Leopold. "At first I couldn't believe my eyes! I've never seen the dogs catch the rabbit in all the years I've been coming here. It's something that just never happens! As soon as I realized something had gone wrong with Flake I hurried up here to the booth. But it was too late."

"Could you see the entrance from where you were standing?"

Barth shook his head. "You see the way these supporting girders stick out to hold the roof. There's a blind spot here so the door to the booth can't really be seen from the stands. Anyone could have entered without being seen."

While Fletcher made notes of the booth's measurements and other facts, and the medical examiner set about removing the knife from the wound, Leopold went down to the track with Sam Barth. "Never had anything like this happen, Captain. I still can't believe it!"

There was barking from a few frustrated dogs as Leopold walked along the edge of the track toward the kennels. One trainer was leading his muzzled greyhound for a trot around the exercise track. "Think we'll be able to finish the rest of the card, Sam?" he asked.

"Not a chance, Matt. They've scratched it all for tonight. We'll try to get another hare controller up from Stamford for tomorrow's card."

"No one seems to be mourning the dead man too much," Leopold observed.

"Aaron Flake was a loner. Stuck pretty much to himself. Behind his back they called him Flakey, of course. He probably had that all his life."

"Was he married?"

"He told people he was divorced but it may not have been true. He came up from the Florida tracks when we started dog racing here. There was some sort of trouble at his last track, but the state investigated and decided he wasn't involved."

"Trouble? Like fixed races?"

"No, something else. I don't know what."

"Have there been any fixed races here?"

"I couldn't say, Captain."

"All right," Leopold said. "I'll talk to you later."

He'd ordered the gates closed shortly after his arrival, but of course the killer had had several minutes to make his escape before the captain's arrival.

Leopold watched the progress of the lines without spotting any familiar faces, then went back to the booth where the medical examiner was just finishing. "What about the weapon?" Leopold asked.

"Standard sort of hunting knife. You can buy them at any sporting goods or department store. Five-inch blade, about nine inches overall. Perfect for hiding in pocket or purse."

"And the program skewered to the body?"

"Beats me! A message of some sort?" He closed his bag and followed the stretcher out.

Fletcher came up the steps from the lower section. "I spotted an old friend of ours in the crowd."

"Who's that?"

"Joyce Train. Used to be a call girl working out of the Harbor Motor Lodge. Remember?"

"How could I forget? She's back in the business, isn't she?"

"So I heard."

"Let's go talk to her," Leopold decided.

They'd been given the use of Sam Barth's private office under the grandstand for questioning, and Fletcher brought Joyce in there. "Hello, Joyce. Enjoying the races?"

"Leopold! So there's been a murder?"

He nodded. "Aaron Flake. Know him?"

"I know him by sight. He wasn't one of my customers, if that's what you mean."

"What can you tell us, Joyce?"

"Nothing. I was out here betting on the dogs like everyone else."

Fletcher perched himself on the edge of the desk. "In your line of work it's good to give the police tips once in a while."

"You're not the vice squad!"

"But they're right down the hall at headquarters. Come on, Joyce. Think hard and give us some information. Who had it in for Flake?"

"I don't know a thing, honest!"

Leopold tried a different approach. "You said he wasn't a customer, and he didn't have a wife on the scene. Any chance he was homosexual?"

She shrugged. "Maybe. I saw him in bars with other men occasionally."

"How occasionally?"

"Last night."

"Who was the other man?"

She glanced away. "It was over at the Sportsman's Lounge. But it wasn't anything like that. This other guy's no queer."

"Suppose you let us decide that. Who was it?"

Joyce Train bit her lip and stalled for time. Leopold knew she would tell them the name, but she wanted to make it look like a difficult decision. "All right," she said finally. "It was Eddie Sargasso, the gambler."

"Sargasso!" Fletcher gave a low whistle. "Man, I'd like to hang something on him!"

"He's here tonight," Joyce added in a low voice.

"Here? At the track?"

She nodded. "You won't say it was me that told, will you?"

"Not unless we have to bring it out in court," Leopold promised. "He didn't see you at the Lounge last night?"

"No. I was in a booth with a—a friend."

"Thanks, Joyce. You've been a big help. We'll remember it." He turned to Fletcher. "Let's go find Eddie Sargasso before he gets away."

Eddie was standing in line with Marie, only three away from the officer taking down names and addresses of the personnel, when Leopold spotted him. He smiled and stuck out his hand. "Captain Leopold! This is a real pleasure!"

"Would you step into the office and have a word with us, Eddie? Your wife too?"

"And lose my place in line?" he asked with a try at lightness.

"You won't have to wait in line," Leopold assured him.

Eddie and Marie followed Leopold into a little office under the grandstand. He knew it belonged to Sam Barth, and wondered where the steward was.

"Now what's on your mind, Captain?"

"The murder of Aaron Flake."

"Terrible thing! Any idea who did it?"

"That's what we're working on. How well did you know him?"

The office door opened and Lieutenant Fletcher came in. That didn't surprise Eddie. He knew Leopold and Fletcher worked together. "Hardly at all," he answered. "I hardly knew him."

"You were having a drink with him last night in the Sportsman's Lounge downtown."

"Yeah? Hey, I guess that's right! Just happened to see him in there. That's the first time we ever talked, you know?"

"You're a gambler, Eddie, the sort who likes to gamble on sure things. There've been some shady races run at this track lately. Not the sort of thing you'd want to gamble on unless you had inside information."

"How do you fix a dog race?"

"That's what I'm asking you. Maybe you do it by bribing the hare operator."

"Not a chance! You saw what happened if the hare isn't controlled just right. The dogs catch it, and there's no race. Those guys aren't licensed because they might be crooks. They're licensed because it takes a certain skill to run the hare at the proper distance from the dogs."

"I don't need any instructions on dog racing," Leopold said. "Suppose you tell me what you and Flake talked about."

"Nothing, I swear! Just barroom chat, that's all."

Leopold turned to Marie. "Were you with your husband at the time of the killing?"

She glanced sideways at Eddie and his heart skipped a beat. They were really out to hang this on him! If only Marie would say the right—

"Not the exact instant," Marie admitted, and his hopes died. "I came up from the lower ticket window just after the race was stopped."

"She was placing a last-minute bet for me," Eddie explained.

"And what were you doing?"

"I was placing a bet too." He knew it sounded foolish, so he explained. "Sometimes people with inside information wait till the last minute to place big bets, so it doesn't cause a run on a certain dog and lower the odds too much. I watch the tote board and if I see a drop in odds during the final minute before a race I usually put a hundred on the dog. The same thing holds with horses. It's just smart betting."

"It's smart betting if you suspect something crooked."

"Well, yeah."

"Why wasn't your wife with you?"

"Sometimes you figure the length of the line wrong and get shut out when the machines lock. I figured with Marie and me in separate lines, at least one of us would make it to the windows in time."

"Did anyone see you there?"

He remembered Joyce. "Girl I know—Joyce Train. I saw her in line just before the board changed."

"But she didn't see you after the race started?"

"Well, no. I was on my way back to our seats."

Fletcher picked that moment to lean across to Leopold and hand him something. It looked to Eddie like an address book. "This was in the dead man's pocket, Captain."

Leopold studied the entry Fletcher had indicated, then passed it along to Eddie. "What do you make of this?"

Marie S., it read, followed by a phone number. Eddie moistened his lips and said, "I don't know."

"Is that your number?"

"Yeah, I guess so."

He turned to Marie. "Mrs. Sargasso, do you have any explanation as to why the dead man had your name and phone number in his address book?"

"I—"

"Shut up, Marie!" Eddie barked.

Leopold leaned forward. "This is murder, Sargasso! And right now you're our prime suspect. You'd better let her talk."

Marie looked at him. "Eddie, we have to tell them what we know."

"Yeah," he agreed reluctantly. "I suppose so."

"Eddie wanted me to meet Flake and strike up an acquaintance. He knew there was something crooked going on at the track, and we figured he'd be a good one to know about it. We'd seen him drinking alone at the bars around town, and I gave it a try, but I didn't get anywhere. I told him my name was Marie Sullivan and he wrote it down, but he never called me."

"How long ago was this?"

"Back in June, about a month ago."

"So last night I tried it," Eddie said. "I figured if he didn't like girls maybe I'd have better luck just chatting with him over a few drinks. But nothing came of it."

"Something came of it," Leopold corrected him. "Aaron Flake was murdered."

"I don't know a thing about that."

Suddenly Marie had a thought. "Eddie, the tickets! We didn't cash them in yet. We've still got them!"

He saw at once what she was driving at. It just might be enough to save their skins. "That's right! The lines were so long we decided to wait till tomorrow night to get our refunds for the canceled race. I've got my hundred-dollar ticket on number four, and you can check the totalizator records to see that the odds on number four took a big drop in the final minute before the race. That was our signal to buy. You got your ticket, Marie?"

She nodded and dug around in her purse, finally producing it. Leopold took the tickets and studied them. "These were bought just before the race?"

"Less than a minute before. We didn't know which dog to bet on before that. And Flake was killed less than a minute into the race."

"I'll agree with that," Leopold said. "There's no way he could have run that rabbit with the knife in his back. It killed him almost instantly."

"Well there! I couldn't have gotten from the ticket window to that booth in anything like two minutes. It's impossible!"

Leopold frowned and said, "Time it, Fletcher." He glanced at Marie. "Where did you buy your tickets?"

"Downstairs."

"Time it from where she was, too. And see if there's a ticket seller closer to Flake's booth."

"Right, Captain."

"Those are the only two grandstand banks of windows," Eddie said. "There's another in the clubhouse, but that's way down at the other end. Besides, this number on the ticket identifies the machine that sold it."

Leopold nodded. "We'll see what Fletcher reports."

Eddie used the few minutes for chatter about the track, and about gambling in general. "There was a time when I'd bet on anything, Captain."

"Want to make a bet on whether I solve this case?"

"I might," Eddie answered carefully.

Fletcher came back shaking his head. "Looks like they're both in the clear, Captain. A fast walk from the upper windows to the booth took me two minutes and twenty-eight seconds. With the crowd here it would have been closer to three minutes. From downstairs where Marie bought her ticket it's even farther—two minutes and forty-five seconds. They couldn't have bought these tickets and still gotten up to the booth in time to stab Flake."

Leopold sighed. "All right, you can go now."

Eddie got to his feet. "I'll lay two-to-one you don't crack this case, Captain."

"I'm not a betting man."

"That's too bad."

After they'd gone Leopold and Fletcher went back to the kennel area, walking beneath the lights past row after row of barking dogs. "They're restless," he told Fletcher. "Unhappy, like me."

"You still think Sargasso's guilty, don't you?"

"He's a two-bit gambler who never did an honest day's work in his life. But we can't get a murder conviction on those grounds."

Up ahead they saw the man from the betting commission and Leopold called to him. "Mr. Wayne, do you have a minute?"

Donald Wayne turned and waited for them to catch up. "Just talking to a few of the owners about what happened," he said.

"Do they have any information?"

"Nothing. No one can imagine Flake having an enemy. He was such a quiet guy."

"How about friends? Did he have any of those?"

"Not many, according to Sam Barth. He knew Flake better than I did, certainly."

"What's going on at this track?" Leopold asked. "They've been fixing races, haven't they?"

"What gives you that idea?"

"Eddie Sargasso told me a lot of money was being bet on certain dogs just before post time. And those dogs usually won."

"I wish he'd make his accusations to me."

"You a friend of Eddie's?"

Donald Wayne nodded. "From the old days, before I was on the betting commission. We used to play poker together."

"But not any more?"

"Matter of fact, he invited me over for a game on Friday night. Don't know if I'll be going now."

"Who else was at these games?"

"Sam Barth, sometimes."

"Mr. Wayne, if there was a fix in at this track, how could it be worked?"

"Oh, lots of ways. They run twelve races a night with eight dogs per race. That's nearly a hundred dogs each night. Of course most dogs race every evening, and travel a circuit through the three New England states that have dog tracks. The owners get to know one another. Sometimes they get to know each other so well that a group of them will get together and take turns winning. The other owners or trainers hold back their dogs by various methods and one man wins. Then it's someone else's turn."

"Is that going on here?"

"To some extent." He spread his hands. "To some extent it probably happens at race tracks—especially harness tracks—too. But that doesn't mean it led to Aaron Flake's death. He wouldn't have been a party to it."

"Except that he's watching the race very carefully through binoculars, every foot of the way. He knows the way greyhounds run, and he recognizes it when they're running different—either too fast or too slow. He could have been blackmailing somebody."

"Yes, I suppose so. But who'd be foolish enough to kill him like that, in the middle of a race? A blackmail victim would more likely choose a dark street after the race, when there was less chance of discovery."

"That's true," Leopold agreed. "It's almost as if the killer *had* to do it during the race."

"And leave that program pinned to his back with the knife," Fletcher reminded them. "If you ask me it's some nut with a grudge against dog tracks."

"Except that Flake unlatched the door for this person."

"Couldn't the latch have been flipped from outside with a piece of plastic or a credit card?" Wayne suggested.

Fletcher shook his head. "I tried that. There's a strip of wood around the jamb that prevents it."

Sam Barth came hurrying up from the direction of the grandstand. "I've been looking for you, Captain. Here's that list of track personnel you requested. Any one of them could have gained admission to the booth."

Leopold glanced at the typewritten sheets. "I think we can rule out the ticket sellers and gate personnel. And any security guards with fixed posts. Likewise the judges, the paddock steward, the starter, and the timekeeper. None of these people could have left their positions during the race. That still leaves stewards like yourself, plus most of the owners and trainers, the veterinarian, and others."

"Plus Flake's friends."

"Yes, if he had any." Leopold was staring up at the grandstand, where the lights were beginning to go out.

"What are you thinking, Captain?" Fletcher asked.

"I'm thinking we should come back here tomorrow night."

Leopold spent much of the following day on the phone to the Florida police. When he'd finished, he thought he had the beginnings of an idea.

"Look here, Fletcher—Aaron Flake once worked at a dog track in Miami where an owner was knifed to death in his trailer."

"The same sort of weapon."

"Exactly. It's just possible that Flake was a blackmailer after all—but blackmailing a murderer instead of a race fixer."

"That still doesn't tell us who did it."

"Were there any fingerprints on the knife or the program?"

Fletcher shook his head. "Wiped clean."

"Blackmail or not, the killer still risked a great deal stabbing Flake during the race, when he knew people would rush to the booth to see what was wrong."

Fletcher brought in two cups of coffee from the temperamental machine in the hall. "Any chance the lever controlling the rabbit could have been turned on automatically, after the killer left the booth?"

"None at all. The starter signaled Flake to release the rabbit. He had to be alive then, even if the killer was standing right behind him in the booth."

Fletcher set the coffee cup on a square piece of cardboard that Leopold used as a coaster. Leopold stared at it in silence for a moment and then said, "You did that to protect the desk, in case the coffee spilled."

"What?"

"Just thinking out loud, Fletcher. I've got an idea who killed Aaron Flake, and I know how we can prove it at the track tonight."

News of the murder had obviously not hurt the dog track's business. By the time Leopold and Fletcher arrived, shortly after the gates opened, lines of people were pouring in.

"Curiosity seekers," Sam Barth said, standing in his red jacket just inside the entrance. "By next week they'll be onto something else."

"Have you seen Eddie Sargasso yet?" Leopold asked.

"Not yet, but he'll be here."

Leopold sent Fletcher to cover the lower-level ticket windows while he took the upstairs ones himself. Sargasso hadn't gone to the clubhouse the previous night, so he probably wouldn't go there tonight. It was just a matter of waiting.

"Looking for killers?" someone asked. It was Joyce Train, with a man the captain didn't know.

"That's right," Leopold said. "I read somewhere they always return to the scene of the crime."

He chatted with her a moment and then glanced back at the lines. Eddie Sargasso was there, with his wife right behind him. Leopold hurried over, edging through the thickening crowd.

"Hello, Captain," Eddie said. "Break the case yet?"

"Just about."

Eddie reached the window and pushed a ticket through. "We're cashing in our tickets on the canceled race last night," he explained.

"I know," Leopold said.

Eddie took his hundred dollars and stepped aside. Then, acting as fast as he could, Leopold's hand shot out to grip Marie Sargasso's wrist. "Not so fast, Marie. I want to see that."

Eddie made a move toward Leopold. "What in hell are you doing?"

"You may not know it, Eddie, but it was your wife who murdered Aaron Flake, and the proof of it is here in her hand."

"You're crazy!" Sargasso growled. "Marie, tell him he's crazy!"

But the life seemed to have gone out of her. "It's true, Eddie," she said simply. "I killed him."

Later, in Sam Barth's office under the grandstand, Leopold explained. "These tickets were the key to it," he said, fanning eight tickets on the previous night's race across the desk. "Marie's alibi, like her husband's, rested on the fact that she was in line, waiting for the odds to change so she could make a last-minute bet on a certain dog. And sure enough, she and Eddie each produced a ticket on the number-four entry. Fletcher timed it and verified they couldn't have bought the tickets and still reached the booth in time to stab Flake."

"So how'd she do it?" Barth asked.

"Simply by purchasing one ticket on each of the eight dogs in the race, as soon as she went downstairs. This gave her time to reach the booth and kill Flake, and still hold a hundred-dollar ticket on whichever dog showed that last-minute odds change. Sure, it cost her eight hundred dollars, but she knew better than anyone else the race would never be completed. She knew she could get her money back on the tickets last night or today. I heard Eddie say they'd do it today because the lines were too long last night. Of course Eddie had no idea his wife was guilty. That was the main reason for her elaborate scheme. Most other people might have killed Flake in an alley, but Marie had to do it in such a way that she'd have a perfect alibi—not only for the police but for her husband!"

"But why did she kill him?" Sam Barth asked.

"We're digging into that. We think Marie killed a man at a Florida dog track years ago and got away with it. Eddie sent her to make Flake's acquaintance as part of their scheme to get inside dope on the fixed races. Flake recognized her from Florida and had some sort of knowledge connecting her with the prior killing. When he tried to blackmail her, she decided to kill him. She knew Eddie usually sent her to buy a last-minute ticket on the races, and she used that as her alibi. She went to the booth, pretending she had a blackmail payment for Flake, and he let her in. While his back was turned controlling the hare, she took the knife from her purse and stabbed him."

"Through the program?" Fletcher asked.

"I saw that coaster under my coffee cup today and I got the idea, Fletcher. The knife blade was sticking through the program when she stabbed him, so it would act as a shield against possible bloodstains. That was the only likely explanation.

"So what did we know? The killer was someone Flake knew— either as a co-worker or an acquaintance. The killer found it necessary to murder Flake during the dog race, even with the risk involved. And the killer had to take great care to avoid even a speck of blood. Whom did that point to?"

"Couldn't it have been Sargasso as well as his wife?"

"Not likely. Eddie was wearing a dark brown jacket yesterday, remember? Likewise, Sam here and all the other track personnel wear dark red blazers. Even Donald Wayne had on a rumpled brown suit, and I think that girl Joyce wore brown too. Dark brown or dark red wouldn't likely show a bloodstain that obviously—not so the killer would find it necessary to use that program trick. But Marie Sargasso was wearing what?—a white pants suit! Even a speck of blood would have been fatal to her."

"There must have been a thousand other women at the track wearing white or light summer colors," Fletcher protested.

"But their names and phone numbers weren't in Flake's address book. And they weren't from Florida as Marie was."

"Why'd she wear white if she was planning the murder?"

Leopold shrugged. "Maybe Eddie liked it on her, and she couldn't attract his suspicion by refusing to wear it. The important thing was that she avoided any blood splattering from the wound by using the program as a guard."

Eddie Sargasso rode down to headquarters in the car with his wife and Leopold. She was silent and her head was bowed. Eddie held her hand all the way, and at one point he said, "You should have taken my bet, Leopold. You solved the case."

"I told you I wasn't a gambler."

"You gambled that she'd break down and confess. You had no real evidence against her."

Leopold thought about it and said, "I suppose there are different sorts of gambling, Eddie. When you put it that way, maybe we're not so different after all."

HIT-AND-RUN

SUSAN DUNLAP

In recent years there have been a number of series procedurals featuring policewomen. The two most prominent female cops are Lillian O'Donnell's Nora Mulcahaney and Dorothy Uhnak's Christy Opara; but a fast-rising star among the newcomers is Susan Dunlap's Berkeley-based Jill Smith, the protagonist of three novels to date: Karma, As a Favor, *and* Not Exactly a Brahmin. *"Hit-and Run" is Jill Smith's first recorded short case—a low-key but intense story about a traffic accident on one of Berkeley's football Saturdays.*

It was four-fifteen Saturday afternoon—a football Saturday at the University of California. For the moment, there was nothing in the streets leading from Memorial Stadium but rain. Sensible Berkeleyans were home, students and alumni were huddled in the stands under sheets of clear plastic, like pieces of expensive lawn furniture, as the Cal Bears and their opponents marched toward the final gun. Then the seventy-five thousand six hundred sixty-two fans would charge gleefully or trudge morosely to their cars and create a near-gridlock all over the city of Berkeley. Then only a fool, or a tourist, would consider driving across town. Then even in a black-and-white—with the pulsers on, and the siren blaring—I wouldn't be able to get to the station.

The conference beat officer Connie Pereira and I had attended—*Indications of the Pattern Behavior of the Cyclical Killer in California*—had let out at three-thirty. We'd figured we just had time to turn in the black-and-white, pick up our own cars, and get home. On the way home, I planned to stop for a pizza. That would be pushing it. But, once I got the pizza in my car, I would be going against traffic. Now, I figured, I could make good time because University Avenue would still be empty.

When the squeal came, I knew I had figured wrong. It was a hit-

and-run. I hadn't handled one of those since long before I'd been assigned to Homicide. But this part of University Avenue was Pereira's beat. I looked at her questioningly; she wasn't on beat now; she could let the squeal go. But she was already reaching for the mike.

I switched on the pulser lights and the siren, and stepped on the gas. The street was deserted. The incident was two blocks ahead, below San Pablo Avenue, on University. There wasn't a car, truck, or bicycle in sight. As I crossed the intersection, I could see a man lying on his back in the street, his herringbone suit already matted with blood. Bent over him was a blond man in a white shirt and jeans.

Leaving Pereira waiting for the dispatcher's reply, I got out of the car and ran toward the two men. The blond man was breathing heavily but regularly, rhythmically pressing on the injured man's chest and blowing into his mouth. He was getting no response. I had seen enough bodies, both dead and dying, in my four years on the force to suspect that this one was on the way out. I doubted the C.P.R. was doing any good. But, once started, it couldn't be stopped until the medics arrived. And despite the lack of reaction, the blond looked like he knew what he was doing.

From across the sidewalk, the pungent smell of brown curry floated from a small, dingy storefront called the Benares Cafe, mixing with the sharp odor of the victim's urine. I turned away, took a last breath of fresh air, and knelt down by the injured man.

The blond leaned over the victim's mouth, blew breath in, then lifted back.

"Did you see the car that hit him?" I asked.

He was pressing on the victim's chest. He waited till he forced air into his mouth again and came up. "A glimpse."

"Where were you then?"

Again he waited, timing his reply with his rising. "Walking on University, a block down." He blew into the mouth again. "He didn't stop. Barely slowed down."

"What kind of car?" I asked, timing my question to his rhythm.

"Big. Silver, with a big, shiny grill."

"What make?"

"Don't know."

"Can you describe the driver?"

"No."

"Man or woman?"

"Don't know."

"Did you see any passengers?"

"No."

"Is there anything else you can tell me about the car?"

He went through an entire cycle of breathing and pressing before he said, "No."

"Thanks."

Now I looked more closely at the victim. I could see the short, gray-streaked brown hair, and the still-dark mustache. I could see the thick eyebrows and the eyes so filled with blood that it might not have been possible to detect the eye color if I hadn't already known it. I took a long look to make sure. But there was no question. Under the blood were the dark brown eyes of Graham Latham.

Behind me, the door of the black-and-white opened, letting out a burst of staccato calls from the dispatcher, then slammed shut. "Ambulance and back-up on the way, Jill," Pereira said as she came up beside me. "It wasn't easy getting anyone off Traffic on a football day."

I stood up and moved away from the body with relief. The blond man continued his work. In spite of the rain, I could see the sweat coming through his shirt.

I relayed his account of the crime, such as it was, to Pereira, then asked her, "Have you ever heard of Graham Latham?"

"Nope. Should I?"

"Maybe not. It's just ironic. When I was first on beat, I handled a hit-and-run. Only that time Latham was the driver. The victim, Katherine Hillman, was left just like he is. She lived—until last week, anyway. I saw her name in the obits. She was one of the guinea pigs they were trying a new electronic pain device on—a last resort for people with chronic untreatable pain."

Pereira nodded.

"I remember her at the trial," I said. "The pain wasn't so bad then. She could still shift around in her wheelchair and get some relief, and she had a boyfriend who helped her. But at the end it must have been bad." I looked over at the body in the street. "From the looks of Graham Latham, he'll be lucky if he can sit up in a wheelchair like she could."

"Be a hard choice," Pereira said, turning back to the black-and-white. She took the red blinkers out of the trunk, then hurried back along the empty street to put them in place.

Despite the cold rain, the sidewalks here weren't entirely empty. On the corner across University, I could see a pair of long pale female legs, shivering under stockings and black satin shorts that almost covered the curve of her buttocks—almost but not quite. Above those shorts, a thick red jacket suggested that, from the waist up, it was winter. The wearer—young, very blonde, with wings of multicolored eye make-up visible from across the street—stood partially concealed behind the building, looking toward Latham's body as if trying to decide whether it could be scooped up, and the cops cleared off, before the free-spending alumni rambled out of Memorial Stadium and drove down University Avenue.

On the sidewalk in front of the Benares Cafe, one of Berkeley's streetpeople—a man with long, tangled, rain-soaked hair that rested on a threadbare poncho, the outermost of three or four ragged layers of clothing—clutched a brown paper bag. Behind him, a tiny woman in a *sari* peered through the cafe window. In a doorway, a man and a woman leaned against a wall, seemingly oblivious to the activity in the street.

Between the Benares Cafe and the occupied doorway was a storefront with boxes piled in the window and the name "Harris" faded on the sign above. There was no indication of what Harris offered to the public. Across the street a mom-and-pop store occupied the corner. Next to it was the Evangelical People's Church— a storefront no larger than the mom-and-pop. Here in Berkeley, there had been more gurus over the years than in most states of India, but splinter Christian groups were rare; Berkeleyans liked their religion a bit more exotic. The rest of the block was taken up by a ramshackle hotel.

I looked back at Graham Latham, still lying unmoving in his herringbone suit. It was a good suit. Latham was an architect in San Francisco, a partner in a firm that had done a stylish low-income housing project for the city. He lived high in the hills above Berkeley. The brown Mercedes parked at the curb had to be his.

Graham Latham wasn't a man who should be found on the same block as the brown-bag clutcher behind him.

I walked toward the streetperson. I was surprised he'd stuck around. He wasn't one who would view the police as protectors.

I identified myself and took his name—John Eskins. "Tell me what you saw of the accident."

"Nothing."

"You were here when we arrived." I let the accusation hang.

"Khan, across the street"—he pointed to the store—"he saw it. He called you guys. Didn't have to; he just did. He said to tell you."

"Okay, but you stick around."

He shrugged.

I glanced toward Pereira. She nodded. In the distance the shriek of the ambulance siren cut through the air. On the ground the blond man was still working on Latham. His sleeves had bunched at the armpits revealing part of a tattoo—"ay" over a heart. In the rain, it looked as if the red of the letters would drip into the heart.

The ambulance screeched to a stop. Two medics jumped out.

The first came up behind the blond man. Putting a hand on his arm, he said, "Okay. We'll take over now."

The blond man didn't break his rhythm.

"It's okay," the medic said, louder. "You can stop now. You're covered."

Still he counted and pressed on Latham's chest, counted and breathed into Latham's unresponsive mouth.

The medic grabbed both arms and yanked him up. Before the blond was standing upright, the other medic was in his place.

"He'll die! Don't let him die! He can't die!" The man struggled to free himself. His hair flapped against his eyebrows; his shirt was soaked. There was blood—Latham's blood—on his face. The rain washed it down, leaving orange lines on his cheeks. "He can't die. It's not fair. You've got to save him!"

"He's getting the best care around," Pereira said.

The blond man leaned toward the action, but the medic pulled him back. Behind us, cars, limited now to one lane, drove slowly, their engines straining in first gear, headlights brightening the back of the ambulance like colorless blinkers. The rain dripped down my hair, under the collar of my jacket, collecting there in a soggy pool.

Turning to me, Pereira shrugged. I nodded. We'd both seen Good Samaritans like him, people who get so involved they can't let go.

I turned toward the store across the street. "Witness called from there. You want me to check it out?"

She nodded. It was her beat, her case. I was just doing her a favor.

I walked across University. The store was typical—a small display of apples, bananas, onions, potatoes, two wrinkled green peppers in front, and the rest of the space taken with rows of cans and boxes, a surprising number of them red, clamoring for the shoppers' notice and failing in their sameness. The shelves climbed high. There were packages of Bisquick, curry, and Garam Masala that the woman in the Benares Cafe wouldn't have been able to reach. In the back was a cooler for milk and cheese, and behind the counter by the door, the one-man bottles of vodka and bourbon— and a small, dark man, presumably Khan.

"I'm Detective Smith," I said, extending my shield. "You called us about the accident?"

"Yes," he said. "I am Farib Khan. I am owning this store. This is why I cannot leave to come to you, you see." He gestured at the empty premises.

I nodded. "But you saw the accident?"

"Yes, yes." He wagged his head side to side in that disconcerting Indian indication of the affirmative. "Mr. Latham—"

"You know him?"

"He is being my customer for a year now. Six days a week."

"Monday through Saturday?"

"Yes, yes. He is stopping on his drive from San Francisco."

"Does he work on Saturdays?" It wasn't the schedule I would have expected of a well-off architect.

"He teaches a class. After his class, he is eating lunch and driving home, you see. And stopping here."

I thought of Graham Latham in his expensive suit, driving his Mercedes. I recalled why he had hit a woman four years ago. It wasn't for curry powder that Graham Latham would be patronizing this ill-stocked store. "Did he buy liquor every day?"

"Yes, yes." Turning behind him, he took a pint bottle of vodka from the shelf. "He is buying this."

So Graham Latham hadn't changed. I didn't know why I would have assumed otherwise. "Did he open it before he left?"

"He is not a bum, not like those who come here not to buy, but to watch, to steal. Mr. Latham is a gentleman. For him, I am putting the bottle in a bag, to take home."

"Then you watched him leave? You saw the accident?"

Again the wagging of his head. "I am seeing, but it is no accident. Mr. Latham, he walks across the street, toward his big car. He is not a healthy man." Khan glanced significantly at the bottle. "So I watch. I am fearing the fall in the street, yes? But he walks straight. Then a car turns the corner, comes at him. Mr. Latham jumps back. He is fast then, you see. The car turns, comes at him. He cannot escape. He is hit. The car speeds off."

"You mean the driver was trying to hit Latham?"

"Yes, yes."

Involuntarily I glanced back to the street. Latham's body was gone now. The witnesses, John Eskin and the C.P.R. man, were standing with Pereira. A back-up unit had arrived. One of the men was checking the brown Mercedes.

Turning back to Khan, I said, "What did the car look like?"

He shrugged. "Old, middle-sized."

"Can you be more specific?"

He half-closed his eyes, trying. Finally, he said, "The day is gray, raining. The car is not new, not one I see in the ads. It is light-colored. Gray? Blue?"

"What about the driver?"

Again, he shrugged.

"Man or woman?"

It was a moment before he said, "All I am seeing is red—a sweater? Yes? A jacket?"

It took only a few more questions to discover that I had learned everything Farib Khan knew. By the time I crossed the street to the scene, Pereira had finished with the witnesses, and one of the back-up men was questioning the couple leaning in the doorway. The witnesses had seen nothing. John Eskins had been in the back of the store at the moment Latham had been hit, and the woman in the Benares Cafe—Pomilla Patel—hadn't seen anything until she heard the car hit him. And the man who stopped to give C.P.R.— Randall Sellinek—hadn't even seen the vehicle drive off. Or so they said.

They stood, a little apart from each other, as if each found the

remaining two unsuitable company. Certainly they were three who
would never come together in any other circumstances. John Eskin
clutched his brown bag, jerking his eyes warily. Pomilla Patel
glanced at him in disgust, as if he alone were responsible for the
decay of the neighborhood. And Randall Sellinek just stood, letting
the cold rain fall on his shirt and run down his bare arms.

I took Pereira aside and relayed what Khan had told me.

She grabbed one back-up man, telling him to call in for more
help. "If it's a possible homicide we'll have to scour the area. We'll
need to question everyone on this block and the ones on either side.
We'll need someone to check the cars and the garbage. Get as many
men as you can."

He raised an eyebrow. We all knew how many that would be.

To me, Pereira said, "You want to take Eskins or Sellinek down
to the station for statements?"

I hesitated. "No. . . . Suppose we let them leave and keep an eye
on them. We have the manpower."

"Are you serious, Jill? It's hardly regulations."

"I'll take responsibility."

Still, she looked uncomfortable. But she'd assisted on too many
of my cases over the years to doubt me completely. "Well, okay.
It's on your head." She moved toward the witnesses. "That's all,
folks. Thanks for your cooperation."

Eskins seemed stunned, but not about to question his good
fortune. He moved west, walking quickly, but unsteadily, toward
the seedy dwellings near the bay. I shook my head. Pereira nodded
to one of the back-up men, and he turned to follow Eskins.

Sellinek gave a final look at the scene of his futile effort and began
walking east, toward San Pablo Avenue and the better neighborhoods beyond. He didn't seem surprised, like Eskins, but then he
hadn't had the same type of contact with us. I watched him cross
the street, then followed. The blocks were short. He came to San
Pablo Avenue, waited for the light, then crossed. I had to run to
make the light.

On the far side of University Avenue the traffic was picking up.
Horns were beeping. The football game was over. The first of the
revelers had made it this far. I glanced back the several blocks to
the scene, wondering if the hooker had decided to wait us out. But
I was too far away to tell.

Sellinek crossed another street, then another. The rain beat down on his white shirt. His blond hair clung to his head. He walked on, never turning to look back.

I let him go five blocks, just to be sure, then caught up with him. "Mr. Sellinek. You remember me, one of the police officers. I'll need to ask you a few more questions."

"Me? Listen, I just stopped to help that man. I didn't want him to die. I wanted him to live."

"I believe you. You knocked yourself out trying to save him. But that still leaves the question of why? Why were you in this neighborhood at all?"

"Just passing through."

"On foot?"

"Yeah, on foot."

"In the rain, wearing just a shirt?"

"So?"

"Tell me again why you decided to give him C.P.R."

"I saw the car hit him. It was new and silver. It had a big, shiny grill. Why are you standing here badgering me? Why aren't you out looking for that car?"

"Because it doesn't exist."

"I *saw* it."

"When?"

"When it hit him."

"But you didn't notice passengers. You couldn't describe the driver."

"The car was too far away. I was back at the corner, behind it. I told you that."

"You didn't look at it when it passed you?"

"No. I was caught up in my own thoughts. I wasn't going to cross the street. There was no reason to look at the traffic. Then the car hit him. He was dying when I got to him—I couldn't let him die."

"I believe that. You didn't intend for him to have something as easy as death."

"What?"

"There wasn't any silver car or shiny grill, Mr. Sellinek." He started to protest, but I held up a hand. "You said you were behind the car and didn't notice it until it hit Latham. You couldn't possibly have seen what kind of grill it had. *You're* the one who ran Latham down."

He didn't say anything. He just stood, letting the rain drip down his face.

"We'll check the area," I said. "We'll find the car you used—maybe not your own car, maybe hot-wired, but there'll be prints. You couldn't have had time to clean them all off. We'll find your red sweater too. When you planned to run Latham down, you never thought you'd have to stop and try to save his life, did you? And once you realized you had to go back to him, you took the sweater off because you were afraid someone might have seen it. Isn't that the way it happened, Mr. Sellinek?"

He still didn't say anything.

I looked at the tattoo on his arm. All of it was visible now—the full name above the heart. It said, "Kay."

"You were Kay Hillman's boyfriend, weren't you? That's why you ran Latham down—because she died last week and you wanted revenge."

His whole body began to shake. "Latham was drunk when he hit Kay. But he got a smart lawyer, he lied in court, he got off with a suspended sentence. What he did to Kay . . . it was just an inconvenience to him. It didn't even change his habits. He still drank when he was driving. He still stopped six days a week at the same store to pick up liquor. Sooner or later he would have run down someone else. It was just a matter of time.

"I wanted revenge, sure. But it wasn't because Kay died. It was for those four years she *lived* after he hit her. She couldn't sit without pain; she couldn't lie down. The pills didn't help. Nothing did. The pain just got worse, month after month." He closed his eyes, squeezing back tears. "I didn't want Latham to die. I wanted him to suffer like Kay did."

Now it was my turn not to say anything.

Sellinek swallowed heavily. "It's not fair," he said. "None of it is fair."

He was right. None of it was fair at all.

THE HALF-INVISIBLE MAN

BILL PRONZINI AND JEFFREY WALLMANN

"The Half-Invisible Man" of this story's title is Patrolman Fred Gallagher, a police officer who feels that he has "done little in his nearly three decades on the metropolitan police force except stand outside hotel and motel rooms, apartments, private chambers in everything from mansions to hovels—glimpsing through doorways every conceivable type of crime man could perpetrate against his fellowman. He was a kind of uninvolved, perpetually detached observer, like one of the morbidly curious who always congregated at the scene of any violent happening—to all concerned a familiar blue uniform instead of a human being." But Fred Gallagher is every bit as good a cop as his superiors; in fact, as he proves here, he is their *superior when it comes to solving a seemingly impossible crime. Bill Pronzini and Jeffrey Wallman have collaborated on numerous short stories, two Western novels, and one crime novel* (Day of the Moon)—*most of which appeared under the joint pseudonym William Jeffrey.*

Patrolman Fred Gallagher stood at his posted position outside the slightly open door of Room 103 in the fashionable Whitewater Motel and listened to Lieutenant Owen Conroy reviewing with Captain of Detectives Philip Fabian the details of the murder that had been committed there earlier that day.

For the past few years Gallagher had been assigned to clerical duties at headquarters, so that he would be readily available as a driver for the ranking officials of the detective squad. He had driven Lieutenant Conroy to the Whitewater in response to this particular squeal and had been stationed on guard in front of Room 103 since their arrival some four hours before. He had during that time seen the body of the dead man, Aaron Maddox; and had silently observed—no one had bothered to speak to him, or it seemed even to look at him—the coming of the lab crew and the assistant medical examiner and the ambulance attendants, their eventual departure, and then the arrival of Captain Fabian.

As he had thought occasionally in the past, he thought now that it was as if he had done little in his nearly three decades on the metropolitan police force except stand outside hotel and motel rooms, apartments, private chambers in everything from mansions to hovels—glimpsing through doorways every conceivable type of crime man could perpetrate against his fellowman. He was a kind of uninvolved, perpetually detached observer, like one of the morbidly curious who always congregated at the scene of any violent happening—to all concerned a familiar blue uniform instead of a human being named Fred Gallagher.

A half-invisible man.

He was lean and fair-skinned, with ordinary features and mild brown eyes. Three weeks earlier he had celebrated his fiftieth birthday—without celebration and completely alone, because he had never married and had no relatives in this city or state. Fifty years old and twenty-seven years a cop, twenty-seven years a patrolman. He had grown up in the tenements of Baltimore and the bunkers of World War II, and had taken and passed his civil service exams shortly after being discharged from the Army.

He possessed a keen native intelligence, but his was the kind of mind which did not easily assimilate academic knowledge; this fact, coupled with a lack of funds, had kept him from considering college. Too, he was a quiet, passive, deferential individual by nature. As a result, the new breed of police officer, with their civic zeal, scientific specialization, university and police academy training, had been consistently promoted over him. Once he had been bitter about it; now he was merely tired and resigned.

He shifted his weight to ease the chronic ache in his legs—owing, of all things, to varicose veins. While the lab crew had been going over the room, Lieutenant Conroy, who was three years Gallagher's junior, had taken notice of him long enough to ask ritualistically and with conscious or unconscious patronage if he wanted a chair.

As always, Gallagher had politely declined. He was tired and resigned, yes—and it was true that the daily donning of his crisply pressed, button-shiny uniform had become a cheerless routine—but he still maintained a certain measure of pride. He would take what life and his chosen profession had dealt to him standing up, not sitting down.

Listening to the lieutenant and the captain talking inside, Gallagher forced his thoughts away from personal reflection and occupied his mind by visualizing the room. It was spacious, low-ceilinged, and no doubt similar to all the other units in the U-shaped motel complex. Three of the walls were paneled in walnut veneer. The fourth, directly opposite the hall entrance, was three-quarters glass window and sliding-glass door, looking out onto a flagstone terrace and center courtyard, and one-quarter built-in wardrobe whose left side abutted the wall separating Room 103 from Room 105.

The wardrobe's lower half consisted of six drawers, and the left half was a closet with its roller door open to reveal nothing but an empty wooden clothes rod. In the center of the room on that side was an extra-wide double bed, and against the outer wall was a long slender writing desk.

The other half of the room, adjoining 101, contained a luggage rack with Maddox's suitcase open on it, a television set on a wall bracket, a single armchair and reading lamp, and the door to the bathroom.

The sound of Conroy's voice told Gallagher that the lieutenant was pacing back and forth on the maroon-colored carpet. Conroy was a small, dark, intense man who had a great deal of nervous energy. Captain Fabian—heavy-set, with gray eyes half-closed as if in constant meditation—was apparently sitting in the armchair. Fabian did not usually come out into the field, but this particular murder case had so mystified Conroy that he'd deemed it necessary to call the captain in for consultation.

Conroy was saying now, "According to the desk clerk, Hedwig, Maddox had just checked in about ten minutes before he was shot. He hadn't had time to do much of anything except open his suitcase and take off his sports jacket."

"How many people heard the shot, Owen?"

"The occupants of the two rooms adjacent, both of whom are definite suspects—Gordon Severin in 105 and Ralph Oakley in

101. The desk clerk, Hedwig, heard it, too; he was the first one to respond."

"Hedwig can see the door to this room from the front desk, right?"

"Right. The angle of the desk in the lobby allows him a clear view of this entire wing, from Rooms 101 to 111."

"Were there any people in the lobby or outside in the courtyard who might've seen something?"

"Not that we've found so far. Quite a few of the rooms are vacant at the moment."

"Okay, go ahead."

"Well, Hedwig came running to investigate the shot and Oakley from Room 101 joined him at the door maybe thirty seconds later. When they couldn't get an answer from in here by beating on the door panel, Hedwig tried the knob; it was locked from the inside. He used his passkey to open up, and they found Maddox sprawled across the bed, shot through the left temple.

"Severin from 105 put in an appearance then, delayed because he says he was taking a shower; he was dressed in a bathrobe and his hair was wet, though that doesn't necessarily corroborate his claim. Anyway, Hedwig locked the door again and called us immediately. He swears no one touched anything in here."

"The sliding-glass door was also locked from the inside?" Fabian asked.

"Right. The safety bolt, the kind the insurance companies require these days, was firmly in place. We checked for jimmy marks, and as you saw there aren't any. As well, there's no handle or lock on the outside and the frame has tight-fitting grooves. There just isn't any way that bolt could have been moved from outside. And with Hedwig at the front desk, there isn't any way the killer could have gone out the hall door and not have been seen."

Gallagher heard Fabian get to his feet and open the bathroom door; then: "What about the window in here?"

"Also closed and locked from the inside," Conroy told him.

The bathroom door clicked shut. "Hedwig and Severin and Oakley all agree that the shot definitely came from *inside* this room?"

"They do, although none of them was able to pinpoint from exactly where in the room."

"And yet you found the murder gun *outside,* on the terrace."

"Yeah, lying about ten feet beyond the locked glass door. You can see why I'm so damned baffled, Phil."

"Well, there's got to be an answer, that much is sure. Anything from Arms Registration on the gun?"

"It isn't registered. It's a .22 caliber Smith and Wesson Target."

"No prints, of course."

"Wiped clean."

"Lab crew didn't find anything at all? In the room?"

"No. They went over the room half a dozen times, and there wasn't a single thing to indicate how the murder was committed. They found a few latent prints belonging to the maid, and also one of Maddox's thumb on the handle inside the glass door. That's it."

"No signs of a struggle?"

"None. Everything was in its place. Oh, the bed was slightly rumpled where Maddox had fallen across it, and his jacket was on the floor of the closet along with a couple of clothes hangers, but otherwise the room was exactly as the maid had left it after preparing it this morning."

"Maddox's print on the sliding-door handle means he must have opened it either for a breath of air or to step out onto the terrace for a look around."

"I considered that," Conroy said, "but there still isn't any way the murderer could have come in through that door, shot Maddox, and then bolted the door on the inside after going out again."

"You searched Severin's and Oakley's rooms and belongings?"

"We did. Same story—not a thing that could even remotely be construed as incriminating or illuminating."

There was the sound of a match being struck, and Gallagher knew Captain Fabian had lit his flame-scarred pipe; he could hear the sound of it drawing, like little gusts of wind from within the room.

Fabian said then, "Oakley and Severin were business associates of the dead man?"

"Yes. The three of them were partners in a small New York investment counseling firm—O.S.M. Consultants. Until two years ago it was called Oakley and Severin Consultants; then Maddox bought a partnership and convinced the other two to streamline the title. He was glib and persuasive, I've been told, a real ball of fire. He'd put together a small fortune through wildcat speculations, and said he was now ready to play it closer to the vest and therefore wanted the respectability of a well-established and conservative firm. If Harrison Caulder's accusations are correct, though, Maddox either changed his mind in midstream or had an ulterior motive from the beginning."

"What about this Caulder?"

"Retired businessman and investor, whose account was handled by Severin before Maddox joined the firm; then Maddox took it over, at Caulder's insistence, because Caulder was impressed by Maddox's energy and drive. Lately, Caulder had become suspicious of the handling of his investments, and yesterday he discovered through a broker in New York that stocks recently bought for him by O.S.M. were on the questionable side, worth nowhere near the money he paid for them.

"Caulder knew the three partners would be staying here at the Whitewater, so he came to confront them last night. Maddox wasn't here yet, but Caulder had words—very strong words—with Oakley and Severin. They begged him not to do anything rash until they had opportunity to talk to Maddox; Oakley told him that if his accusations were valid, Maddox was the only one who could have engineered any fraud."

"Just how would his alleged fraud benefit Maddox personally?"

"The way I got it, by buying these non-Board stocks he could arrange kickbacks from the quasi-legitimate companies involved— all of which were siphoned into his own pocket. So if true, he was not only cheating O.S.M. clients but milking the firm itself of its reputation. From what Oakley told me, reputation is the lifeblood of any investment counseling or brokerage outfit, and this kind of duplicity could mean total ruin. In other words, even though Oakley and Severin were innocent in the matter, and made restitution, their firm could still go under."

A few moments of silence. Then the striking of another match reached Gallagher's ears; Fabian's pipe had gone out. Gallagher lifted one glossy black shoe, then the other, to alleviate the pain in his legs.

Captain Fabian said at length, "How long have Severin and Oakley been here at the Whitewater?"

"Two days."

"For what reason?"

"They came to try to persuade a couple of large investors who lived in this area to transfer their accounts to O.S.M. They had to settle for the Whitewater instead of one of the larger downtown hotels because of the state political convention now going on."

"Why didn't Maddox come with them initially?"

"He was working with another client in Albany."

"Was Caulder here at the time of the shooting?"

"He says he wasn't, but he can't prove it," Conroy answered. "He'd been here about an hour before Maddox's arrival, for another talk with Oakley and Severin, and then claims to have gone for a walk in the neighborhood to work off some of his steam before seeing Maddox; he returned shortly after we arrived. I've got men out now checking for possible corroborative witnesses."

"Tell me something about Oakley and Severin and Caulder—your impressions, any personal facts you were able to dig out."

"Well, Ralph Oakley is sixty-one, a widower without children—sententious, ultra-conservative. His hobby is solving acrostics and cryptograms and the like, which may or may not mean anything; I learned that from Severin. I got the feeling Oakley never quite approved of Maddox, but was shrewd enough to realize he and Severin had to have fresh and enthusiastic blood if the firm was to attract new prospects; that was why they allowed Maddox to buy in."

"Caulder's accusations must have hit him hard, then."

"Right. And Severin as well, although he's a quiet and introspective type who doesn't display much of what he feels or thinks. He's forty-eight, and lives on Long Island with his wife. Pretty much of a homebody, doesn't drink or smoke; Oakley says Severin makes knickknacks out of wood and things in his spare time. In his own way he's just as conservative as Oakley; and he also didn't seem to approve of Maddox.

"Caulder, on the other hand, is waspish and highly excitable. He worked himself into a rage while I was interviewing him, the usual flap about police harassment. He's divorced and fifty-five, something of a swinger to hear him tell it, and prides himself on being neat and well-dressed; those latter two facts, he says, are additional reasons why he took to Maddox at first, since Maddox was the same way. Caulder was a manufacturer of remote-controlled electronic devices before his retirement, and there might be an angle in that, I suppose; but if so, I just can't see how."

"Anything else, Owen?"

"So far, not a thing, Captain."

Gallagher flexed his shoulder muscles—his back had begun to hurt along with his legs—then glanced into the expensively appointed, plant-festooned lobby. It was deserted now, as was the hallway in both directions; other patrolmen were on duty out front to keep out rubberneckers and reporters, and Hedwig, Oakley, Severin, and Caulder were being detained in the motel lounge for further questioning.

There was nothing to distract Gallagher's attention; his mind wandered back and forth over the conversation which he had just overheard and which was being partially replayed in Room 103.

After a time he heard the captain exhale heavily and say that further speculation seemed pointless and it was time he personally interviewed the suspects. Gallagher straightened up in an attitude of attention as Fabian and Lieutenant Conroy emerged into the hallway.

The captain flicked eyes over him. "Hold the fort, Gallagher. We'll be back directly."

"Yes, sir." And then, on impulse: "Would it be all right if I stayed inside the room instead of out here in the hall?"

Conroy shrugged. "Suit yourself."

Gallagher watched his two superiors walk down into the lobby, on their way to the lounge, then he turned slowly to enter the empty room.

When Fabian and Conroy returned an hour later, Gallagher was standing patiently by the door, just inside Room 103.

The captain was saying, ". . . after interrogating the three of them I'm forced to agree that there's not a damned thing to point to any one as the killer. They all have motives, but no apparent opportunity, and while I hate to admit it I can't for the life of me figure out how the murder could have been committed. I've got the feeling one of them is guilty, same as you, Owen—but which one?"

Gallagher said quietly, "Gordon Severin, sir, in Room 105."

Fabian and Conroy stopped abruptly, turned, and Gallagher saw disbelief register on their faces—not so much because of *what* he had said, he thought, as because *he* had said it. But they were looking at him now, really looking at him.

The captain asked, "What did you say?"

"That Gordon Severin murdered Aaron Maddox, sir."

"How the hell can you make a statement like that?"

Gallagher drew a deep breath and released it slowly, his eyes steady on theirs."I couldn't help overhearing you and the lieutenant talking over all the details of the case a while ago, sir, and I got to thinking about some of the things you said. They sort of formed a pattern in my mind, and an idea came to me, and I checked it out while you were gone. It's the right answer, all right."

They kept on staring at him.

"I'm not sure I understand all that business about investment counseling and stock fraud," Gallagher said, "but it wouldn't seem that Caulder's accusations triggered the murder. He confronted Severin and Oakley just last night, as you said, and this is a crime that must have been planned some time in advance. It could be Severin had found out on his own what Maddox was doing to O.S.M. clients and to the firm itself, decided to kill him, then maybe try and cover up Maddox's fraud before any of their people found out; too late for that after Caulder came, but not too late to carry out his plan for murdering Maddox. Whatever Severin's motive, I guess it will come out sooner or later."

He paused. "Anyway, the important thing is that Severin is the killer. What proves it is the fact that he's the occupant of Room 105."

"What does Room 105 have to do with it?" Conroy demanded. "How could Severin have gotten from there into here to kill Maddox and then back again?"

"He didn't, sir. He shot Maddox from his room, from Number 105."

The two officials exchanged incredulous glances, as if they thought perhaps Gallagher had gone quietly mad. Fabian said, "For God's sake, man—murdered him through a solid wall?"

"Yes, sir, exactly—through a solid wall. If you'll come over here with me, I can show you how he did it."

He led them across to the built-in wardrobe, glanced into the empty closet, then returned his gaze to Conroy.

"Sir," he said, "you mentioned earlier that you'd found Maddox's sports jacket on the closet floor. Well, that struck me as being pretty odd, because of something else you mentioned—that Maddox, like Caulder, was neat and well-dressed. I'm something of a neat man myself, and neat people would never drop an expensive sports jacket on the *floor* of a closet.

"Also, you said everything in this room was as the maid had left it when she cleaned this morning; and yet there were clothes hangers on the closet floor as well. I asked myself why both the sports jacket *and* the hangers should be there—the only two things out of place. And that's when the idea came to me."

Gallagher reached into the closet and took hold of the wooden clothes rod, which was attached to the wardrobe walls inside wooden ring brackets. The rod was loose, and he was able to jerk free the end in the left-hand bracket. That end, when he brought the rod out within Conroy's and Fabian's vision, had a round threaded puncture in it—the kind a small wood tap would make.

Inside the left-hand ring was a neatly drilled hole, slightly larger than the circumference of the rod; through the hole, which penetrated both closet and room walls, they could see the wooden end of another clothes rod—the one in the closet of Room 105.

Captain Fabian said in amazement, "Well, I'm damned. Thorough as the lab crew is, there was just no reason for them to have thought of removing this rod; hell, it's something you look at but never really see in the first place."

Yeah, Gallagher thought, *something you look at but never really see.* He said, "The way it would seem, Severin removed the rod in his own closet, in Room 105, then drilled the hole; he knew from the reservations that Maddox would occupy this room, 103, and he had two days to do the job and to dispose of wood shavings and the brace and bit he'd have used. You said yourself, Lieutenant, that his hobby was making knickknacks out of wood, so this kind of thing would've been no problem for him. With the rod in his closet back in place, there'd be no indication to the maid that anything was out of the ordinary when she came in to clean.

"Just before Maddox arrived, he must have turned on his shower and wet his hair and got into a bathrobe. He removed his rod again, drove the tap into the end of the rod in 103, then drew it through the hole into his closet. When he did that, the hangers naturally fell off and onto the floor. Severin waited in his closet then, I'd say, peering through the hole; as soon as Maddox came here and rolled back the door to hang up his jacket, Severin inserted the muzzle of the .22 and shot him. Maddox dropped the jacket, staggered back, and fell back across the bed.

"Severin then slid the rod of 103 back through the hole and fit it into place in the brackets, and then unscrewed the tap. He opened the sliding door in his room and skidded the murder gun out onto the terrace after first wiping off his prints, turned off the shower, and joined Oakley and Hedwig in this room."

When Gallagher had finished speaking, there was a long, tense, meditative pause. Conroy broke it by saying, "By God, it fits, it all fits."

Fabian said in a grim voice, "Let's go get Severin."

Conroy turned to Gallagher and grasped him briefly by the arm. "Man, you've done a fine piece of detective work here."

"See to it you get a departmental citation," the captain said perfunctorily, and he and Conroy crossed to the door. Then, as if in afterthought: "You'd better stay here and keep an eye on things. We'll call you if we need you."

"Yes, sir."

They hurried out, and Gallagher listened to their footsteps retreating along the hall. A departmental citation, he thought; a handshake from the commissioner and maybe his name in the local papers—maybe. But that would be all. No promotion, even if he wasn't already too old for it. His "fine piece of detective work" would be considered a lucky fluke, nothing more, and would be quickly forgotten.

Fabian and Conroy and all the others—this was the worst of it—would continue to look at him without looking at him, without seeing *him;* the words and actions of the captain and the lieutenant a moment ago had told him that plainly enough. And in another twelve years there would be a gold watch at his retirement dinner, and a meager patrolman's pension, and three months afterward no one would really remember the person whose name was Fred Gallagher. The half-invisible man would have vanished completely.

He started slowly across the room, acutely conscious of the ache in his legs, and looked down at the padded armchair. He looked at it for a long time, then he thought: *No, that much is all I've got left to hang onto; I won't let them take my pride too.*

Gallagher went out into the hall, closing the door behind him, and stood there waiting stiffly for the return of his superiors.

NIGHTSHADE

ED McBAIN

*The 87th Precinct series by Ed McBain (Evan Hunter), which
began in 1956 with* Cop Hater *and continues to the present,
have been widely and justly praised as the finest police
procedurals by an American. (They may well be the finest of all
procedurals, past and present.) McBain's research into actual
police methods is meticulous, up-to-date, and vividly incorpo-
rated into his stories; and his understanding of the "cop mind"
is acute. "Nightshade" is among the best of the shorter works
about the 87th Precinct; in the words of Ellery Queen, it tells of
"one night in the lives and deaths of detectives Steve Carella,
Cotton Hawes, Bert Kling, Meyer Meyer, and the rest of the
squad . . . one night that is a microcosm of a metropolis—a
mosaic of murder, vandalism, ghosts(!), bombing, theft, of
missing persons, junkies, pushers, drunk-and-disorderlies, burglars, muggers . . ."*

The morning hours of the night come imperceptibly here.

It is a minute before midnight on the peeling face of the hanging
wall clock, and then it is midnight, and then the minute hand
moves visibly and with a lurch into the new day. The morning
hours have begun, but scarcely anyone has noticed. The stale coffee
in soggy cardboard containers tastes the same as it did thirty
seconds ago, the spastic rhythm of the clacking typewriters continues unabated, a drunk across the room shouts that the world is full
of brutality, and cigarette smoke drifts up toward the face of the
clock where, unnoticed and unmourned, the old day has already
been dead for two minutes.

Then the telephone rings.

The men in this room are part of a tired routine, somewhat
shabby about the edges, as faded and as gloomy as the room itself,
with its cigarette-scarred desks and its smudged green walls. This

could be the office of a failing insurance company were it not for
the evidence of the holstered pistols hanging from belts on the
backs of wooden chairs painted a darker green than the walls. The
furniture is ancient, the typewriters are ancient, the building itself
is ancient—which is perhaps only fitting since these men are
involved in what is an ancient pursuit, a pursuit once considered
honorable. They are law enforcers. They are, in the mildest words
of the drunk still hurling epithets from the grilled detention cage
across the room, dirty rotten pigs.

The telephone continues to ring.

The little girl lying in the alley behind the theater was wearing a
belted white trench coat wet with blood. There was blood on the
floor of the alley, and blood on the metal fire door behind her, and
blood on her face and matted in her blonde hair, blood on her
miniskirt and on the lavender tights she wore. A neon sign across
the street stained the girl's ebbing life juices green and then orange,
while from the open knife wound in her chest the blood sprouted
like some ghastly night flower, dark and rich, red, orange, green,
pulsing in time to the neon flicker—a grotesque psychedelic light
show, and then losing the rhythm, welling up with less force and
power.

She opened her mouth, she tried to speak, and the scream of an
ambulance approaching the theater seemed to come from her mouth
on a fresh bubble of blood. The blood stopped, her life ended, the
girl's eyes rolled back into her head.

Detective Steve Carella turned away as the ambulance attendants
rushed a stretcher into the alley. He told them the girl was dead.

"We got here in seven minutes," one of the attendants said.

"Nobody's blaming you," Carella answered.

"This is Saturday night," the attendant complained. "Streets are
full of traffic. Even *with* the damn siren."

Carella walked to the unmarked sedan parked at the curb. Detective Cotton Hawes, sitting behind the wheel, rolled down his
frostrimed window and said, "How is she?"

"We've got a homicide," Carella answered.

The boy was eighteen years old, and he had been picked up not
ten minutes ago for breaking off car aerials. He had broken off

twelve on the same street, strewing them behind him like a Johnny Appleseed planting radios; a cruising squad car had spotted him as he tried to twist off the aerial of a 1966 Cadillac. He was drunk or stoned or both, and when Sergeant Murchison at the muster desk asked him to read the Miranda-Escobedo warning signs on the wall, printed in both English and Spanish, he could read neither.

The arresting patrolman took the boy to the squadroom upstairs, where Detective Bert Kling was talking to Hawes on the telephone. Kling signaled for the patrolman to wait with his prisoner on the bench outside the slatted wooden rail divider, and then buzzed Murchison at the desk downstairs.

"Dave," he said, "we've got a homicide in the alley of the Eleventh Street Theater. You want to get it rolling?"

"Right," Murchison said, and hung up.

Homicides are a common occurrence in this city, and each one is treated identically, the grisly horror of violent death reduced to routine by a police force that would otherwise be overwhelmed by statistics. At the muster desk upstairs Kling waved the patrolman and his prisoner into the squadroom. Sergeant Murchison first reported the murder to Captain Frick, who commanded the 87th Precinct, and then to Lieutenant Byrnes, who commanded the 87th Detective Squad. He then phoned homicide, who in turn set into motion an escalating process of notification that included the police laboratory, the Telegraph, Telephone and Teletype Bureau at headquarters, the medical examiner, the district attorney, the district commander of the detective division, the chief of detectives, and finally the police commissioner himself. Someone had thoughtlessly robbed a young woman of her life, and now a lot of sleepy-eyed men were being shaken out of their beds on a cold October night.

Upstairs, the clock on the squadroom wall read 12:30 A.M. The boy who had broken off twelve car aerials sat in a chair alongside Bert Kling's desk. Kling took one look at him and yelled to Miscolo in the clerical office to bring in a pot of strong coffee. Across the room the drunk in the detention cage wanted to know where he was. In a little while they would release him with a warning to try to stay sober till morning.

But the night was young.

They arrived alone or in pairs, blowing on their hands, shoulders hunched against the bitter cold, breaths pluming whitely from their lips. They marked the dead girl's position in the alleyway, they took her picture, they made drawings of the scene, they searched for the murder weapon and found none, and then they stood around speculating on sudden death. In this alleyway alongside a theater the policemen were the stars and the celebrities, and a curious crowd thronged the sidewalk where a barricade had already been set up, anxious for a glimpse of these men with their shields pinned to their overcoats—the identifying Playbills of law enforcement, without which you could not tell the civilians from the plainclothes cops.

Monoghan and Monroe had arrived from homicide, and they watched dispassionately now as the assistant medical examiner fluttered around the dead girl. They were both wearing black overcoats, black mufflers, and black fedoras; both were heavier men than Carella who stood between them with the lean look of an overtrained athlete, a pained expression on his face.

"He done some job on her," Monroe said.

Monoghan made a rude sound.

"You identified her yet?" Monroe asked.

"I'm waiting for the M.E. to get through," Carella answered.

"Might help to know what she was doing here in the alley. What's that door there?" Monoghan asked.

"Stage entrance."

"Think she was in the show?"

"I don't know," Carella said.

"Well, what the hell," Monroe said, "they're finished with her pocketbook there, ain't they? Why don't you look through it? You finished with that pocketbook there?" he yelled to one of the lab technicians.

"Yeah, anytime you want it," the technician shouted back.

"Go on, Carella, take a look."

The technician wiped the blood off the dead girl's bag, then handed it to Carella. Monoghan and Monroe crowded in on him as he twisted open the clasp.

"Bring it over to the light," Monroe said.

The light, with a metal shade, hung over the stage door. So violently had the girl been stabbed that flecks of blood had even dotted the enameled white underside of the shade. In her bag they found a driver's license identifying her as Mercy Howell of 1113 Rutherford Avenue, Age 24, Height 5′ 3″, Eyes Blue. They found an Actors Equity card in her name, as well as credit cards for two of the city's largest department stores. They found an unopened package of Virginia Slims, and a book of matches advertising an art course. The found a rat-tailed comb. They found seventeen dollars and forty-three cents. They found a package of Kleenex, and an appointment book. They found a ballpoint pen with shreds of tobacco clinging to its tip, an eyelash curler, two subway tokens, and an advertisement for a see-through blouse, clipped from one of the local newspapers.

In the pocket of her trench coat, when the M.E. had finished with her and pronounced her dead from multiple stab wounds in the chest and throat, they found an unfired Browning .25 caliber automatic. They tagged the gun and the handbag, and they moved the girl out of the alleyway and into the waiting ambulance for removal to the morgue. There was now nothing left of Mercy Howell but a chalked outline of her body and a pool of her blood on the alley floor.

"You sober enough to understand me?" Kling asked the boy.

"I was never drunk to begin with," the boy answered.

"Okay then, here we go," Kling said. "In keeping with the supreme court decision in Miranda versus Arizona we are not permitted to ask you any questions until you are warned of your right to counsel and your privilege against self-incrimination."

"What does that mean?" the boy asked. "Self-incrimination?"

"I'm about to explain that to you now," Kling said.

"This coffee stinks."

"First, you have the right to remain silent if you so choose," Kling said. "Do you understand that?"

"I understand it."

"Second, you do not have to answer any police questions if you don't want to. Do you understand that?"

"What the hell are you asking me if I understand for? Do I look like a moron or something?"

"The law requires that I ask whether or not you understand these specific warnings. *Did* you understand what I just said about not having to answer?"

"Yeah, yeah, I understood."

"All right. Third, if you do decide to answer any questions, the answers may be used as evidence against you, do you—?"

"What the hell did I do, break off a couple of lousy car aerials?"

"Did you understand that?"

"I understood it."

"You also have the right to consult with an attorney before or during police questioning. If you do not have the money to hire a lawyer, a lawyer will be appointed to consult with you."

Kling gave this warning straight-faced even though he knew that under the criminal procedure code of the city for which he worked, a public defender could not be appointed by the courts until the preliminary hearing. There was no legal provision for the courts *or* the police to appoint counsel during questioning, and there were certainly no police funds set aside for the appointment of attorneys. In theory, a call to the Legal Aid Society should have brought a lawyer up there to the old squadron within minutes, ready and eager to offer counsel to any indigent person desiring it. But in practice, if this boy sitting beside Kling told him in the next three seconds that he was unable to pay for his own attorney and would like one provided, Kling would not have known just what to do— other than call off the questioning.

"I understand," the boy said.

"You've signified that you understand all the warnings," Kling said, "and now I ask you whether you are willing to answer my questions without an attorney here to counsel you."

"Go fly a kite," the boy said. "I don't want to answer nothing."

So that was that.

They booked him for a criminal mischief, a class-A misdemeanor defined as intentional or reckless damage to the property of another person, and they took him downstairs to a holding cell, to await transport to the criminal courts building for arraignment.

The phone was ringing again, and a woman was waiting on the bench just outside the squadroom.

The watchman's booth was just inside the metal stage door. An electric clock on the wall behind the watchman's stool read 1:10

A.M. The watchman was a man in his late seventies who did not at all mind being questioned by the police. He came on duty, he told them, at 7:30 each night. The company call was for 8:00, and he was there at the stage door waiting to greet everybody as they arrived to get made up and in costume. Curtain went down at 11:20, and usually most of the kids were out of the theater by 11:45 or, at the latest, midnight. He stayed on till 9:00 the next morning, when the theater box office opened.

"Ain't much to do during the night except hang around and make sure nobody runs off with the scenery," he said, chuckling.

"Did you happen to notice what time Mercy Howell left the theater?" Carella asked.

"She the one got killed?" the old man asked.

"Yes," Hawes said. "Mercy Howell. About this high, blonde hair, blue eyes."

"They're all about that high, with blonde hair and blue eyes," the old man said, and chuckled again. "I don't know hardly none of them by name. Shows come and go, you know. Be a hell of a chore to have to remember all the kids who go in and out that door."

"Do you sit here by the door all night?" Carella asked.

"Well, no, not all night. What I do, I lock the door after everybody's out and then I check the lights, make sure just the work light's on. I won't touch the switchboard, not allowed to, but I can turn out lights in the lobby, for example, if somebody left them on, or down in the toilets—sometimes they leave lights on down in the toilets. Then I come back here to the booth, and read or listen to the radio. Along about two o'clock I check the theater again, make sure we ain't got no fires or nothing, and then I come back here and make the rounds again at four o'clock, and six o'clock, and again about eight. That's what I do."

"You say you lock this door?"

"That's right."

"Would you remember what time you locked it tonight?"

"Oh, must've been about ten minutes to twelve. Soon as I knew everybody was out."

"How do you know when they're out?"

"I give a yell up the stairs there. You see those stairs there? They go up to the dressing rooms. Dressing rooms are all upstairs in this house. So I go to the steps, and I yell, 'Locking up! Anybody here?' And if somebody yells back, I know somebody's here, and I say, 'Let's shake it, honey,' if it's a girl, and if it's a boy, I say, 'Let's hurry it up, sonny.' " The old man chuckled again. "With this show it's sometimes hard to tell which's the girls and which's the boys. I manage, though," he said, and again chuckled.

"So you locked the door at ten minutes to twelve?"

"Right."

"And everybody had left the theater by that time?"

" 'Cept me, of course."

"Did you look out into the alley before you locked the door?"

"Nope. Why should I do that?"

"Did you hear anything outside *while* you were locking the door?"

"Nope."

"Or at any time *before* you locked it?"

"Well, there's always noise outside when they're leaving, you know. They got friends waiting for them, or else they go home together, you know—there's always a lot of chatter when they go out."

"But it was quiet when you locked the door?"

"Dead quiet," the old man said.

The woman who took the chair beside Detective Meyer Meyer's desk was perhaps thirty-two years old, with long straight black hair trailing down her back, and wide brown eyes that were terrified. It was still October, and the color of her tailored coat seemed suited to the season, a subtle tangerine with a small brown fur collar that echoed an outdoors trembling with the colors of autumn.

"I feel sort of silly about this," she said, "but my husband insisted that I come."

"I see," Meyer said.

"There are ghosts," the woman said.

Across the room Kling unlocked the door to the detention cage and said, "Okay, pal, on your way. Try to stay sober till morning, huh?"

"It ain't one thirty yet," the man said. "The night is young." He stepped out of the cage, tipped his hat to Kling, and hurriedly left the squadroom.

Meyer looked at the woman sitting beside him, studying her with new interest because, to tell the truth, she had not seemed like a nut when she first walked into the squadroom. He had been a detective for more years than he chose to count, and in his time had met far too many nuts of every stripe and persuasion. But he had never met one as pretty as Adele Gorman with her well-tailored, fur-collared coat, and her Vassar voice and her skillfully applied eye makeup, lips bare of color in her pale white face, pert and reasonably young and seemingly intelligent—but apparently a nut besides.

"In the house," she said. "Ghosts."

"Where do you live, ma'am?" he asked. He had written her name on the pad in front of him, and now he watched her with his pencil poised and recalled the lady who had come into the squadroom only last month to report a gorilla peering into her bedroom from the fire escape outside. They had sent a patrolman over to make a routine check, and had even called the zoo and the circus (which coincidentally was in town, and which lent at least some measure of credibility to her claim), but there had been no gorilla on the fire escape, nor had any gorilla recently escaped from a cage. The lady came back the next day to report that her visiting gorilla had put in another appearance the night before, this time wearing a top hat and carrying a black cane with an ivory head. Meyer had assured her that he would have a platoon of cops watching her building that night, which seemed to calm her at least somewhat. He had then led her personally out of the squadroom and down the iron-runged steps, and through the high-ceilinged muster room, and past the hanging green globes on the front stoop, and onto the sidewalk outside the station house. Sergeant Murchison, at the muster desk, shook his head after the lady was gone, and muttered, "More of them outside than in."

Meyer watched Adele Gorman now, remembered what Murchison had said, and thought: *Gorillas in September, ghosts in October.*

"We live in Smoke Rise," she said. "Actually, it's my father's house, but my husband and I are living there with him."

"The address?"

"MacArthur Lane—number three hundred seventy-four. You take the first access road into Smoke Rise, about a mile and a half east of Silvermine Oval. The name on the mailbox is Van Houten.

That's my father's name. Willem Van Houten." She paused and studied him, as though expecting some reaction.

"Okay," Meyer said, and ran a hand over his bald pate. He looked up and said, "Now, you were saying, Mrs. Gorman—"

"That we have ghosts."

"Uh-huh. What kind of ghosts?"

"Ghosts. Poltergeists. Shades. I don't know," she said, and shrugged. "What kinds of ghosts are there?"

"Well, they're your ghosts, so suppose you tell me," Meyer said.

The telephone on Kling's desk rang. He lifted the receiver and said, "Eighty-seventh, Detective Kling."

"There are two of them," Adele said.

"Male or female?"

"One of each."

"Yeah," Kling said into the telephone, "go ahead."

"How old would you say they were?"

"Centuries, I would guess."

"No, I mean—"

"Oh, how old do they look? Well, the man—"

"You've seen them?"

"Oh, yes, many times."

"Uh-huh," Meyer said.

"I'll be right over," Kling said into the telephone. "You stay there." He slammed down the receiver, opened his desk drawer, pulled out a holstered revolver, and hurriedly clipped it to his belt. "Somebody threw a bomb into a store-front church. One-seven-three-three Culver Avenue. I'm heading over."

"Right," Meyer said. "Get back to me."

"We'll need a couple of meat wagons. The minister and two others were killed, and it sounds as if there're a lot of injured."

"Will you tell Dave?"

"On the way out," Kling said, and was gone.

"Mrs. Gorman," Meyer said, "as you can see, we're pretty busy here just now. I wonder if your ghosts can wait till morning."

"No, they can't," Adele said.

"Why not?"

"Because they appear precisely at two forty-five A.M., and I want someone to see them."

"Why don't you and your husband look at them?" Meyer said.

"You think I'm a nut, don't you?" Adele said.

"No, no, Mrs. Gorman, not at all."

"Oh, yes you do," Adele said. "I didn't believe in ghosts either—until I saw these two."

"Well, this is all very interesting, I assure you, Mrs. Gorman, but really we do have our hands full right now, and I don't know what we can do about these ghosts of yours, even if we did come over to take a look at them."

"They've been stealing things from us," Adele said, and Meyer thought: *Oh, we have got ourselves a prime lunatic this time.*

"What sort of things?"

"A diamond brooch that used to belong to my mother when she was alive. They stole that from my father's safe."

"What else?"

"A pair of emerald earrings. They were in the safe, too."

"When did these thefts occur?"

"Last month."

"Isn't it possible the jewelry's been mislaid?"

"You don't mislay a diamond brooch and a pair of emerald earrings that are locked inside a wall safe."

"Did you report these thefts?"

"No."

"Why not?"

"Because I knew you'd think I was crazy. Which is just what you're thinking right this minute."

"No, Mrs. Gorman, but I'm sure you can appreciate the fact that we—uh—can't go around arresting ghosts," Meyer said, and tried a smile.

Adele Gorman did not smile back. "Forget the ghosts," she said, "I was foolish to mention them. I should have known better." She took a deep breath, looked him squarely in the eye, and said, "I'm here to report the theft of a diamond brooch valued at six thousand dollars, and a pair of earrings worth thirty-five hundred dollars. Will you send a man to investigate tonight, or should I ask my father to get in touch with your superior officer?"

"Your father? What's he got to—"

"My father is a retired surrogate's court judge," Adele said.

"I see."

"Yes, I hope you do."

"What time did you say these ghosts arrive?" Meyer asked, and sighed heavily.

Between midnight and 2:00 the city does not change very much. The theaters have all let out, and the average Saturday night revelers, good citizens from Bethtown or Calm's Point, Riverhead or Majesta, have come into the Isola streets again in search of a snack or a giggle before heading home. The city is an ants' nest of after-theater eateries ranging from chic French cafés to pizzerias to luncheonettes to coffee shops to hot-dog stands to delicatessens, all of them packed to the ceilings because Saturday night is not only the loneliest night of the week, it is also the night to howl. And howl they do, these good burghers who have put in five long hard days of labor and who are anxious now to relax and enjoy themselves before Sunday arrives, bringing with it the attendant boredom of too much leisure, anathema for the American male.

The crowds shove and jostle their way along The Stem, moving in and out of bowling alleys, shooting galleries, penny arcades, strip joints, night clubs, jazz emporiums, souvenir shops, lining the sidewalks outside plate-glass windows in which go-go girls gyrate, or watching with fascination as a roast beef slowly turns on a spit. Saturday night is a time for pleasure for the good people of Isola and environs, with nothing more on their minds than a little enjoyment of the short respite between Friday night at 5:00 and Monday morning at 9:00.

But along around 2:00 A.M., the city begins to change.

The good citizens have waited to get their cars out of parking garages (more garages than there are barber shops) or have staggered their way sleepily into subways to make the long trip back to the outlying sections, the furry toy dog won in the Pokerino palace clutched limply, the laughter a bit thin, the voice a bit croaked, a college song being sung on a rattling subway car, but without much force or spirit. Saturday night has ended, it is really Sunday morning already, and the morning hours are truly upon the city—and now the denizens appear.

The predators approach, with the attendant danger of the good citizens getting mugged and rolled. The junkies are out in force, looking for cars foolishly left unlocked and parked on the streets, or—lacking such fortuitious circumstance—experienced enough to force the side vent with a screwdriver, hook the lock button with a wire hanger, and open the door that way. There are pushers peddling their dream stuff, from pot to speed to hoss, a nickel bag or a twenty-dollar deck; fences hawking their stolen goodies, anything from a transistor radio to a refrigerator, the biggest bargain basement in town; burglars jimmying windows or forcing doors with a celluloid strip, this being an excellent hour to break into apartments, when the occupants are asleep and the street sounds are hushed.

But worse than any of these are the predators who roam the night in search of trouble. In cruising wedges of three or four, sometimes high but more often not, they look for victims—a taxicab driver coming out of a cafeteria, an old woman poking around garbage cans for hidden treasures, a teenage couple necking in a parked automobile—it doesn't matter. You can get killed in this city at any time of the day or night, but your chances for extinction are best after 2:00 A.M. because, paradoxically, the night people take over in the morning. There are neighborhoods that terrify even cops in this lunar landscape, and there are certain places the cops will not enter unless they have first checked to see that there are two doors, one to get in by, and the other to get out through, fast, should someone decide to block the exit from behind.

The Painted Parasol was just such an establishment.

They had found in Mercy Howell's appointment book a notation that read: *Harry, 2:00 a.m. The Painted Parasol;* and since they knew this particular joint for exactly the kind of hole it was, and since they wondered what connection the slain girl might have had with the various unappetizing types who frequented the place from dusk till dawn, they decided to hit it and find out. The front entrance opened on a long flight of stairs that led down to the main room of what was not a restaurant, and not a club, though it combined features of both. It did not possess a liquor license, and so it served only coffee and sandwiches; but occasionally a rock singer would plug in his amplifier and guitar and whack out a few numbers for the patrons. The back door of the—hangout?—opened onto a sidestreet alley. Hawes checked it out, reported back to Carella, and they both made a mental floor plan just in case they needed it later.

Carella went down the long flight of steps first, Hawes immedi-

ately behind him. At the bottom of the stairway they moved
through a beaded curtain and found themselves in a large room
overhung with an old Air Force parachute painted in a wild psychedelic pattern. A counter on which rested a coffee urn and trays
of sandwiches in Saran Wrap was just opposite the hanging beaded
curtain. To the left and right of the counter were perhaps two dozen
tables, all of them occupied. A waitress in a black leotard and black
high-heeled patent-leather pumps was swiveling between and around
the tables, taking orders.

There was a buzz of conversation in the room, hovering, cap-
tured in the folds of the brightly painted parachute. Behind the
counter a man in a white apron was drawing a cup of coffee from
the huge silver urn. Carella and Hawes walked over to him. Carella
was almost six feet tall, and he weighed one hundred and eighty
pounds, with wide shoulders and a narrow waist and the hands of
a street brawler. Hawes was six feet two inches tall, and he weighed
one hundred and ninety-five pounds bone-dry, and his hair was a
fiery red with a white streak over the left temple where he had once
been knifed while investigating a burglary. Both men looked like
exactly what they were—fuzz.

"What's the trouble?" the man behind the counter asked.

"No trouble," Carella said. "This your place?"

"Yeah. My name is Georgie Bright, and I already been visited,
thanks. Twice."

"Oh? Who visited you?"

"First time a cop named O'Brien, second time a cop named
Parker. I already cleared up that whole thing that was going on
downstairs."

"What whole thing going on downstairs?"

"In the men's room. Some kids were selling pot down there, it
got to be a regular neighborhood supermarket. So I done what
O'Brien suggested, I put a man down there outside the toilet door,
and the rule now is only one person goes in there at a time. Parker
came around to make sure I was keeping my part of the bargain. I
don't want no narcotics trouble here. Go down and take a look if
you like. You'll see I got a man watching the toilet."

"Who's watching the man watching the toilet?" Carella asked.

"That ain't funny," Georgie Bright said, looking offended.

"Know anybody named Harry?" Hawes asked.

"Harry who? I know a lot of Harrys."

"Any of them here tonight?"

"Maybe."

"Where?"

"There's one over there near the bandstand. The big guy with the light hair."

"Harry what?"

"Donatello."

"Make the name?" Carella asked Hawes.

"No," Hawes said.

"Neither do I."

"Let's talk to him."

"You want a cup of coffee or something?" Georgie Bright asked.

"Yeah, why don't you send some over to the table?" Hawes said, and followed Carella across the room to where Harry Donatello was sitting with another man. Donatello was wearing gray slacks, black shoes and socks, a white shirt open at the throat, and a double-breasted blue blazer. His long blondish hair was combed straight back from the forehead, revealing a sharply defined widow's peak. He was easily as big as Hawes, and he sat with his hands folded on the table in front of him, talking to the man who sat opposite him. He did not look up as the detectives approached.

"Is your name Harry Donatello?" Carella asked.

"Who wants to know?"

"Police officers," Carella said, and flashed his shield.

"I'm Harry Donatello. What's the matter?"

"Mind if we sit down?" Hawes asked, and before Donatello could answer, both men sat, their backs to the empty bandstand and the exit door.

"Do you know a girl named Mercy Howell?" Carella asked.

"What about her?"

"Do you know her?"

"I know her. What's the beef? She underage or something?"

"When did you see her last?"

The man with Donatello, who up to now had been silent, suddenly piped, "You don't have to answer no questions without a lawyer, Harry. Tell them you want a lawyer."

The detectives looked him over. He was small and thin, with black hair combed sideways to conceal a receding hairline. He was badly in need of a shave. He was wearing blue trousers and a striped shirt.

"This is a field investigation," Hawes said dryly, "and we can ask anything we damn please."

"Town's getting full of lawyers," Carella said. "What's *your* name, counselor?"

"Jerry Riggs. You going to drag *me* in this, whatever it is?"

"It's a few friendly questions in the middle of the night," Hawes said. "Anybody got any objections to that?"

"Getting so two guys can't even sit and talk together without getting shook down," Riggs said.

"You've got a rough life, all right," Hawes said, and the girl in the black leotard brought their coffee to the table, and then hurried off to take another order. Donatello watched her jiggling as she swiveled across the room.

"So when's the last time you saw the Howell girl?" Carella asked again.

"Wednesday night," Donatello said.

"Did you see her tonight?"

"No."

"Were you supposed to see her tonight?"

"Where'd you get that idea?"

"We're full of ideas," Hawes said.

"Yeah, I was supposed to meet her here ten minutes ago. Dumb broad is late, as usual."

"What do you do for a living, Donatello?"

"I'm an importer. You want to see my business card?"

"What do you import?"

"Souvenir ashtrays."

"How'd you get to know Mercy Howell?"

"I met her at a party in The Quarter. She got a little high, and she done her thing."

"What thing?"

"The thing she does in that show she's in."

"Which is what?"

"She done this dance where she takes off all her clothes."

"How long have you been seeing her?"

"I met her a couple of months ago. I see her on and off, maybe once a week, something like that. This town is full of broads, you know—a guy don't have to get himself involved in no relationship with no specific broad."

"What was your relationship with *this* specific broad?"

"We have a few laughs together, that's all. She's a swinger, little Mercy," Donatello said, and grinned at Riggs.

"Want to tell us where you were tonight between eleven and twelve?"

"Is this still a *field* investigation?" Riggs asked sarcastically.

"Nobody's in custody yet," Hawes said, "so let's cut the legal jazz, okay? Tell us where you were, Donatello."

"Right here," Donatello said. "From ten o'clock till now."

"I suppose somebody saw you here during that time."

"A *hundred* people saw me."

A crowd of angry black men and women were standing outside the shattered window of the storefront church. Two fire engines and an ambulance were parked at the curb. Kling pulled in behind the second engine, some ten feet away from the hydrant. It was almost 2:30 A.M. on a bitterly cold October night, but the crowd looked and sounded like a mob at an afternoon streetcorner rally in the middle of August. Restless, noisy, abrasive, anticipative, they ignored the penetrating cold and concentrated instead on the burning issue of the hour—the fact that a person or persons unknown had thrown a bomb through the plate-glass window of the church.

The beat patrolman, a newly appointed cop who felt vaguely uneasy in this neighborhood even during his daytime shift, greeted Kling effusively, his pale white face bracketed by earmuffs, his gloved hands clinging desperately to his nightstick. The crowd parted to let King through. It did not help that he was the youngest man on the squad, with the callow look of a country bumpkin on his unlined face; it did not help that he was blonde and hatless; it did not help that he walked into the church with the confident youthful stride of a champion come to set things right. The crowd knew he was fuzz, and they knew he was Whitey, and they knew, too, that if this bombing had taken place on Hall Avenue crosstown and downtown, the police commissioner himself would have arrived behind a herald of official trumpets.

This, however, was Culver Avenue, where a boiling mixture of Puerto Ricans and Blacks shared a disintegrating ghetto, and so the car that pulled to the curb was not marked with the commissioner's distinctive blue-and-gold seal, but was instead a green Chevy convertible that belonged to Kling himself; and the man who stepped out of it looked young and inexperienced and inept despite the confident stride he affected as he walked into the church, his shield pinned to his overcoat.

The bomb had caused little fire damage, and the firemen already had the flames under control, their hoses snaking through and around the overturned folding chairs scattered around the small room. Ambulance attendants picked their way over the hoses and around the debris, carrying out the injured—the dead could wait.

"Have you called the bomb squad?" Kling asked the patrolman.

"No," the patrolman answered, shaken by the sudden possibility that he had been derelict in his duty.

"Why don't you do that now?" Kling suggested.

"Yes, sir," the patrolman answered, and rushed out. The ambulance attendants went by with a moaning woman on a stretcher. She was still wearing her eyeglasses, but one lens had been shattered and blood was running in a steady rivulet down the side of her nose. The place stank of gunpowder and smoke and charred wood. The most serious damage had been done at the rear of the small store, farthest away from the entrance door. Whoever had thrown the bomb must have possessed a good pitching arm to have hurled it so accurately through the window and across the fifteen feet to the makeshift altar.

The minister lay across his own altar, dead. Two women who had been sitting on folding chairs closest to the altar lay on the floor, tangled in death, their clothes still smoldering. The sounds of the injured filled the room, and then were suffocated by the overriding siren-shriek of the second ambulance arriving. Kling went outside to the crowd.

"Anybody here witness this?" he asked.

A young man, black, wearing a beard and a natural hair style, turned away from a group of other youths and walked directly to Kling.

"Is the minister dead?" he asked.

"Yes, he is," Kling answered.

"Who else?"

"Two women."

"Who?"

"I don't know yet. We'll identify them as soon as the men are through in there." Kling turned again to the crowd. "Did anybody see what happened?" he asked.

"I saw it," the young man said.

"What's your name, son?"

"Andrew Jordan."

Kling took out his pad. "All right, let's have it."

"What good's this going to do?" Jordan asked. "Writing all this stuff in your book?"

"You said you saw what—"

"I saw it, all right. I was walking by, heading for the pool room up the street, and the ladies were inside singing, and this car pulled up and a guy got out, threw the bomb, and ran back to the car."

"What kind of a car was it?"

"A red Volkswagen."

"What year?"

"Who can tell with those VWs?"

"How many people in it?"

"Two. The driver and the guy who threw the bomb."

"Notice the license-plate number?"

"No. They drove off too fast."

"Can you describe the man who threw the bomb?"

"Yeah. He was white."

"What else?" Kling asked.

"That's all," Jordan replied. "He was white."

There were perhaps three dozen estates in all of Smoke Rise, a hundred or so people living in luxurious near-seclusion on acres of valuable land through which ran four winding, interconnected, private roadways. Meyer Meyer drove between the wide stone pillars marking Smoke Rise's western access road, entering a city within a city, bounded on the north by the River Harb, shielded from the River Highway by stands of poplars and evergreens on the south—exclusive Smoke Rise, known familiarly and derisively to the rest of the city's inhabitants as "The Club."

MacArthur Lane was at the end of the road that curved past the Hamilton Bridge. Number 374 was a huge graystone house with a slate roof and scores of gables and chimneys jostling the sky, perched high in gloomy shadow above the Harb. As he stepped from the car, Meyer could hear the sounds of river traffic, the hooting of tugs, the blowing of whistles, the eruption of a squawk box on a destroyer midstream. He looked out over the water. Reflected lights glistened in shimmering liquid beauty—the hanging globes on the bridge's suspension cables, the dazzling reds and greens of signal lights on the opposite shore, single illuminated window slashes in apartment buildings throwing their mirror images onto the black surface of the river, the blinking wing lights of an airplane overhead moving in watery reflection like a submarine. The air was cold, and a fine piercing drizzle had begun several minutes ago.

Meyer shuddered, pulled the collar of his coat higher on his neck, and walked toward the old gray house, his shoes crunching on the driveway gravel, the sound echoing away into the high surrounding bushes.

The stones of the old house oozed wetness. Thick vines covered the walls, climbing to the gabled, turreted roof. He found a doorbell set over a brass escutcheon in the thick oak doorjamb, and pressed it. Chimes sounded somewhere deep inside the house. He waited.

The door opened suddenly.

The man looking out at him was perhaps seventy years old, with piercing blue eyes; he was bald except for white thatches of hair that sprang wildly from behind each ear. He wore a red smoking jacket and black trousers, a black ascot around his neck, and red velvet slippers.

"What do you want?" he asked immediately.

"I'm Detective Meyer of the Eighty-seventh—"

"Who sent for you?"

"A woman named Adele Gorman came to the—"

"My daughter's a fool," the man said. "We don't need the police here." And he slammed the door in Meyer's face.

The detective stood on the doorstep feeling somewhat like a horse's neck. A tugboat hooted on the river. A light snapped on upstairs, casting an amber rectangle into the dark driveway. He looked at the luminous dial of his watch. It was 2:35 A.M. The drizzle was cold and penetrating. He took out his handkerchief, blew his nose, and wondered what he should do next. He did not like ghosts, and he did not like lunatics, and he did not like nasty old men who did not comb their hair and who slammed doors in a person's face. He was about to head back for his car when the door opened again.

"Detective Meyer?" Adele Gorman said. "Do come in."

"Thank you," he said, and stepped into the entrance foyer.

"You're right on time."

"Well, a little early actually," Meyer said. He still felt foolish. What the hell was he doing in Smoke Rise investigating ghosts in the middle of the night?

"This way," Adele said, and he followed her through a somberly paneled foyer into a vast dimly lighted living room. Heavy oak beams ran overhead, velvet draperies hung at the window, the room was cluttered with ponderous old furniture. He could believe there were ghosts in this house, he could believe it.

A young man wearing dark glasses rose like a specter from the sofa near the fireplace. His face, illuminated by the single standing floor lamp, looked wan and drawn. Wearing a black cardigan sweater over a white shirt and dark slacks, he approached Meyer unsmilingly with his hand extended—but he did not accept Meyer's hand when it was offered in return.

Meyer suddenly realized that the man was blind.

"I'm Ralph Gorman," he said, his hand still extended. "Adele's husband."

"How do you do, Mr. Gorman," Meyer said, and took his hand. The palm was moist and cold.

"It was good of you to come," Gorman said. "These apparitions have been driving us crazy."

"What time is it?" Adele asked suddenly, and looked at her watch. "We've got five minutes," she said. There was a tremor in her voice. She looked suddenly very frightened.

"Won't your father be here?" Meyer asked.

"No, he's gone up to bed," Adele said. "I'm afraid he's bored with the whole affair, and terribly angry that we notified you."

Meyer made no comment. Had he known that Willem Van Houten, former surrogate's court judge, had not wanted the police to be notified, Meyer would not have been here either. He debated leaving now, but Adele Gorman had begun to talk again.

". . . is in her early thirties, I would guess. The other ghost, the male, is about your age—forty or forty-five, something like that."

"I'm thirty-seven," Meyer said.

"Oh."

"The bald head fools a lot of people."

"Yes."

"I was bald at a very early age."

"Anyway," Adele said, "their names are Elisabeth and Johann, and they've probably been—"

"Oh, they have names, do they?"

"Yes. They're ancestors, you know. My father is Dutch, and there actually were an Elisabeth and Johann Van Houten in the family centuries ago, when Smoke Rise was still a Dutch settlement."

"They're Dutch. Um-huh, I see," Meyer said.

"Yes. They always appear wearing Dutch costumes. And they also speak Dutch."

"Have you heard them, Mr. Gorman?"

"Yes," Gorman said. "I'm blind, you know—" he added, and hesitated, as though expecting some comment from Meyer. When none came, he said, "But I have heard them."

"Do you speak Dutch?"

"No. My father-in-law speaks it fluently, though, and he identified the language for us, and told us what they were saying."

"What *did* they say?"

"Well, for one thing, they said they were going to steal Adele's jewelry, and they did just that."

"Your *wife's* jewelry? But I thought—"

"It was willed to her by her mother. My father-in-law keeps it in his safe."

"Kept, you mean."

"No, keeps. There are several pieces in addition to the ones that were stolen. Two rings and also a necklace."

"And the value?"

"Altogether? I would say about forty thousand dollars."

"Your ghosts have expensive taste."

The floor lamp in the room suddenly began to flicker. Meyer glanced at it and felt the hackles rising at the back of his neck.

"The lights are going out, Ralph," Adele whispered.

"Is it two forty-five?"

"Yes."

"They're here," Gorman whispered. "The ghosts are here."

Mercy Howell's roommate had been asleep for nearly four hours when they knocked on her door. But she was a wily young lady, hip to the ways of the big city, and very much awake as she conducted her own little investigation without so much as opening the door a crack. First she asked them to spell their names slowly. Then she asked them their shield numbers. Then she asked them to hold their shields and I.D. cards close to the door's peephole, where she could see them. Still unconvinced, she said through the locked door, "You just wait there a minute."

They waited for closer to five minutes before they heard her approaching the door again. The heavy steel bar of a Fox lock was lowered noisily to the floor, a safety chain rattled on its track, the tumblers of one lock clicked open, and then another, and finally the girl opened the door.

"Come in," she said. "I'm sorry I kept you waiting. I called the station house and they said you were okay."

"You're a very careful girl," Hawes said.

"At this hour of the morning? Are you kidding?" she said.

She was perhaps twenty-five, with her red hair up in curlers, her face cold-creamed clean of makeup. She was wearing a pink quilted robe over flannel pajamas, and although she was probably a very pretty girl at 9:00 A.M., she now looked about as attractive as a Buffalo nickel.

"What's your name, Miss?" Carella asked.

"Lois Kaplan. What's this all about? Has there been another burglary in the building?"

"No, Miss Kaplan. We want to ask you some questions about Mercy Howell. Did she live here with you?"

"Yes," Lois said, and suddenly looked at them shrewdly. "What do you mean *did*? She still *does.*"

They were standing in the small foyer of the apartment, and the foyer went so still that all the night sounds of the building were clearly audible all at once, as though they had not been there before but had only been summoned up now to fill the void of silence. A toilet flushed somewhere, a hot-water pipe rattled, a baby whimpered, a dog barked, someone dropped a shoe. In the foyer, now filled with noise, they stared at each other wordlessly, and finally Carella drew a deep breath and said, "Your roommate is dead. She was stabbed tonight as she was leaving the theater."

"No," Lois said, simply and flatly. "No, she isn't."

"Miss Kaplan—"

"I don't give a damn what you say, Mercy isn't dead."

"Miss Kaplan, she's dead."

"Oh, God," Lois said, and burst into tears.

The two men stood by feeling stupid and big and awkward and helpless. Lois Kaplan covered her face with her hands and sobbed into them, her shoulders heaving, saying over and over again, "I'm sorry, oh, God, please, I'm sorry, please, oh poor Mercy, oh my God," while the detectives tried not to watch.

At last the crying stopped and she looked up at them with eyes that had been knifed, and said softly, "Come in. Please," and led them into the living room. She kept staring at the floor as she talked. It was as if she could not look them in the face, not these men who had brought her the dreadful news.

"Do you know who did it?" she asked.

"No. Not yet."

"We wouldn't have wakened you in the middle of the night if—"

"That's all right."

"But very often, if we get moving on a case fast enough, before the trail gets cold—"

"Yes, I understand."

"We can often—"

"Yes, before the trail gets cold," Lois said.

"Yes."

The apartment went silent again.

"Would you know if Miss Howell had any enemies?" Carella asked.

"She was the sweetest girl in the world," Lois said.

"Did she argue with anyone recently? Were there any—"

"No."

"—any threatening telephone calls or letters?"

Lois Kaplan looked up at them. "Yes," she said. "A letter."

"A *threatening* letter?"

"We couldn't tell. It frightened Mercy, though. That's why she bought the gun."

"What kind of gun?"

"I don't know. A small one."

"Would it have been a .25 caliber Browning?"

"I don't know guns."

"Was this letter mailed to her, or delivered personally?"

"It was mailed to her. At the theater."

"When?"

"A week ago."

"Did she report it to the police?"

"No."

"Why not?"

"Haven't you seen *Rattlesnake?*" Lois said.

"What do you mean?" Carella asked.

"*Rattlesnake*. The musical. The show Mercy was in."

"No, I haven't."

"But you've heard of it."

"No."

"Where do you live, for God's sake? On the moon?"

"I'm sorry, I just haven't—"

"Forgive me," Lois said immediately. "I'm not usually—I'm trying very hard to—I'm sorry. Forgive me."

"That's all right," Carella said.

"Anyway, it's a big hit now but—well, there was trouble in the beginning, you see. Are you *sure* you don't know about this? It was in all the newspapers."

"I guess I missed it," Carella said. "What was the trouble about?"

"Don't *you* know about this either?" she asked Hawes.

"No, I'm sorry."

"About Mercy's dance?"

"No."

"Well, in one scene Mercy danced the title song without any clothes on. Because the idea was to express—the hell with what the idea was. The point is that the dance wasn't at all obscene, it wasn't even sexy! But the police *missed* the point and closed the show down two days after it opened. The producers had to go to court for a writ or something to get the show opened again."

"Yes, I remember it now," Carella said.

"What I'm trying to say is that nobody involved with *Rattlesnake* would report *anything* to the police. Not even a threatening letter."

"If she bought a pistol," Hawes said, "she would have *had* to go to the police. For a permit."

"She didn't have a permit."

"Then how'd she get the pistol? You can't buy a handgun without first—"

"A friend of hers sold it to her."

"What's the friend's name?"

"Harry Donatello."

"An importer," Carella said.

"Of souvenir ashtrays," Hawes said.

"I don't know what he does for a living," Lois said, "but he got the gun for her."

"When was this?"

"A few days after she received the letter."

"What did the letter say?" Carella asked.

"I'll get it for you," Lois said, and went into the bedroom. They heard a dresser drawer opening, the rustle of clothes, what might have been a tin candy box being opened. Lois came back into the room. "Here it is," she said.

There didn't seem much point in trying to preserve latent prints on a letter that had already been handled by Mercy Howell, Lois Kaplan, and the Lord knew how many others. But nonetheless Carella accepted the letter on a handkerchief spread over the palm of his hand, and then looked at the face of the envelope. "She should have brought this to us. It's written on hotel stationery, we've got an address without lifting a finger."

The letter had indeed been written on stationery from The Addison Hotel, one of the city's lesser-known fleabags, some two blocks north of the Eleventh Street Theater, where Mercy Howell had worked. There was a single sheet of paper in the envelope. Carella unfolded it. Lettered on the paper in pencil were the words:

Put on Your Close, Miss! The Avenging Angel

***

The lamp went out, the room was black.

At first there was no sound but the sharp intake of Adele

Gorman's breath. And then, indistinctly, as faintly as though carried on a swirling mist that blew in wetly from some desolated shore, there came the sound of garbled voices, and the room grew suddenly cold. The voices were those of a crowd in endless debate, rising and falling in cacaphonous cadence, a mixture of tongues that rattled and rasped. There was the sound, too, of a rising wind, as though a door to some forbidden landscape had been sharply and suddenly blown open to reveal a host of corpses incessantly pacing, involved in formless dialogue.

The voices rose in volume now, carried on that same chill penetrating wind, louder, closer, until they seemed to overwhelm the room, clamoring to be released from whatever unearthly vault contained them. And then, as if two of those disembodied voices had succeeded in breaking away from the mass of unseen dead, bringing with them a rush of bone-chilling air from some world unknown, there came a whisper at first, the whisper of a man's voice, saying the single word "Ralph!"—sharp-edged and with a distinctive foreign inflection.

"Ralph!"—and then a woman's voice joining it saying, "Adele!"—pronounced strangely and in the same cutting whisper.

"Adele!"—and then "Ralph!" again, the voices overlapping, unmistakably foreign, urgent, rising in volume until the whispers commingled to become an agonizing groan—and then the names were lost in the shrilling echo of the wind.

Meyer's eyes played tricks in the darkness. Apparitions that surely were not there seemed to float on the crescendo of sound that saturated the room. Barely perceived pieces of furniture assumed amorphous shapes as the male voice snarled and the female voice moaned above it.

And then the babel of other voices intruded again, as though calling these two back to whatever grim mossy crypt they had momentarily escaped. The sound of the wind became more fierce, and the voices receded, and echoed, and were gone.

The lamp sputtered back into dim illumination. The room seemed perceptibly warmer, but Meyer was covered with a cold clammy sweat.

"Now do you believe?" Adele Gorman asked.

Detective Bob O'Brien was coming out of the men's room down

the hall when he saw the woman sitting on the bench just outside the squadroom. He almost went back into the toilet, but he was an instant too late; she had seen him, so there was no escape.

"Hello, Mr. O'Brien," she said and performed an awkward little half-rising motion, as though uncertain whether she should stand to greet him or accept the deference due a lady. The clock on the squadroom wall read 3:02 A.M. but the lady was dressed as though for a brisk afternoon's hike in the park—brown slacks, low-heeled walking shoes, beige car coat, a scarf around her head. She was perhaps fifty-five, with a face that once must have been pretty, save for the overlong nose. Green-eyed, with prominent cheek-bones and a generous mouth, she executed her abortive rise, then fell into step beside O'Brien as he walked into the squadroom.

"Little late in the night to be out, isn't it, Mrs. Blair?" O'Brien asked. He was not an insensitive cop, but his manner now was brusque and dismissive. Faced with Mrs. Blair for perhaps the seventeenth time in a month, he tried not to empathize with her loss because, truthfully, he was unable to assist her, and his inability to do so was frustrating.

"Have you seen her?" Mrs. Blair asked.

"No," O'Brien said. "I'm sorry, Mrs. Blair, but I haven't."

"I have a new picture—perhaps that will help."

"Yes, perhaps it will," he said.

The telephone was ringing. He lifted the receiver and said, "Eighty-seventh, O'Brien here."

"Bob, this's Bert Kling over on Culver—the church bombing."

"Yeah, Bert."

"Seems I remember seeing a red Volkswagen on that hot-car bulletin we got yesterday. You want to dig it out and let me know where it was snatched?"

"Yeah, just a second," O'Brien said, and began scanning the sheet on his desk.

"Here's the new picture," Mrs. Blair said. "I know you're very good with runaways, Mr. O'Brien—the kids all like you and give you information. If you see Penelope, all I want you to do is tell her I love her and am sorry for the misunderstanding."

"Yeah, I will," O'Brien said. Into the phone he said, "I've got two red VWs, Bert, a sixty-four and a sixty-six. You want both?"

"Shoot," Kling said.

"The sixty-four was stolen from a guy named Art Hauser. It was parked outside eight-six-one West Meridian."

"And the sixty-six?"

"Owner is a woman named Alice Cleary. Car was stolen from a parking lot on Fourteenth."

"North or South?"

"South. Three-o-three South."

"Right. Thanks, Bob," Kling said, and hung up.

"And ask her to come home to me," Mrs. Blair said.

"Yes, I will," O'Brien said. "If I see her, I certainly will."

"That's a nice picture of Penny, don't you think?" Mrs. Blair asked. "It was taken last Easter. It's the most recent picture I have. I thought it would be helpful to you."

O'Brien looked at the girl in the picture, and then looked up into Mrs. Blair's green eyes, misted now with tears, and suddenly wanted to reach across the desk and pat her hand reassuringly, the one thing he could not do with any honesty. Because whereas it was true that he was the squad's runaway expert, with perhaps fifty snapshots of teenagers crammed into his bulging notebook, and whereas his record of finds was more impressive than any other cop's in the city, uniformed or plainclothes, there wasn't a damn thing he could do for the mother of Penelope Blair, who had run away from home last June.

"You understand—" he started to say.

"Let's not go into that again, Mr. O'Brien," she said, and rose.

"Mrs. Blair—"

"I don't want to hear it," Mrs. Blair said, walking quickly out of the squadroom. "Tell her to come home. Tell her I love her," she said, and was gone down the iron-runged steps.

O'Brien sighed and stuffed the new picture of Penelope into his notebook. What Mrs. Blair did not choose to hear again was the fact that her runaway daughter Penny was twenty-four years old, and there was not a single agency on God's green earth, police or otherwise, that could force her to go home again if she did not choose to.

Fats Donner was a stool pigeon with a penchant for Turkish baths. A mountainous white Buddha of a man, he could usually be found at one of the city's steam emporiums at any given hour of the day, draped in a towel and reveling in the heat that saturated his flabby body. Bert Kling found him in an all-night place called Steam-Fit.

Kling sent the masseur into the steam room to tell Donner he was there, and Donner sent word out that he would be through in five minutes, unless Kling wished to join him. Kling did not wish to join him. He waited in the locker room, and in seven minutes' time, Donner came out, draped in his customary towel, a ludicrous sight at any time, but particularly at 3:30 A.M.

"Hey!" Donner said. "How you doing?"

"Fine," Kling said. "How about yourself?"

"Comme-ci, comme-ca," Donner said and made a seesawing motion with one fleshy hand.

"I'm looking for some stolen heaps," Kling said, getting directly to the point.

"What kind?" Donner said.

"Volkswagens. A sixty-four and a sixty-six."

"What color?"

"Red."

"Both of them?"

"Yes."

"Where were they heisted?"

"One from in front of eight-six-one West Meridian. The other from a parking lot on South Fourteenth."

"When was this?"

"Both last week sometime. I don't have the exact dates."

"What do you want to know?"

"Who stole them."

"You think it's the same guy on both?"

"I don't know."

"What's so important about these heaps?"

"One of them may have been used in a bombing tonight."

"You mean the church over on Culver?"

"That's right."

"Count me out," Donner said.

"What do you mean?"

"There's a lot of guys in this town who're in *sympathy* with what happened over there tonight. I don't want to get involved."

"Who's going to know whether you're involved or not?" Kling asked.

"The same way *you* get information, they get information."

"I need your help, Donner."

"Yeah, well, I'm sorry on this one," Donner said, and shook his head.

"In that case I'd better hurry downtown to High Street."

"Why? You got another source down there?"

"No, that's where the D.A.'s office is."

Both men stared at each other—Donner in a white towel draped around his belly, sweat still pouring from his face and his chest even though he was no longer in the steam room, and Kling looking like a slightly tired advertising executive rather than a cop threatening a man with revelation of past deeds not entirely legal. They stared at each other with total understanding, caught in the curious symbiosis of law breaker and law enforcer, an empathy created by neither man, but essential to the existence of both. It was Donner who broke the silence.

"I don't like being coerced," he said.

"I don't like being refused," Kling answered.

"When do you need this?"

"I want to get going on it before morning."

"You expect miracles, don't you?"

"Doesn't everybody?"

"Miracles cost."

"How much?"

"Twenty-five if I turn up one heap, fifty if I turn up both."

"Turn them up first. We'll talk later."

"And if somebody breaks my head later?"

"You should have thought of that before you entered the profession," Kling said. "Come on, Donner, cut it out. This is a routine bombing by a couple of punks. You've got nothing to be afraid of."

"No?" Donner asked. And then, in a very professional voice, he uttered perhaps the biggest understatement of the decade. "Racial tensions are running high in this city right now."

"Have you got my number at the squadroom?"

"Yeah, I've got it," Donner said glumly.

"I'm going back there now. Let me hear from you soon."

"You mind if I get dressed first?" Donner asked.

The night clerk at The Addison Hotel was alone in the lobby when Carella and Hawes walked in. Immersed in an open book on the desk in front of him, he did not look up as they approached. The lobby was furnished in faded Victorian: a threadbare Oriental rug, heavy curlicued mahogany tables, ponderous stuffed chairs with sagging bottoms and soiled antimacassars, two spittoons resting alongside each of two mahogany paneled supporting columns. A genuine Tiffany lampshade hung over the registration desk, one leaded glass panel gone, another badly cracked. In the old days The Addison had been a luxury hotel. It now wore its past splendor with all the style of a dance-hall girl in a moth-eaten mink she'd picked up in a thrift shop.

The clerk, in contrast to his antique surroundings, was a young man in his mid-twenties, wearing a neatly pressed brown tweed suit, a tan shirt, a gold and brown rep tie, and eyeglasses with tortoise-shell rims. He glanced up at the detectives belatedly, squinting after the intense concentration of peering at print, and then he got to his feet.

"Yes, gentlemen," he said. "May I help you?"

"Police officers," Carella said. He took his wallet from his pocket, and opened it to where his detective's shield was pinned to a leather flap.

"Yes, sir."

"I'm Detective Carella, this is my partner, Detective Hawes."

"How do you do? I'm the night clerk—my name is Ronald Sanford."

"We're looking for someone who may have been registered here two weeks ago," Hawes said.

"Well, if he was registered here two weeks ago," Sanford said, "chances are he's still registered. Most of our guests are residents."

"Do you keep stationery in the lobby here?" Carella asked.

"Sir?"

"Stationery. Is there any place here in the lobby where someone could walk in off the street and pick up a piece of stationery?"

"No, sir. There's a writing desk there in the corner, near the staircase, but we don't stock it with stationery, no, sir."

"Is there stationery in the rooms?"

"Yes, sir."

"How about here at the desk?"

"Yes, of course, sir."

"Is there someone at this desk twenty-four hours a day?"

"Twenty-four hours a day, yes, sir. We have three shifts. Eight to four in the afternoon. Four to midnight. And midnight to eight A.M."

"You came on at midnight, did you?"

"Yes, sir."

"Any guests come in after you started your shift?"

"A few, yes, sir."

"Notice anybody with blood on his clothes?"

"Blood? Oh, no, sir."

"Would you have noticed?"

"What do you mean?"

"Are you pretty aware of what's going on around here?"

"I try to be, sir. At least, for most of the night. I catch a little nap when I'm not studying, but usually—"

"What do you study?"

"Accounting."

"Where?"

"At Ramsey U."

"Mind if we take a look at your register?"

"Not at all, sir."

He walked to the mail rack and took the hotel register from the counter there. Returning to the desk he opened it and said, "All of our present guests are residents, with the exception of Mr. Lambert in two hundred and four, and Mrs. Grant in seven hundred and one."

"When did they check in?"

"Mr. Lambert checked in—last night, I think it was. And Mrs. Grant has been here four days. She's leaving on Tuesday."

"Are these the actual signatures of your guests?"

"Yes, sir. All guests are asked to sign the register, as required by state law."

"Have you got that note, Cotton?" Carella asked, and then turned again to Sanford. "Would you mind if we took this over to the couch there?"

"Well, we're not supposed—"

"We can give you a receipt for it, if you like."

"No, I guess it'll be all right."

They carried the register to a couch upholstered in faded red velvet. With the book supported on Carella's lap they unfolded the note that Mercy Howell had received, and began to compare the signatures of the guests with the only part of the note that was not written in block letters—the words, *The Avenging Angel*.

There were fifty-two guests in the hotel. Carella and Hawes went through the register once, and then started through it again.

"Hey," Hawes said suddenly.

"What?"

"Look at this one."

He took the note and placed it on the page so that it was directly above one of the signatures:

Put on Your Close, Miss!
The Avenging Angel
Timothy Allen Ames

"What do you think?" he asked.

"Different handwriting," Carella said.

"Same initials," Hawes said.

Detective Meyer Meyer was still shaken. He did not like ghosts. He did not like this house. He wanted to go home to his wife Sarah. He wanted her to stroke his hand and tell him that such things did not exist. How could he believe in poltergeists, shades, Dutch spirits? Ridiculous!

But he had heard them, and he had felt their chilling presence, and had almost thought he'd seen them, if only for an instant. He turned with fresh shock now toward the hall staircase and the sound of descending footsteps. Eyes wide, he waited for whatever new manifestation might present itself. He was tempted to draw his revolver, but he was afraid such an act would appear foolish to the Gormans. He had come here a skeptic, and he was now at least *willing* to believe, and he waited in dread for whatever was coming down those steps with such ponderous footfalls—some ghoul trailing winding sheets and rattling chains? Some specter with a bleached skull for a head and long bony fingers?

Willem Van Houten, wearing his red velvet slippers and his red smoking jacket, his hair still jutting wildly from behind each ear, his blue eyes fierce, came into the living room and walked directly to where his daughter and son-in-law were sitting.

"Well?" he asked. "Did they come again?"

"Yes, Daddy," Adele said.

"What did they want this time?"

"I don't know. They spoke Dutch again."

Van Houten turned to Meyer. "Did *you* see them?" he asked.

"No, sir, I did not," Meyer said.

"But they were *here*," Gorman protested, and turned his blank face to his wife. "I heard them."

"Yes, darling," Adele assured him. "We *all* heard them. But it was like that other time, don't you remember? When we could hear them even though they couldn't quite break through."

"Yes, that's right," Gorman said, and nodded. "This happened once before, Detective Meyer." He was facing Meyer now, his head tilted quizzically, the sightless eyes covered with their black glasses. When he spoke his voice was like that of a child seeking reassurance. "But you *did* hear them, didn't you, Detective Meyer?"

"Yes," Meyer said. "I heard them, Mr. Gorman."

"And the wind?"

"Yes, the wind, too."

"And felt them. It—it gets so cold when they appear. You did feel their presence, didn't you?"

"I felt something," Meyer said.

Van Houten suddenly asked, "Are you satisfied?"

"About what?" Meyer said.

"That there are ghosts in this house? What's why you're here, isn't it? To ascertain—"

"He's here because I asked Adele to notify the police," Gorman said.

"Why did you do that?"

"Because of the stolen jewelry," Gorman said. "And because—" He paused. "Because I've lost my sight, yes, but I wanted to—to make sure I wasn't losing my mind as well."

"You're perfectly sane, Ralph," Van Houten said.

"About the jewelry—" Meyer said.

"They took it," Van Houten said.

"Who?"

"Johann and Elisabeth. Our friendly neighborhood ghosts."

"That's impossible, Mr. Van Houten."

"Why is it impossible?"

"Because ghosts—" Meyer started, and hesitated.

"Yes?"

"Ghosts—well, ghosts don't go around stealing jewelry. I mean, what use would they have for it?" he said lamely, and looked at the Gormans for corroboration. Neither of the Gormans seemed to be in a substantiating mood. They sat on the sofa near the fireplace, both looking glum.

"They want us out of this house," Van Houten said. "It's as simple as that."

"How do you know?"

"Because they said so."

"When?"

"Before they stole the necklace and the earrings."

"They told this to you?"

"To me and to my children. All three of us were here."

"But I understand the ghosts speak only Dutch."

"Yes, I translated for Ralph and Adele."

"And then what happened?"

"What do you mean?"

"When did you discover the jewelry was missing?"

"The instant they were gone."

"You mean you went to the safe?"

"Yes, and opened it, and the jewelry was gone."

"We had put it in the safe not ten minutes before that," Adele said. "We'd been to a party, Ralph and I, and we got home very late, and Daddy was still awake, reading, sitting in that chair you're in this very minute. I asked him to open the safe, and he did, and he put the jewelry in and closed the safe and . . . and then *they* came and . . . and made their threats."

"What time was this?"

"The usual time. The time they always come. Two forty-five in the morning."

"And you say the jewelry was put into the safe at what time?"

"About two thirty," Gorman said.

"And when was the safe opened again?"

"Immediately after they left. They only stay a few moments. This time they told my father-in-law they were taking the necklace and the earrings with them. He rushed to the safe as soon as the lights came on again—"

"Do the lights always go off?"

"Always," Adele said. "It's always the same. The lights go off, and the room gets very cold, and we hear these strange voices arguing." She paused. "And then Johann and Elisabeth come."

"Except that this time they didn't come," Meyer said.

"And one other time," Adele said quickly.

"They want us out of this house," Van Houten said, "that's all there is to it. Maybe we ought to leave. Before they take *everything* from us."

"Everything? What do you mean?"

"The rest of my daughter's jewelry. And some stock certificates. Everything that's in the safe."

"Where *is* the safe?" Meyer asked.

"Here. Behind this painting." Van Houten walked to the wall opposite the fireplace. An oil painting of a pastoral landscape hung there in an ornate gilt frame. The frame was hinged to the wall. Van Houten swung the painting out as though opening a door, and revealed the small, round, black safe behind it. "Here."

"How many people know the combination?" Meyer asked.

"Just me," Van Houten said.

"Do you keep the number written down anywhere?"

"Yes."

"Where?"

"Hidden."

"Where?"

"I hardly think that's any of your business, Detective Meyer."

"I'm only trying to find out whether some other person could have got hold of the combination somehow."

"Yes, I suppose that's possible," Van Houten said. "But highly unlikely."

"Well," Meyer said, and shrugged. "I don't really know what to say. I'd like to measure the room, if you don't mind, get the dimensions, placement of doors and windows, things like that. For my report." He shrugged again.

"It's rather late, isn't it?" Van Houten said.

"Well, I *got* here rather late," Meyer said, and smiled.

"Come, Daddy, I'll make us all some tea in the kitchen," Adele said. "Will you be long, Detective Meyer?"

"It may take a while."

"Shall I bring you some tea?"

"Thank you, that would be nice."

She rose from the couch and then guided her husband's hand to her arm. Walking slowly beside him, she led him past her father and out of the room. Van Houten looked at Meyer once again, nodded briefly, and followed them out. Meyer closed the door behind them and immediately walked to the standing floor lamp.

The woman was sixty years old, and she looked like anybody's grandmother, except that she had just murdered her husband and three children. They had explained her rights to her, and she had told them she had nothing to hide and would answer any questions they asked her. She sat in a straight-backed squadroom chair, wearing a black cloth coat over blood-stained nightgown and robe, her handcuffed hands in her lap, her hands unmoving on her black leather pocketbook.

O'Brien and Kling looked at the police stenographer, who glanced up at the wall clock, noted the time of the interrogation's start as 3:55 A.M., and then signaled that he was ready whenever they were.

"What is your name?" O'Brien asked.

"Isabel Martin."

"How old are you, Mrs. Martin?"

"Sixty."

"Where do you live?"

"On Ainsley Avenue."

"Where on Ainsley?"

"Six hundred fifty-seven Ainsley."

"With whom do you live there?"

"With my husband Roger, and my son Peter, and my daughters Anne and Abigail."

"Would you like to tell us what happened tonight, Mrs. Martin?" Kling asked.

"I killed them all," she said. She had white hair, a fine aquiline nose, brown eyes behind rimless spectacles. She stared straight ahead of her as she spoke, looking neither to her right nor to her left, seemingly alone with the memory of what she had done not a half hour before.

"Can you give us some of the details, Mrs. Martin?"

"I killed *him* first."

"Who do you mean, Mrs. Martin?"

"My husband."

"When was this?"

"When he came home."

"What time was that, do you remember?"

"A little while ago."

"It's almost four o'clock now," Kling said. "Would you say this was at, what, three thirty or thereabouts?"

"I didn't look at the clock," she said. "I heard his key in the door, and I went in the kitchen, and there he was."

"Yes?"

"There's a meat cleaver I keep on the sink. I hit him with it."

"Why did you do that, Mrs. Martin?"

"Because I wanted to."

"Were you arguing with him, is that it?"

"No. I just went over to the sink and picked up the cleaver, and then I hit him with it."

"Where did you hit him, Mrs. Martin?"

"On his head and on his neck and I think on his shoulder."

"You hit him three times with the cleaver?"

"I hit him a lot of times. I don't know how many."

"Were you aware that you were hitting him?"

"Yes, I was aware."

"You knew you were striking him with a cleaver."

"Yes, I knew."

"Did you intend to kill him with the cleaver?"

"I intended to kill him with the cleaver."

"And afterwards, did you know you had killed him?"

"I knew he was dead, yes."

"What did you do then?"

"My oldest child came into the kitchen. Peter. My son. He yelled at me, he wanted to know what I'd done, he kept yelling at me and yelling at me. I hit him, too—to get him to shut up. I hit him only once, across the throat."

"Did you know what you were doing at the time?"

"I knew what I was doing. He was *another* one, that Peter."

"What happened next, Mrs. Martin?"

"I went in the back bedroom where the two girls sleep, and I hit Annie with the cleaver first, and then I hit Abigail."

"Where did you hit them, Mrs. Martin?"

"On the face. Their faces."

"How many times?"

"I think I hit Annie twice, and Abigail only once."

"Why did you do that, Mrs. Martin?"

"Who would take care of them after I was gone?" Mrs. Martin asked of no one.

There was a long pause, then Kling asked, "Is there anything else you want to tell us?"

"There's nothing more to tell. I done the right thing."

The detectives walked away from the desk. They were both pale. "Man," O'Brien whispered.

"Yeah," Kling said. "We'd better call the night D.A. right away, get him to take a full confession from her."

"Killed four of them without batting an eyelash," O'Brien said, and shook his head, and went back to where the stenographer was typing up Mrs. Martin's statement.

The telephone was ringing. Kling walked to the nearest desk and lifted the receiver. "Eighty-seventh, Detective Kling," he said.

"This is Donner."

"Yeah, Fats."

"I think I got a lead on one of those heaps."

"Shoot."

"This would be the one heisted on Fourteenth Street. According to the dope I've got it happened yesterday morning. Does that check out?"

"I'll have to look at the bulletin again. Go ahead, Fats."

"It's already been ditched," Donner said. "If you're looking for it try outside the electric company on the River Road."

"Thanks, I'll make a note of that. Who stole it, Fats?"

"This is strictly *entre nous,*" Donner said. "I don't want *no* tie-in with it *never.* The guy who done it is a mean little guy—rip out his mother's heart for a dime. He hates blacks, killed one in a street rumble a few years ago, and managed to beat the rap. I think maybe some officer was on the take, huh, Kling?"

"You can't square homicide in this city, and you know it, Fats."

"Yeah? I'm surprised. You can square damn near anything else for a couple of bills."

"What's his name?"

"Danny Ryder. Three-five-four-one Grover Avenue. You won't find him there now, though."

"Where *will* I find him now?"

"Ten minutes ago he was in an all-night bar on Mason, place called Felicia's. You going in after him?"

"I am."

"Take your gun," Donner said.

There were seven people in Felicia's when Kling got there at 4:45. He cased the bar through the plate-glass window fronting the place, unbuttoned the third button of his overcoat, reached in to clutch the butt of his revolver, worked it out of the holster once and then back again, and went in through the front door.

There was the immediate smell of stale cigarette smoke and beer and sweat and cheap perfume. A Puerto Rican girl was in whispered consultation with a sailor in one of the leatherette-lined booths. Another sailor was hunched over the juke box, thoughtfully considering his next selection, his face tinted orange and red and green from the colored tubing. A tired, fat, fifty-year old blonde sat at the far end of the bar, watching the sailor as though the next button he pushed might destroy the entire world. The bartender was polishing glasses. He looked up when Kling walked in and immediately smelled the law.

Two men were seated at the opposite end of the bar.

One of them was wearing a blue turtleneck sweater, gray slacks, and desert boots. His brown hair was clipped close to his scalp in a military cut. The other man was wearing a bright orange team jacket, almost luminous, with the words *Orioles, S.A.C.* lettered across its back. The one with the crewcut said something softly, and the other one chuckled. Behind the bar a glass clinked as the bartender replaced it on the shelf. The juke box erupted in sound, Jimi Hendrix rendering *All Along the Watchtower*.

Kling walked over to the two men.

"Which one of you is Danny Ryder?" he asked.

The one with the short hair said, "Who wants to know?"

"Police officer," Kling said, and the one in the orange jacket whirled with a pistol in his hand. Kling's eyes opened wide in surprise, and the pistol went off.

There was no time to think, there was hardly time to breathe. The explosion of the pistol was shockingly close, the acrid stink of cordite was in Kling's nostrils. The knowledge that he was still alive, the sweet rushing clean awareness that the bullet had somehow missed him was only a fleeting click of intelligence accompanying what was essentially a reflexive act.

Kling's .38 came free of its holster, his finger was inside the trigger guard and around the trigger, he squeezed off his shot almost before the gun had cleared the flap of his overcoat, fired into the orange jacket and threw his shoulder simultaneously against the chest of the man with the short hair, knocking him backward off his stool. The man in the orange jacket, his face twisted in pain, was leveling the pistol for another shot.

Kling fired again, squeezing the trigger without thought of rancor, and then whirled on the man with the short hair, who was crouched on the floor against the bar.

"Get *up!*"

"Don't shoot!"

"Get *up!*"

He yanked the man to his feet, hurled him against the bar, thrust the muzzle of his pistol at the blue turtleneck sweater, ran his hands under the armpits and between the legs, while the man kept saying over and over again, "Don't shoot, please don't shoot."

He backed away from him and leaned over the one in the orange jacket.

"Is this Ryder?" he asked.

"Yes."

"Who're you?"

"Frank Pasquale. Look, I—"

"Shut up, Frank," Kling said. "Put your hands behind your back. Move!"

He had already taken his handcuffs from his belt. He snapped them onto Pasquale's wrists, and only then became aware that Jimi Hendrix was still singing, the sailors were watching with pale white faces, the Puerto Rican girl was screaming, the fat faded blonde had her mouth open, the bartender was frozen in midmotion, the tip of his bar towel inside a glass.

"All right," Kling said. He was breathing harshly. "All right," he said again, and wiped his forehead.

Timothy Allen Ames was a potbellied man of forty, with a thick black mustache, a mane of long black hair, and brown eyes sharply alert at 5:05 in the morning. He answered the door as though he'd been already awake, asked for identification, then asked the detectives to wait a moment, closed the door, and came back shortly afterward, wearing a robe over his striped pajamas.

"Is your name Timothy Ames?" Carella asked.

"That's me," Ames said. "Little late to be paying a visit, ain't it?"

"Or early, depending how you look at it," Hawes said.

"One thing I can do without at five A.M. is humorous cops," Ames said. "How'd you get up here, anyway? Is that little jerk asleep at the desk again?"

"Who do you mean?" Carella asked.

"Lonnie Sanford, or whatever his name is."

"Ronald—Ronnie Sanford."

"Yeah, him. Always giving me trouble."

"What kind of trouble?"

"About broads," Ames said. "Acts like he's running a nunnery here, can't stand to see a guy come in with a girl. I notice he ain't got no compunctions about letting *cops* upstairs, though, no matter *what* time it is."

"Never mind Sanford, let's talk about you," Carella said.

"Sure, what would you like to know?"

"Where were you between eleven twenty and twelve tonight?"

"Right here."

"Can you prove it?"

"Sure. I got back here about eleven o'clock, and I been here ever since. Ask Sanford downstairs—no, he wasn't on yet. He don't come on till midnight."

"Who *else* can we ask, Ames?"

"Listen, you going to make trouble for me?"

"Only if you're in trouble."

"I got a broad here. She's over eighteen, don't worry. But, like, she's a junkie, you know? But I know you guys, and if you want to make trouble—"

"Where is she?"

"In the john."

"Get her out here."

"Look, do me a favor, will you? Don't bust the kid. She's trying to kick the habit, she really is. I been helping her along."

"How?"

"By keeping her busy," Ames said, and winked.

"Call her."

"Bea, come out here!" Ames shouted.

There were a few moments of hesitation, then the bathroom door opened. The girl was a tall plain brunette wearing a short terrycloth robe. She sidled into the room cautiously, as though expecting to be struck in the face at any moment. Her brown eyes were wide with expectancy. She knew fuzz, she knew what it was like to be arrested on a narcotics charge, and she had listened to the conversation from behind the closed bathroom door; and now she waited for whatever was coming, expecting the worst.

"What's your name, Miss?" Hawes asked.

"Beatrice Norden."

"What time did you get here tonight, Beatrice?"

"About eleven."

"Was this man with you?"

"Yes."

"Did he leave here at any time tonight?"

"No."

"Are you sure?"

"I'm positive. He picked me up about nine o'clock—"

"Where do you live, Beatrice?"

"Well, that's the thing, you see," the girl said. "I been put out of my room."

"So where'd he pick you up?"

"At my girlfriend's house. You can ask her, she was there when he came. Her name is Rosalie Dawes. Anyway, Timmy picked me up at nine, and we went out to eat, and we came up here around eleven."

"I hope you're telling us the truth, Miss Norden," Carella said.

"I swear to God, we been here all night," Beatrice answered.

"All right, Ames," Hawes said, "we'd like a sample of your handwriting."

"My *what?*"

"Your handwriting."

"What for?"

"We collect autographs," Carella said.

"Gee, these guys really break me up," Ames said to the girl. "Regular night-club comics we get in the middle of the night."

Carella handed him a pencil and then tore a sheet from his pad. "You want to write this for me?" he said. "The first part's in block lettering."

"What the hell is block lettering?" Ames asked.

"He means *print* it," Hawes said.

"Then why didn't he say so?"

"Put on your clothes, Miss," Carella said.

"What for?" Beatrice said.

"That's what I want him to write," Carella explained.

"Oh."

"Put on your clothes, Miss," Ames repeated, and lettered it onto the sheet of paper. "What else?" he asked, looking up.

"Now sign it in your own handwriting with the following words: The Avenging Angel."

"What the hell is this supposed to be?" Ames asked.

"You want to write it, please?"

Ames wrote the words, then handed the slip of paper to Carella.

He and Hawes compared it with the note that had been mailed to
Mercy Howell:

Put on Your Clothes, Miss.
The Avenging Angel
Put on Your Close, Miss!
The Avenging Angel

"So?" Ames asked.
"So you're clean," Hawes said.

At the desk downstairs, Ronnie Sanford was still immersed in
his accounting textbook. He got to his feet again as the detectives
came out of the elevator, adjusted his glasses on his nose, and said,
"Any luck?"

"Afraid not," Carella answered. "We're going to need this register for a while, if that's okay."

"Well—"

"Give him a receipt for it, Cotton," Carella said. It was late, and
he didn't want a debate in the lobby of a rundown hotel. Hawes
quickly made out a receipt in duplicate, signed both copies, and
handed one to Sanford.

"What about this torn cover?" Hawes asked belatedly.

"Yeah," Carella said. There was a small rip on the leather
binding of the book. He fingered it briefly now, then said, "Better
note that on the receipt, Cotton." Hawes took back the receipt and,
on both copies, jotted the words "Small rip on front cover." He
handed the receipts back to Sanford.

"Want to just sign these, Mr. Sanford?" he said.

"What for?" Sanford asked.

"To indicate we received the register in this condition."

"Oh, sure," Sanford said. He picked up a ballpoint pen from its desk holder, and asked, "What do you want me to write?"

"Your name and your title, that's all."

"My title?"

"Night Clerk, The Addison Hotel."

"Oh, sure," Sanford said, and signed both receipts. "This okay?" he asked. The detectives looked at what he had written.

"You like girls?" Carella asked suddenly.

"What?" Sanford asked.

"Girls," Hawes said.

"Sure. Sure, I like girls."

"Dressed or naked?"

"I—I don't know what you mean, sir."

"Where were you tonight between eleven twenty and midnight?" Hawes asked.

"Getting—getting ready to come to—to work," Sanford said.

"You sure you weren't in the alley of the Eleventh Street Theater stabbing a girl named Mercy Howell?"

"What? No—no, of course not. I was—I was home—getting dressed—" Sanford took a deep breath and decided to get indignant. "Listen, what's this all about?" he said.

"It's all about this," Carella said, and turned one of the receipts so that Sanford could read the signature:

Ronald Sanford
Night Clerk
The Addison Hotel

"Get your hat," Hawes said. "Study hall's over."

It was 5:25 when Adele Gorman came into the room with Meyer's cup of tea. He was crouched near the air-conditioning unit recessed into the wall to the left of the drapes; he glanced up when he heard her, then rose.

"I didn't know what you took," she said, "so I brought everything."

"Thank you," he said. "Just a little sugar is fine."

"Have you measured the room?" she asked, and put the tray down on the table in front of the sofa.

"Yes, I think I have everything I need now," Meyer said. He put a spoonful of sugar into the tea, stirred it, then lifted the cup to his mouth. "Hot," he said.

Adele Gorman was watching him silently. She said nothing. He kept sipping his tea. The ornate clock on the mantelpiece ticked in a swift whispering tempo.

"Do you always keep this room so dim?" Meyer asked.

"Well, my husband is blind, you know," Adele said. "There's really no need for brighter light."

"Mmm. But your father reads in this room, doesn't he?"

"I beg your pardon?"

"The night you came home from that party. He was sitting in the chair over there near the floor lamp. Reading. Remember?"

"Oh. Yes, he was."

"Bad light to read by."

"Yes, I suppose it is."

"I think maybe those bulbs are defective," Meyer said.

"Do you think so?"

"Mmm. I happened to look at the lamp, and there are three one-hundred-watt bulbs in it, all of them burning. You should be getting a lot more light with that much wattage."

"Well, I really don't know about such—"

"Unless the lamp is on a rheostat, of course."

"I'm afraid I don't even know what a rheostat is."

"It's an adjustable resistor. You can dim your lights or make them brighter with it. I thought maybe the lamp was on a rheostat, but I couldn't find a control knob anywhere in the room." Meyer paused. "You wouldn't know if there's a rheostat control in the house, would you?"

"I'm sure there isn't," Adele said.

"Must be defective bulbs then," Meyer said, and smiled. "Also, I think your air conditioner is broken."

"No, I'm sure it isn't."

"Well, I was just looking at it, and all the switches are turned to the 'On' position, but it isn't working. So I guess it's broken. That's a shame, too, because it's such a nice unit. Sixteen thousand BTUs. That's a lot of cooling power for a room this size. We've got one of those big old price-fixed apartments on Concord, my wife and I, with a large bedroom, and we get adequate cooling from a half-ton unit. It's a shame this one is broken."

"Yes. Detective Meyer, I don't wish to appear rude, but it is late—"

"Sure," Meyer said. "Unless, of course, the air conditioner's on a remote switch, too. So that all you have to do is turn a knob in another part of the house and it comes on." He paused. "*Is* there such a switch somewhere, Mrs. Gorman?"

"I have no idea."

"I'll just finish my tea and run along," Meyer said. He lifted the cup to his lips, sipped the tea, glanced at her over the rim, took the cup away from his mouth, and said, "But I'll be back."

"I hardly think there's any need for that," Adele said.

"Well, some jewelry's been stolen—"

"The ghosts—"

"Come off it, Mrs. Gorman."

The room went silent.

"Where are the loudspeakers, Mrs. Gorman?" Meyer asked. "In the false beams up there? They're hollow—I checked them out."

"I think perhaps you'd better leave," Adele said slowly.

"Sure," Meyer said. He put the cup down, and got to his feet.

"I'll show you out," Adele said.

They walked to the front door and out into the driveway. The night was still. The drizzle had stopped, and a thin layer of frost covered the grass rolling away toward the river. Their footsteps crunched on the gravel as they walked toward the automobile.

"My husband was blinded four years ago," Adele said abruptly. "He's a chemical engineer, there was an explosion at the plant, he could have been killed. Instead, he was only blinded." She hesitated an instant, then said again, "Only blinded," and there was such a sudden cry of despair in those two words that Meyer wanted to put his arm around her, console her the way he might his daughter, tell her that everything would be all right come morning.

But instead he leaned on the fender of his car, and she stood beside him looking down at the driveway gravel, her eyes not meeting his. They could have been conspirators exchanging secrets in the night, but they were only two people who had been thrown together on a premise as flimsy as the ghosts that inhabited this house.

"He gets a disability pension from the company," Adele said, "they've really been quite kind to us. And, of course, I work. I teach school, Detective Meyer. Kindergarten. I love children." She paused. She would not raise her eyes to meet his. "But—it's sometimes very difficult. My father, you see—"

Meyer waited. He longed suddenly for dawn, but he waited patiently, and heard her catch her breath as though committed to go ahead now however painful the revelation might be, compelled to throw herself on the mercy of the night before the morning sun broke through.

"My father's been retired for fifteen years. He gambles, Detective Meyer. He's a horse player. He loses large sums of money."

"Is that why he stole your jewels?" Meyer asked.

"You know, don't you?" Adele said simply, and raised her eyes to his. "Of course you know. It's quite transparent, his ruse, a shoddy little show really, a performance that would fool no one but—no one but a blind man." She brushed at her cheek; he could not tell whether the cold air had caused her sudden tears. "I really don't care about the theft; the jewels were left to me by my mother, and after all it was my father who bought them for her, so it's—it's really like returning a legacy. I really don't care about that part of it. I'd have *given* the jewelry to him if only he'd asked, but he's such a proud man. A proud man who steals from me and pretends that ghosts are committing the crime.

"And my husband, in his dark universe, listens to the sounds my father puts on tape and visualizes things he cannot quite believe and so he asks me to notify the police because he needs an impartial observer to contradict the suspicion that someone is stealing pennies from his blind man's cup. That's why I came to you, Detective Meyer. So that you would arrive here tonight and perhaps be fooled as I was fooled at first, and perhaps say to my husband, 'Yes, Mr. Gorman, there *are* ghosts in your house.'"

She suddenly placed her hand on his sleeve. The tears were streaming down her face, she had difficulty catching her breath. "Because you see, Detective Meyer, there *are* ghosts in this house, there really and truly are. The ghost of a proud man who was once a brilliant judge and who is now a gambler and a thief; and the ghost of a man who once could see, and who now trips and falls in the darkness."

On the river a tugboat hooted. Adele Gorman fell silent. Meyer opened the door of his car and got in behind the wheel.

"I'll call your husband tomorrow," he said gruffly. "Tell him I'm convinced something supernatural is happening here."

"And will you be back, Detective Meyer?"

"No," he said. "I won't be back, Mrs. Gorman."

In the squadroom they were wrapping up the night. Their day had begun at 7:45 P.M. yesterday, and they had been officially relieved at 5:45 A.M.; but they had not left the office yet because there were questions still to be asked, reports to be typed, odds and ends to be put in place before they could go home. And since the relieving detectives were busy getting *their* approaching workday organized, the squadroom at 6:00 A.M. was busier than it might have been on any given afternoon, with two teams of cops getting in each other's way.

In the interrogation room, Carella and Hawes were questioning young Ronald Sanford in the presence of the assistant district attorney who had come over earlier to take Mrs. Martin's confession, and who now found himself listening to another one when all he wanted to do was go home to sleep. Sanford seemed terribly shocked that they had been able to notice the identical handwriting in *The Addison Hotel* and *The Avenging Angel*—he couldn't get over it. He thought he had been very clever in misspelling the word "clothes," because then they'd think an illiterate had written it, not someone studying to be an accountant.

He could not explain why he had killed Mercy Howell. He got all mixed up when he tried to explain that. It had something to do with the moral climate of America, and people exposing themselves in public, people like that shouldn't be allowed to pollute others, to foist their filth on others, to intrude on the privacy of others who were trying so very hard to make something of themselves, studying accounting by day and working in a hotel by night, what right had these people to ruin it for everybody else?

Frank Pasquale's tune, sung in the clerical office to Kling and O'Brien, was not quite so hysterical, but similar to Sanford's nonetheless. He had gotten the idea together with Danny Ryder. They had decided between them that the Blacks in America were taking jobs away from decent hardworking people who only wanted to be left alone, what right did they have to force themselves on everybody else? So they had decided to bomb the church, just to show them they couldn't get away with it, not in America. He didn't seem terribly concerned over the fact that his partner was lying stonecold dead on a slab at the morgue, or that their little Culver Avenue expedition had cost three people their lives, and had severely injured a half dozen others. All he wanted to know, repeatedly, was whether his picture would be in the paper.

At his desk Meyer started to type up a report on the Gorman ghosts, then decided the hell with it. If the lieutenant asked him where he'd been half the night, he would say he had been out looking for trouble in the streets. The Lord knew there was enough of *that* around, any night. He pulled the report forms and their separating sheets of carbon paper from the ancient typewriter, and noticed that Detective Hal Willis was pacing the room, waiting to get at the desk the moment he vacated it.

"Okay, Hal," he said, "it's all yours."

"*Finalmente!*" Willis, who was not Italian, said.

The telephone rang.

The sun was up when they came out of the building and walked past the hanging green "87" globes and down the low flat steps to the sidewalk. The park across the street shimmered with early-morning autumn brilliance, the sky above it was clear and blue.

They walked toward the diner on the next block, Meyer and O'Brien ahead of the others, Carella, Hawes, and Kling bringing up the rear. They were tired, and exhaustion showed in their eyes, in the set of their mouths, in the pace they kept. They talked without animation, mostly about their work, their breaths feathery and white on the cold morning air.

When they reached the diner, they took off their overcoats and ordered hot coffee and cheese Danish and toasted English muffins. Meyer said he thought he was coming down with a cold. Carella told him about some cough medicine his wife had given one of the children. O'Brien, munching on a muffin, glanced across the diner and saw a young girl in one of the booths. She was wearing blue jeans and a bright colored Mexican serape, and she was talking to a boy wearing a Navy pea jacket.

"I think I see somebody," he said, and he moved out of the booth past Kling and Hawes, who were talking about the newest regulation on search and seizure.

The girl looked up when he approached the booth.

"Miss Blair?" he said. "Penelope Blair?"

"Yes," the girl answered. "Who are you?"

"Detective O'Brien," he said, "Eighty-seventh Precinct. Your mother was in last night, Penny. She asked me to tell you—"

"Flake off, cop," Penelope Blair said. "Go stop a riot somewhere."

O'Brien looked at her silently for a moment. Then he nodded, turned away, and went back to the table.

"Anything?" Kling asked.

"You can't win 'em all," O'Brien said.